REFLECTIONS ON MEANING

Reflections on Meaning

PAUL HORWICH

CLARENDON PRESS · OXFORD

*This book has been printed digitally and produced in a standard specification
in order to ensure its continuing availability*

OXFORD
UNIVERSITY PRESS

Great Clarendon Street, Oxford OX2 6DP

Oxford University Press is a department of the University of Oxford.
It furthers the University's objective of excellence in research, scholarship,
and education by publishing worldwide in

Oxford New York

Auckland Cape Town Dar es Salaam Hong Kong Karachi
Kuala Lumpur Madrid Melbourne Mexico City Nairobi
New Delhi Shanghai Taipei Toronto
With offices in
Argentina Austria Brazil Chile Czech Republic France Greece
Guatemala Hungary Italy Japan South Korea Poland Portugal
Singapore Switzerland Thailand Turkey Ukraine Vietnam

Oxford is a registered trade mark of Oxford University Press
in the UK and in certain other countries

Published in the United States
by Oxford University Press Inc., New York

ISBN 0-19-925125-8

Printed and bound by CPI Antony Rowe, Eastbourne

Preface

The aim of this book is to explain how mere noises, marks, gestures, and mental/neural symbols, are able to capture the world—that is, how words and sentences (in whatever medium) come to *mean* what they do, to *stand* for certain things, to be *true* or *false* of reality.

The answer I will be expounding is a working-out of Wittgenstein's idea that the meaning of a term is nothing more than its *use*. He compared the words of a language to pieces in a game: just as the queen in chess qualifies as such, not because of its shape, but by virtue of the rules that specify its unique role, e.g. its initial position, and how it is permitted to move, similarly, each word derives its meaning and representational potential—its 'life'—not from its internal physical nature, but from a pattern of use, an implicitly followed rule, that governs the circumstances in which sentences containing it are to be accepted. And just as there is no limit to the variety of forms that may be taken by rules even within a single game, so too our rules for the uses of different words vary dramatically in character and content. Therefore, it would be wrong for us to demand a neat, uniform analysis of meaning in terms of some naturalistic (e.g. causal) relation between words and the things to which they refer—we should expect no theory of the simple form

> w means DOG = w bears relation R to dogs.
> w means RED = w bears relation R to red things.
> w means ATOM = w bears relation R to atoms.
> . . . and so on.

Nonetheless, there may well be, in the case of each word, a specific fact that determines which particular rule for its use we are implicitly observing, and that thereby fixes what we mean by it.

Theories of meaning that are more-or-less inspired by these ideas—that is, so called 'use theories', 'functional role theories', and 'conceptual role theories'—have been subjected to a variety of objections that are widely taken to be devastating. There is, for example, Quine's argument that no objective line can be drawn between those uses of a word that are essential to its meaning and those that are not. There is Davidson's worry (pressed by Fodor and Lepore) that the compositionality of meaning could not be accommodated, since the uses of sentences are not determined by the uses of their component words. There is Kripke's suggestion that dispositions for the use of a word could not explain why one *ought* apply it to some things but not others. And there are frequent allegations of crass behaviourism, rampant holism, and knee-jerk reductionism. My hope is to convince the reader that, armed with a proper understanding of where and how these criticisms apply, it is possible to design a use-theoretic account that escapes them.

Although initial versions of the following chapters were written as autonomous essays, they have been assembled and revised so as to comprise a genuine book—one that is focused on articulating and defending this conception of language. The first chapter sets the stage by summarizing the main philosophical debates in the area. The second presents my positive, neo-Wittgensteinian proposal, elaborating the ideas just sketched. Its central thesis is that the meaning of a word is the *law*—the implicitly followed rule—governing its overall use. The third chapter contrasts that position with the more familiar one mentioned above (developed in different ways by Fodor, Dretske, Millikan, Jacob, and Papineau), to the effect that there *is* a uniform account of how words relate to what they stand for. Applying one of the central morals of this discussion, the fourth chapter aims to specify the nature of *vagueness*. Its main claims are, first, that the so-called 'borderline cases' of a term are those for which its law of use dictates that we can confidently apply neither it nor its negation and, second, that any such applications are nonetheless true or false. The fifth chapter defends my picture of meaning against the charge that it fails to accommodate its *normative* import. I argue that how a word *should* be used *derives from* its meaning (not the other way around). The sixth chapter delves into epistemology, examining the relationship between meaning-constituting rules of word-use and our fundamental canons of justification for belief, and finding it not to be as intimate as many theorists have claimed. The seventh chapter, in a more empirical spirit, considers all these matters from the perspective of Chomskian psycho-linguistics. And the eighth chapter offers an unorthodox anti-Davidsonian account of the way in which the meanings of complex expressions depend on the meanings of their component words.

The theory that is developed in these discussions is the one suggested in my 1998 book, *Meaning*. But the material presented here contains a host of improved formulations, new arguments, extensions of the position, responses to criticism, and also a few (relatively minor) changes of mind. There is no need to have looked at the earlier work in order to understand this one. But nor is there much overlap, apart from main conclusions. Indeed, I believe that these conclusions are better expressed and better supported here than before. So I'm hopeful that those who have read that book will still find this one worthwhile.

My gratitude to the many colleagues who have given me comments and criticism will emerge at appropriate points in the following pages. However, I want straightaway to record a special indebtedness to those whose published reactions to my previous efforts in this area focused attention on some of the problems that most needed to be addressed. For this vital stimulus I would like to thank Paul Boghossian (2003), Noam Chomsky (2003), Michael Devitt (2002), Hartry Field (2001), Jerry Fodor and Ernie Lepore (2002), Allan Gibbard (2002), Anil Gupta (2003), Bob Hale and Crispin Wright (2000), Jerry Katz (2004), Mark Sainsbury (2002), Stephen Schiffer (2000), and Tim Williamson (1997).

Contents

1

The Space of Issues and Options

1. INTRODUCTION

Each expression of a language surely *means* something—there is some fact as to what it means; but the nature of such facts is notoriously obscure and controversial. Consider the term "dog". It possesses a distinctive literal meaning in English, and this feature is closely associated with various others—for example, that we use the word to help articulate certain thoughts; that it is appropriately translated into the Italian "cane" and the German "Hund"; and that we should try to apply it to dogs and only to dogs. But such characteristics range from the puzzling to the downright mysterious. Does thought itself take place in language? How might 'little' meanings (like that of "dog") combine into 'bigger' ones (like that of "dogs bark")? What is it about that word's meaning that enables it to reach out through space and time, and latch on to a particular hairy animal in ancient China? And there is a ramified profusion of further questions, as we shall see. So it isn't surprising that philosophy abounds with theories that aim to demystify these matters, to say what it is for a word or a sentence to have a meaning.

This introductory chapter aims to map the terrain of alternative suggestions. To that end I will mention the central issues that must be confronted in developing a decent account of meaning, together with the various positions that might be taken with respect to them, and some of the arguments that can be given for and against these positions. Be warned, however, that the immediately following discussions are cryptic and sketchy—something of a mad dash through the literature. They are intended merely to provide an orienting background to the line of thought that will be elaborated at a more reasonable speed in the rest of this work.

2. MEANING SCEPTICISM

It is sometimes maintained that the expressions of a language really do not, as we might naively think, possess meanings—but accounts of this sceptical kind may be more or less radical. At the most extreme there is a theory that, as far as I know, has never been seriously proposed, namely, that there are no semantic phenomena at all, that no word stands for anything, and that no sentence is true or false. Such a view is hardly credible: for no one who understands the word "dog" could doubt that it picks out dogs (if there are any dogs); and no one who understands the sentence "dogs bark" could doubt that it expresses a truth if and only if dogs bark; and so on. However, there are less radical forms of meaning-scepticism that *do* have adherents.

For example, one might deny (with Quine[1]) that there are any facts concerning the meanings or referents of *foreign* expressions (including the expressions of compatriots, who *seem* to be speaking the same language as oneself). This is not as chauvinistic as it may initially sound; for it amounts to a general and unbiased scepticism about the objectivity of translation. Quine's position is based on his 'indeterminacy thesis': namely, that linguistic behaviour at home and abroad—which he takes to provide the only facts with the *potential* to establish the correctness of any proposed translation

---

[1] Quine, W. V. (1962), *Word and Object*; idem (1990), *Pursuit of Truth*.

manual—will in fact be consistent with many such proposals; so we can rarely fix what a foreigner (or any other person) means by his words. But a number of counters to this argument have appeared in the literature. One response (pioneered by Chomsky[2]) is that the failure of the phenomena of word-usage to settle how an expression should be translated would not result in there being *no fact of the matter*, but merely in a familiar *underdetermination of theory by data* (i.e. in a difficulty of discovering what the facts of translation are). Another common strategy of reply (e.g. Horwich[3]) is to argue that Quine has adopted too narrow a view—too behaviouristic—of what the non-semantic meaning-constituting features of word-use may be; that they actually include, not merely assent–dissent dispositions, but also (for example) causal relations amongst such dispositions; and that once such further evidence is taken into account, the alleged indeterminacy disappears. To illustrate using Quine's famous case: although we may be prepared to assent and dissent, in the same environmental circumstances, to "There's a rabbit" and "There's an undetached rabbit-part", we tend to assent to the second as a consequence of having assented to the first, not vice versa; and that causal fact can be a ground for deciding which of two co-assertible foreign sentences should be translated into one and which into the other.

A different and relatively mild form of semantic scepticism would countenance facts about what refers to what and about the truth conditions of sentences, but would renounce any finer-grained notion of meaning, such as Fregean 'sense'. Thus there would be no respect in which co-referential terms (such as "Hesperus" and "Phosphorus") would differ in meaning. One

[2] Chomsky, N. (1975), "Quine's Empirical Assumptions" in Davidson and Hintikka (eds.), *Words and Objections*; idem (1987), "Reply to Review Discussion of *Knowledge of Language*", *Mind and Language* 2: 178–97.

[3] Horwich, P. G. (1998), *Meaning*, chap. 9.

source of this scepticism might be a Millian/Russellian rejection (Salmon,[4] Donnellan,[5] Crimmins & Perry,[6] Lycan,[7] Soames[8]) of the argument typically offered in support of fine-grained meanings: namely, Frege's argument that they are needed in order to accommodate our intuition that (for example) 'believing Hesperus is Phosphorus' is not the same thing as 'believing Hesperus is Hesperus'. But it remains hard to see much wrong with that reasoning.[9]

Another widespread motivation for embracing the mild form of scepticism is the Davidsonian view that *compositionality* (the dependence of our understanding of sentences on our understanding of their component words) requires that fine-grained meanings be abandoned in favour of mere truth conditions and their coarse-grained determinants.[10] But again one might well prefer a Fregean point of view: one might suppose that the state of understanding a complex expression is *identical* to the state of understanding its various parts and appreciating how they are combined with one another. In that case compositionality will have a trivial explanation, and there will be no pressure to adopt Davidson's truth conditional account of it.[11]

---

[4] Salmon, N. (1986), *Frege's Puzzle*.

[5] Donnellan, K. (1989), "Belief and the Identity of Reference" in French, Uehling, and Wettstein (eds.), *Midwest Studies in Philosophy, vol. 13, Contemporary Perspectives in the Philosophy of Language II* 275–88.

[6] Crimmins, M., and Perry, J. (1989), "The Prince and the Phone Booth: Reporting Puzzling Beliefs", *Journal of Philosophy* 86: 685–711.

[7] Lycan, W. (1990), "On Respecting Puzzles About Belief Ascriptions [A Reply to Devitt]", *Pacific Philosophical Quarterly* 71: 182–8.

[8] Soames, S. (2002), *Beyond Rigidity: The Unfinished Agenda of Naming and Necessity*.

[9] Frege, G. (1952), "On Sense and Reference", *Translations from the Philosophical Writings of Gottlob Frege*, P. Geach and M. Black (eds.). For a defence of Frege's argument, see S. Schiffer (2004), *The Things We Mean*.

[10] Davidson, D. (1984), *Truth and Interpretation*. There is some controversy as to whether Davidson himself advocates an *elimination* of meaning in favour of truth conditions, or an *analysis* of meaning in terms of truth conditions. For reasons given in chap. 8 fn. 5, I myself favour the second of these interpretations.

[11] This point of view is elaborated slightly in section 5 of the present chapter and developed more fully in chap. 8.

Finally there is a so-called 'non-factualist' form of meaning-scepticism, which Kripke[12] takes Wittgenstein[13] to be urging. The idea is that although we may properly and usefully attribute meanings to someone's words, we should not think of these attributions as reporting *genuine* ('robust') facts about that person, but rather as implementing some quite different speech act—something along the lines of 'expressing our recommendation that his words be taken at face value'. Of course, there is a perfectly legitimate *deflationary* sense of "fact" in which "p" is trivially equivalent to "It is a fact that p"; and when we attribute a meaning we obviously suppose there to be a 'fact', in *that* sense, as to what is meant. Thus non-factualism faces the problem of specifying what makes certain facts 'genuine' or 'robust' ones; and this has not so far been satisfactorily resolved. For example, it might be tempting to identify them as those facts that enter into causal/explanatory relations. But then— since it is pretty clear that a word's meaning helps to explain the circumstances in which sentences containing it are accepted— the Kripkensteinian position would be pretty clearly false. Alternatively, it might be said that the 'genuine'/'robust' facts are those that are constituted by physical facts. But in that case non-factualism would boil down to a familiar form of anti-reductionism, and one would be hard-pressed to see anything sceptical about it.

3. REDUCTIONISM

Amongst *non*-sceptical accounts of meaning, some are reductionist, others are not: some aim to identify underlying non-semantic facts in virtue of which an expression possesses its meaning; others take this to be impossible and aim for no more than an *epistemological* story—a specification of which

---

[12] Kripke, S. (1982), *Wittgenstein: On Rules and Private Language*.
[13] Wittgenstein, L. (1953), *Philosophical Investigations*.

non-semantic data would tend to justify the tentative ascription of a given meaning.

Reductionist theories are typically motivated by a general sentiment to the effect that, since we humans are fundamentally physical beings, i.e. made of atoms, all our characteristics—including our understanding of languages—must somehow be constituted out of physical facts about us. However, many philosophers are unconvinced by this line of thought—arguing that the majority of familiar properties (e.g. 'red', 'chair', 'democracy', etc.) resist strict analysis in physical terms, and therefore that the way in which empirical facts are admittedly somehow grounded in the physical need not meet the severe constraints of a reductive account. In response to this point, it may be observed that although some weak form of physical grounding might suffice for *certain* empirical properties, others—those with a rich and regular array of physical effects—call for strict reduction. Otherwise, given the causal autonomy of the physical, those effects would be mysteriously overdetermined. In particular, the fact that the meaning of each word is the core-cause of its overall use (i.e. of all the non-semantic facts concerning the acceptance of sentences containing it) would be explanatorily anomalous unless meaning-facts were themselves reducible to non-semantic phenomena. However, as plausible as these considerations might be, the only solid argument for semantic reductionism would be an articulation and defence of some specific theory of that form. Conversely, the best anti-reductionist argument is that no such account has been found despite strenuous attempts to construct one.

Reductionist approaches of various stripes will be the focus in what follows; so I won't dwell on them now. As for *anti*-reductionist proposals, amongst the most prominent in contemporary analytic philosophy are those due to McGinn, McDowell, Davidson, and Kripke. McGinn[14] argues that our not having

---

[14] McGinn, C. (1984), *Wittgenstein on Meaning*.

managed to devise a plausible reductive account of 'understand-ing' should be no more surprising or embarrassing than our inability to give such an account of other psychological features, like bravery or kindness. McDowell[15] gives this perspective a Wittgensteinian gloss: since our puzzlement about meaning is merely an artefact of self-inflicted mystification, the illumina-tion we need will have to come from a rooting out of confusions rather than from the development of a reductive theory, and so there is not the slightest reason to expect there to be such a thing. Davidson[16] combines that anti-reductionist metaphysics with a neo-Quinean epistemology of interpretation: the most plausible translation manual for a foreign speaker's language is the one that optimizes overlap between the circumstances in which her sentences are held true and the circumstances in which we hold true the sentences into which hers are to be translated. And Kripke[17] sketches a superficially similar idea (on behalf of Wittgenstein): it is reasonable to tentatively suppose that some-one means PLUS by a symbol of hers when she deploys it more or less as we deploy the word "plus". But note that in Kripke's view, unlike Davidson's, such norms are not to be regarded as specify-ing the evidence for a species of 'genuine' fact.

4. LANGUAGE AND THOUGHT

A further bone of contention is the relationship between overt, public languages, such as English and Chinese, and the psycho-logical states of belief, desire, intention, and other forms of thought, which these languages are used to articulate and

---

[15] McDowell, J. (1984), "Wittgenstein on Following a Rule", *Synthese* 58(3): 325–63; idem (1994), *Mind and World*.

[16] Davidson, D. (1984), *Truth and Interpretation*. His non-reductionist view of truth conditions is combined (as noted above) with a truth conditional analysis of meaning.

[17] Kripke, S. (1982), *Wittgenstein: On Rules and Private Language*.

communicate. The central issue here is whether or not thinking itself invariably takes place within a language (or language-like symbol-system). Is it the case, for example, that the state of 'believing that dogs bark' consists in accepting (perhaps unconsciously) some mental sentence whose meaning is DOGS BARK? The overall shape of any account of meaning will depend on how this question is answered.[18]

Consider, to begin with, the philosophers who would *deny* that thinking is inevitably linguistic. Within that group there are those (such as Grice[19]) who maintain that the meanings of public-language sentences derive (in virtue of our intentions and conventions) from the propositional contents of the beliefs, etc. that they are typically used to express. Thus "dogs bark" means what it does because of our practice of uttering it in order to convey the belief that dogs bark. But this approach fails to address the problem of how certain configurations of the mind/brain come to instantiate the intentions and beliefs they do. Then we find those—arguably Wittgenstein[20] and Quine[21]— who would solve this problem by supposing that public language meanings are 'prior' (in a certain sense) to the contents of thoughts, i.e. that one can see how a given state of the mind/brain comes to possess the conceptual content it does by reference to the meaning (independently explained) of the public expression with which it is correlated.

Alternatively, there are theorists who maintain that all human thinking takes place within a mental language—either a universal 'Mentalese' or else a mental form of English, Italian, etc. (depending on the speaker). Of these theorists, many (e.g.

---

[18] I will use expressions in capital letters to name meanings. Thus, "DOG" names the meaning of the English word "dog"; "I AM HUNGRY" names the literal English meaning of "I am hungry", etc.

[19] Grice, P. (1957), "Meaning", *Philosophical Review* 66: 377–88; idem (1969), "Utterer's Meaning and Intention", *Philosophical Review* 78.

[20] Wittgenstein, L. (1953), *Philosophical Investigations*.

[21] See his *Word and Object*.

Fodor,[22] Schiffer,[23] Loar,[24] Sperber and Wilson,[25] Neale[26]) advocate a two-stage theory: first, an account of how the terms of a mental language come to mean what they do; and, second, a neo-Gricean account of how the meanings of someone's overt public language derive from those contents.

However, as we shall see in the appendix to Chapter 2, it might be argued that the agreements and explicit intentions invoked by Grice *rely* on public language meaning, and so cannot constitute it; that the link between a sound and its mental associate is fixed at an early age; and that their common meaning derives from the joint possession of the same meaning-constituting property, e.g. the same basic use, or the same causal correlations with external properties. Therefore, it is best to suppose that there is a *single* way in which meaning is constituted, applying equally well to both mental and overt languages. Such an approach would obviously have to be non-Gricean. And it would be especially compelling if each of us thinks largely in our own *public* language. From this point of view—suggested by Gilbert Harman,[27] and argued in Chapter 7—it seems especially clear that there can be no substantial difference between an account of the contents of thoughts and an account of the literal semantic meanings of the sentences that express them.

5. COMPOSITIONALITY

It is uncontroversial that, apart from idioms, the meaning of any complex expression-type (such as a sentence) depends on

[22] Fodor, J. (1975), *The Language of Thought*; idem (1987), *Psychosemantics*; idem (2001), "Language, Thought, and Compositionality", *Mind and Language* 1–15.
[23] Schiffer, S. (1972), *Meaning*; idem (1987), *Remnants of Meaning*; idem (2003), *The Things We Mean*.   [24] Loar, B. (1981), *Mind and Meaning*.
[25] Sperber, D., and Wilson, D. (1995), *Relevance*.
[26] Neale, S. (2004), "This, That, and the Other", in *Descriptions and Beyond*.
[27] Harman, G. (1982), "Conceptual Role Semantics", *Notre Dame Journal of Formal Logic* 28: 252–6; idem (1987), "(Non-solipsistic) Conceptual Role Semantics", in E. Lepore (ed.), *New Directions in Semantics*.

the meanings of its component words and on how those words have been combined with one another. But there is little consensus on how this obvious fact should be incorporated within a full story about meaning.

A common assumption is that compositionality puts a *severe* constraint on an adequate account of how an expression's meaning is engendered. For it requires that the facts in virtue of which a given sentence means what it does be implied by the structure of the sentence together with the facts in virtue of which the words mean what they do. And, given certain further commitments that one could well have, this condition may be difficult to satisfy.

For example, verificationists (e.g. Schlick[28]) maintain that the meaning of each sentence consists in the way in which we would go about establishing whether or not it is true (—from which it follows that no untestable hypothesis could be meaningful). And they go on to say (in light of compositionality) that the meaning of each *word* must consist in the constant 'contribution' it makes to the various 'methods of verification' of the various sentences in which it appears. But this point of view suffers from the fact that no one has ever been able to spell out what these contributing characteristics are. In addition, it is hard to see why one should not be able to construct sentences that, despite being neither verifiable nor falsifiable, nonetheless possess meanings in virtue of their familiar structures and the familiar meanings of their parts. Thus compositionality and verificationism do not sit well together.

Davidson's influential thesis (mentioned in section 2) is that compositionality may be accommodated only by identifying the meanings of sentences with truth conditions and the meanings of words with reference conditions; for one will then be in a position to derive the former meanings from the latter by exploiting the methods deployed in Tarski's definitions of truth.

---

[28] Schlick, M. (1959), "Positivism and Realism" in A. J. Ayer, *Logical Positivism*.

And this idea sparked energetic research programmes aimed towards extending the types of linguistic construction (e.g. to those involving adverbs, indexicals, modalities, etc.) for which this treatment may be given, and towards finding a notion of 'truth condition' that is strong enough to determine (or replace) meaning. Doubts about whether such problems can be solved tended to be dismissed with the response that since natural languages are evidently compositional, and since there is no alternative to the truth-conditional way of accommodating that characteristic, there *must* be solutions, and so our failing to find them can only be due to a lack of ingenuity.[29]

In a similar vein, Fodor and Lepore[30] also brandish a 'substantive compositionality constraint'. In their case, the aim is to knock out various accounts of word meaning. For example, they argue that the meaning of a term cannot be an associated *stereotype*, since the stereotypes associated with words (e.g. with "pet" and "fish") do not determine the stereotypes associated with the complexes (e.g. "pet fish") in which those words appear. Clearly this argument presupposes that there is a certain *uniformity* in how the meanings of expressions are constituted, i.e. that whatever sort of thing (e.g. an associated stereotype, or a reference/ truth condition) provides the meanings of *words* must also provide the meanings of the *complexes* formed from them.

An alternative picture—one that will be developed in Chapter 8—would oppose this uniformity assumption (including the Davidsonian implementation of it). Indeed, it would oppose giving any *general* account—covering the meanings of complexes as well as words—of the sort that could leave open the question of whether the former could be determined by the latter. Instead, its account of complexes would *presuppose*

---

[29] See chap. 8 for elaboration of the difficulties confronting Davidson's account of compositionality.

[30] Fodor, J., and Lepore, E. (1991), "Why Meaning (Probably) Isn't Conceptual Role", *Mind and Language* 6: 328–43; idem (1996), "The Pet Fish and the Red Herring: Why Concepts Arn't Prototypes", *Cognition* 58(2): 243–76.

compositionality; for it would say that the meaning of a complex expression is *constituted* by the facts concerning its structure and the meanings of its words. For example, the property, 'x means THEAETETUS FLIES', would be constituted by the property, 'x is an expression that results from applying a function-term that means FLIES to an argument-term that means THEAETETUS'. In that case, *any* reductive account of word-meanings—no matter how poor it is—will induce a reductive account of complex-meanings that trivially complies with the principle of compositionality. Thus that principle cannot help us to decide how the meanings of *words* are constituted.

6. NORMATIVITY

Focusing now on what *does* engender the meaning of a word, we find a much debated division between theories that favour analyses in *evaluative* terms and those that do not. There is an intimate relation (emphasized by Kripke[31]) between what a word means and how it *should* be used: for example, if a word means DOG then one ought to aim to apply it only to dogs; therefore one should not apply it to something observed swinging from tree to tree. And many philosophers (e.g. Gibbard,[32] Brandom,[33] Lance and Hawthorne[34]) have drawn the conclusion that meaning must somehow be explicated in terms of what one ought and ought not to say—hence, that meaning is *constitutionally* evaluative. Thus it could be, for example, that the meaning of "not" is partially engendered by the fact that one ought not to accept instances of "p and not p".

---

[31] See his *Wittgenstein: On Rules and Private Language*.
[32] Gibbard, A. (1994), "Meaning and Normativity", *Philosophical Issues 5: Truth and Rationality*, E. Villanueva (ed.), 95–115.
[33] Brandom, R. (1994), *Making It Explicit*.
[34] Lance, M., and Hawthorne, J. (1997), *The Grammar of Meaning: Normativity and Semantic Content*.

In opposition to this conclusion it can be argued that the 'factual' effects of a word's meaning (namely, someone's disposition to accept certain sentences containing it) would be difficult to explain if meaning were evaluative rather than 'factual'. And in opposition to the *reasoning* behind that conclusion, it can be argued that the evaluative *import* of a meaning-property isn't enough to make that property *constitutionally* evaluative. Killing, for example, has evaluative import; one ought not to do it. And this could well be a *basic* evaluative fact—not explicable on the basis of more fundamental ones. But we may nevertheless give an account of killing in wholly non-evaluative language. So why not take the same view of meaning?

The answer, perhaps, is that, unlike killing, meaning is a matter of *implicitly following rules* (Wittgenstein,[35] Brandom); for the patterns of word-use that a speaker displays are the result of corrective molding by his community. But even if one concedes that meaning is constitutionally *regulative*—i.e. a matter of rule following—this is not to say that attributions of meaning are *evaluative*. No doubt, the notion of 'its being *right* to follow a certain rule' is evaluative. But the notion of 'a person's *actually* following that rule' surely lies on the other side of the 'fact'/value divide.

Moreover, it would remain to be seen whether meaning is *fundamentally* regulative—for one might aspire to analyse rule-following in entirely non-normative, naturalistic terms. Some philosophers (e.g. Kripke and Brandom, in the works just cited) contend that this is impossible. They argue that any analysis of 'implicitly following rule R' would have to depend on an a priori specification of the naturalistic conditions in which an action would qualify as *mistaken*, and that such an account cannot be supplied. But there are others (e.g. Blackburn[36]) who maintain that the required account *can* be supplied. And yet others, (e.g. myself, in Chapter 5 of this book) who reject the

---

[35] Wittgenstein, L. (1953), *Philosophical Investigations*.
[36] Blackburn, S. (1984), "The Individual Strikes Back", *Synthese* 58: 281–301.

requirement, claiming that the relevant notion of 'mistake' is defined in terms of 'following rule R', rather than vice versa, and proposing analyses that do not satisfy it. Thus one might suppose that S implicitly follows R when, as a result of corrective reinforcement, it is an 'ideal law' that S conforms with that rule—where the notion of 'ideal' is the non-normative, naturalistic one that is often deployed in scientific models, e.g. the ideal gas laws.

7. INDIVIDUALISM

According to some philosophers (again following Kripke) a consequence of these *normativity* considerations is that meaning is an essentially *social* phenomenon; so a 'private language' is impossible. For the implicit rule-following which must be involved in a person's meaning something allegedly depends on activities of correction displayed within his linguistic community. And this conclusion is independently supported by the observation (Kripke,[37] Evans,[38] Putnam,[39] Burge[40]) that we in fact do interpret people, not merely on the basis of their own idiosyncratic usage of words, but also on the basis of what their community means. Thus if a girl, reporting what she has learned at school, says "Kripke discovered other worlds", we take her to be referring *not* to whichever individual satisfies some definite description that she happens to associate with the name—there may be no such description, or it may pick out the wrong guy—but rather to *Kripke*, i.e. the person her teacher was referring to, who was in turn referring to the same person as

[37] Kripke, S. (1980), *Naming and Necessity.*

[38] Evans, G. (1973), "The Causal Theory of Names", *Proceedings of the Aristotelian Society*, Suppl. vol. 47: 187–208.

[39] Putnam, H. (1975), "The Meaning of "Meaning" ", in his *Mind, Language and Reality: Philosophical Papers, vol. 2.*

[40] Burge, T. (1979), "Individualism and the Mental", *Midwest Studies in Philosophy* 4: 73–121.

his source of the name was referring to, and so on. And when Putnam—a self-confessed incompetent with tree-names—says, pointing to a big shrub, "Is that an elm?", we take him to have asked whether it's an *elm*, i.e. whether it's what the experts would call "an elm". His own defective practice with the word does not fix what he means by it. (See section (h) of Chapter 2 for further discussion.)

Opposed to this conception, however, there are a number of philosophers (e.g. Chomsky,[41] Crane,[42] Segal[43]) who maintain that there *is* a kind of meaning, better suited to psychological explanation, whereby what each person means is constituted by facts about that person alone and is conceptually (though not causally) *in*dependent of what other people do. These theorists could either deny that this individualistic brand of meaning is constitutionally regulative; or they could accept that it is, but regard the rules as sustained by *self*-correction. They may allow that we *also* have a notion of communal meaning, and that this is the notion that is typically deployed in ordinary language when we speak of what someone means. But, if so, they will contend that it is derived (e.g. by a sort of *averaging*) from the more fundamental notion of idiolectal meaning—so that communal meaning is not appropriate for explaining a particular person's thoughts and actions.

8. EXTERNALISM

Alongside the distinction between 'communal' and 'individual-istic' accounts, there is a distinction between those theories according to which what we mean by our words (at least *certain* words) depends on the physical environment of their deployment, and those according to which meanings are wholly "in the head".

[41] Chomsky, N. (1986), *Knowledge of Language*.
[42] Crane, T. (1991), "All the Difference in the World", *Philosophical Quarterly* 41: 1–25.   [43] Segal, G. (2000), *A Slim Book about Narrow Content*.

The former ('externalist') perspective came to prominence with Putnam's[44] famous thought experiment. Since Oscar's physical duplicate on Twin Earth is surrounded by a liquid that, despite its superficial appearance, isn't really water, we are reluctant to say that the doppelganger's word "water" refers to the same thing as our word does—even though, since he and Oscar are intrinsically identical, their internal uses of it are exactly the same. Thus it would seem that the facts that provide certain terms with their meanings must include aspects of the outside world.

On the other hand, it has been argued (Fodor[45], White,[46] Jackson and Pettit,[47] Chalmers[48]) that words like "water" have a certain *indexical* character—that their reference depends (as in the case of "I", "our", and "here"), not merely on their fixed meanings in English, but also on the *context* of their use. One method of implementing this idea would be to suppose that the meaning of "water" is constituted by an acceptance of

$$x \text{ is water } \leftrightarrow x \text{ has the underlying nature, if any, of the stuff in } our \text{ seas, rivers, lakes and rain.}$$

In this way (as Putnam himself appreciated) the usual twin-earth intuitions may be somewhat reconciled with internalism. Twin-Oscar would *mean* the same as Oscar, but would *refer* to something different.

9. DEFLATIONISM

An especially prominent form of externalist view is one that explains the meaning of a word in terms of its reference, which

[44] Putnam, H. (1975), "The Meaning of "Meaning" ", in his *Mind, Language and Reality: Philosophical Papers, vol. 2.*   [45] See his *Psychosemantics.*

[46] White, S. (1991), "Narrow Content and Narrow Interpretation", in S. White (ed.), *The Unity of the Self.*

[47] Jackson, F., and Pettit, P. (1993), "Some Content is Narrow", in J. Heil and A. Mele (eds.), *Mental Causation.*

[48] Chalmers, D. (2002), "The Components of Content", in D. Chalmers (ed.), *Philosophy of Mind: Classical and Contemporary Readings.*

is then explained in terms of one or another naturalistic relation between the word and some aspect of the world (Devitt[49]). More specifically, Stampe[50] and Fodor[51] have developed (each in their own way) the idea that

$$w \text{ means } F \equiv w \text{ is causally correlated with fs,}$$

where the lower-case "f" is to be replaced by a predicate (e.g. "dog") and the capital "F" is to be replaced by a name of the concept that the predicate expresses (e.g. "DOG"). Alternatively, Millikan,[52] Dretske,[53] Papineau,[54] Neander,[55] and Jacob[56] have offered versions of the idea that

$$w \text{ means } F \equiv \text{ the (evolutionary) function of } w \text{ is to} \\ \text{indicate the presence of fs.}$$

However, a good case can be made that the relational form exemplified by all such accounts, viz.

$$w \text{ means } F \equiv R(w, f)$$

is incorrect, and that the motivation for implicitly insisting on it is defective. For the reason one might be drawn to such an account is that meaning has truth-theoretic import; if a word means DOG, then it is true of *dogs*; so sentences containing it are about *dogs*. And, in general,

$$w \text{ means } F \rightarrow (x)(w \text{ is true of } x \leftrightarrow fx).$$

But this implies—assuming some reductive analysis of 'w is true of x' as 'wCx'—that whatever constitutes the meaning-fact

---

[49] Devitt, M. (1996), *Coming To Our Senses.*

[50] Stampe, D. W. (1977), "Toward a Causal Theory of Linguistic Representation", *Midwest Studies In Philosophy* 42–63, P. French, T. Uehling, and H. Wettstein (eds.), 42–63.   [51] See his *Psychosemantics.*

[52] Millikan, R. (1984), *Language, Thought and Other Biological Categories.*

[53] Dretske, F. (1986), "Misrepresentation", in Radu Bogan (ed.), *Belief: Form, Content, and Function.* New York: Oxford University Press, 1986.

[54] Papineau, D. (1987), *Reality and Representation.*

[55] Neander, K. (1995), "Misrepresenting and Malfunctioning", *Philosophical Studies* 79: 109–41.   [56] Jacob, P. (1997), *What Minds Can Do.*

must entail '(x)(wCx ↔ fx)', and so must indeed be an instance
of the form, 'R(w, f)'. However (as we shall see in detail in
Chapter 3)[57] this line of thought is undermined by the plausibility
of *deflationism* with respect to truth and reference: namely, the
idea that these are non-naturalistic, logical notions—mere
devices of generalization. For, if that is correct, then the presumption that 'w is true of x' has some reductive analysis would be
mistaken.

Thus the import of deflationism is that we should not require
a reductive theory of meaning to have the *relational* form

$$w \text{ means } F \equiv R(w, f)$$

Nor—which comes to the same thing—should we expect,
given some proposed reductive analysis of a specific meaning-
property, to be able to *explain* why it holds (e.g. why a word
with *this* particular use must mean DOG, and must be true of
that set of objects). And nor—again equivalently—should we
require an account that will enable us to *read off* what each
word means from information about its use. Consequently, our
inability to devise a theory that does satisfy such constraints—
an inability which has been convincingly demonstrated by
Kripke,[58] Boghossian,[59] and Loewer[60]—should not tempt us
to doubt (as they do) the prospects for a reductionist account.
It should rather confirm what we might well have already
recognized—that these constraints should never have been
imposed in the first place.

The legitimate basic requirement on an adequate analysis of
a meaning-property is exactly what one would expect from
consideration of reductions elsewhere—i.e. in biology, physics,

---

[57] See also my "Meaning, Use and Truth" (1995), *Mind* 104-414, 1995,
355–68.   [58] See his *Wittgenstein: On Rules and Private Language*.
[59] Boghossian, P. (1989), "The Rule Following Considerations", *Mind*
XCVIII (392): 507–50.
[60] Loewer, B. (1997), "A Guide to Naturalizing Semantics", in B. Hale and
C. Wright (eds.), *A Companion to the Philosophy of Language*.

etc.—namely, that the alleged underlying property must contribute to explanations of the *symptoms* of the superficial property. Thus 'being magnetic' reduces to having a certain microstructure in virtue of the fact that something's possession of that microstructure explains why it exhibits the attraction–repulsion behaviour that is symptomatic of being magnetic. Similarly, 'U(w)' provides a good analysis of 'w means F' if and only if 'U(w)' contributes to explanations of the symptoms of meaning F. But the symptoms of a word's meaning F are its having a certain overall use (that of the word "f"). Therefore, 'U(w)' constitutes the meaning of "f" just in case it explains (in conjunction with extraneous factors) the differing circumstances in which all the various sentences containing "f" are accepted. And there is no reason why the satisfaction of this adequacy condition should dictate analyses that take the relational form.

10. PROMISING DIRECTIONS

The preceding survey of alternative views of meaning suggests that there are reasonable prospects for an account that is (a) non-sceptical, (b) reductive, (c) applicable to both overt and mental languages, (d) focused in the first instance on word-meaning and trivially extendable to sentence-meaning, (e) not evaluative or fundamentally regulative, (f) applicable to both communal languages and idiolects, (g) internalist, and (h) deflationist, in the sense of not having to take the form of a relational account, 'w means F $\equiv$ R(w, f)', which would incorporate a naturalistic analysis of truth.

These features are characteristic of so-called *use* theories of meaning, deriving from the work of Wittgenstein[61] and Sellars,[62] and also known as "conceptual (or functional) role semantics"

---

[61] See his *Philosophical Investigations*.
[62] Sellars, W. (1969), "Language as Thought and as Communication", *Philosophy and Phenomenological Research* 29: 506–27.

(see Field,[63] Block,[64] Harman,[65] Peacocke,[66] and Wright[67]). According to the version of it that I favour, and which will be developed in subsequent chapters, the meaning of each word, w, is engendered by its 'basic acceptance property'—that is, by the fact that w's overall use stems from the acceptance (in certain circumstances) of specified sentences containing it. A singular virtue of this proposal is that we have a plausible model— namely inference—of how such a property might, in conjunction with other factors, explain a word's *overall* use (i.e. the acceptance-facts regarding every sentence containing the word). Consequently, we can see how the just mentioned condition on an adequate account of meaning constitution might be met.

Given the enormous variety of things that are done with language, we should not expect there to be much similarity between the basic acceptance properties of different predicates. Perhaps those of colour words resemble each other to a fair degree; and similarly there could well be resemblances within species names, numerical predicates, evaluations, mental terms, etc.; but as we move from one such type to another there is likely to be a considerable divergence of structure. In particular, there is no reason to anticipate that the basic acceptance property of predicate "f" will generally have the form 'R(w, f)'. Indeed, one might question whether it *ever* will.

Nonetheless it will not be hard to account for a word's referential and normative character. We have the pair of fundamental schemata:

$$w \text{ means } F \rightarrow (x)(w \text{ is true of } x \leftrightarrow fx),$$

[63] Field, H. (1977), "Logic, Meaning and Conceptual Role", *Journal of Philosophy* 69: 379–409.

[64] Block, N. (1986), "Advertisment for a Semantics for Psychology", *Midwest Studies in Philosophy* 10, (eds.) P. French, T. Uehling, and H. Wettstein.

[65] Harman, G. (1982), "Conceptual Role Semantics", *Notre Dame Journal of Formal Logic* 28: 252–6; idem (1987), "(Non-solipsistic) Conceptual Role Semantics", in E. Lepore (ed.), *New Directions in Semantics*.

[66] Peacocke, C. (1992), *A Study of Concepts*.

[67] Wright, C. (2001), *Rails to Infinity*.

where F is what, in the present context, we mean by our predicate "f"; and

$$(x)(w \text{ is true of } x \leftrightarrow fx) \rightarrow \text{one's goal should be that}$$
of *accepting the application of w to x only if fx.*

Therefore, once we have established (on the basis of the above-mentioned adequacy condition) that a word's meaning F is constituted by its having a certain basic acceptance property, then its principal referential and normative characteristics are trivially accommodated.

Two further features of this proposal are worth emphasizing (and will be treated in greater depth in the next chapter). First it is 'non-holistic' in the sense that it incorporates an objective separation between those sentences that are held true as a matter of meaning and those sentences whose acceptance is not required by meaning alone. This anti-Quinean[68] distinction is drawn on the basis of explanatory priority: the meaning-constituting uses are those that are responsible for the others. Thus one may rebut the claim that 'use theories' inevitably lead, for better (Block,[69] Harman[70]) or for worse (Fodor and Lepore[71]), to holism. Second the theory is 'non-atomistic' in the following sense: it implies that the existence of words with certain meanings requires the existence of further words with certain different meanings. After all, the meaning of a word can be engendered by the acceptance of some particular sentence containing it only if the *other* words in that sentence are understood appropriately. This is not the extreme and implausible view (condemned by

---

[68] Quine, W. V. (1953), "Two Dogmas of Empiricism", in his *From a Logical Point of View.*

[69] Block, N. (1994–5), "An Argument for Holism", *Proceedings of the Aristotelian Society* 95: 151–69.

[70] Harman, G. (1993), "Meaning Holism Defended" in Fodor and Lepore 1993a, *Holism: A Consumer Update Grazer, Philosophische Studien* 46: 163–71.

[71] Fodor, L., and Lepore, E. (1991), *Holism.*

Dummett[72]) that the meaning of every word depends on the meanings of every other word in the language. What is required, rather, is that there be a limited stock of interrelated basic meanings on which all others asymmetrically depend.

11. FURTHER PROBLEMS

This introductory survey provides no more than the briefest of discussions of some of the many important issues and options confronting a theorist of the nature of meaning. And those dimensions of controversy that I have mentioned are merely the most central ones; there are others that have not yet been considered, but which any satisfactory account must come to grips with. Let me end by listing four of them that will be taken up in the next chapter.

(I) It is not unnatural to think that whenever a word is used the speaker invests it with a certain meaning, and that if he uses the same word (i.e. sound-type) on another occasion, then he may or may not decide to invest it with the same meaning. It may seem, therefore, that the meaning of an unambiguous word-*type* should be explained in terms of the uniform meaning given to its various *tokens*; similarly the meanings of *ambiguous* word–types should be explained in terms of the several meanings distributed amongst its tokens. But this tempting picture is at odds with the various accounts we have been considering. For example, according to Fodor's theory, the meaning of a type is engendered by a causal correlation between its tokens and exemplifications of a certain property. And the other accounts also attribute meaning, in the first instance, to word-types. Thus we must address the following couple of questions. Can there be a reductive account (perhaps a modification of one of those discussed above) that applies initially to word-*tokens*? And if, on

---

[72] Dummett, M. (1991), *The Logical Basis of Metaphysics*.

the contrary, *type*-meaning is indeed primary, then how—given the phenomenon of *ambiguity*—are we to account for the meanings of specific *tokens*?

(II) We have been concentrating on our notion of 'the meaning of a word in a given language'. But there are other meanings of "meaning" that also stand in need of explication, especially:

(a) *What the speaker means* on a given occasion by some word—where this is some temporary modification of its meaning in the language as a whole. The notion of meaning in which "The President" may be used, in virtue of the speaker's local intentions, to mean "The current President of France".

(b) *What is said*, in a given context, by the utterance of some sentence, *the proposition expressed* by a sentence-token. The notion of meaning in which "I am hungry" means different things depending, *not* on the speaker's intentions, but on *who* is speaking, and on *when* the utterance is performed.

(c) *The conventional pragmatic content* of a term, its *illocutionary force* (going beyond the *de dicto* propositional constituent that is expressed by it). The respect of meaning in which "but" differs from "and", and in which "I promise to go" engenders a specific obligation.

(d) *The full information conveyed* by the making of a given utterance, i.e. its 'conversational implicature', that which the hearer may infer from the speaker's deciding, in the circumstances, to say what he does. The respect of meaning in which "There's no milk left" can mean "Would you buy some?".

(e) *The non-literal meanings* of an expression, including metaphorical and ironic meanings.

It is not implausible that the kind of meaning on which I have been focusing here (and on which I will continue to focus in subsequent chapters) is fundamental, i.e. that the other kinds are best explained in terms of it. But this assumption may be justified only on the basis of defensible concrete proposals (Grice,[73] Sperber and Wilson,[74] Neale,[75] Recanati[76]).

(III) On the face of it, an expression's having a certain meaning consists in its standing in the relation, 'x means y', to an entity of a special kind—a meaning-entity. Consequently, one would expect a reductive theory of any particular meaning-fact to be the product of two more basic theories: first, an analysis of the general meaning-relation; and second, an analysis of the particular meaning-entity involved. But it is not obvious how to square this expectation with any of the reductive proposals discussed above, since they do not appear to be divisible into components of this sort. In light of this tension, it would seem that at least one of the following theses must be defended: (1) that meaning-facts do not in fact have the just-mentioned apparent structure; or (2) that their reduction does not in fact require analyses of their constituents; or (3) that some form of non-semantic 'grounding' of them, weaker than reduction, is the most that can be expected; or (4) that certain analysantia of the sort considered above (e.g. that such-and-such sentences containing w are accepted underived) can in fact be factored into one part that analyses the meaning-relation and another that analyses a particular meaning-entity. In the next chapter I will be defending a version of the fourth strategy: meaning-entities are identified with basic acceptance properties, and the meaning-relation is reduced to the relation of exemplification between words and those properties.

(IV) According to Quine's thesis of radical indeterminacy there are few foreign expressions whose correct translations into English are grounded in objective facts. But even if Quine is

---

[73] Grice, P. (1989), *Studies in the Way of Words*.
[74] Sperber, D., and Wilson, D., *Relevance*.
[75] Neale, S. (2003), *Descriptions* idem, "This, That, and the Other".
[76] Recanati, F. (2004), *Literal Meaning*.

99 per cent wrong (for the reasons mentioned in section 2), it may be that the correct translations of *some* expressions are nonetheless indeterminate. For example, Brandom[77] and Field[78] have argued that a language's words for the two square-roots of minus one may be used so similarly that there will be no properties that might constitute the distinctive meaning of one of them (and thereby constitute its translation into "i" rather than "−i") that are not also possessed by the other. But any such prospect is a threat to semantic reductionism. For it is not easy to see how that doctrine, in any of its specific forms, can be reconciled with the concession that there is even a *single* term whose meaning is not constituted by non-semantic facts.

What is plain from the above review is that research into the nature of meaning must confront a formidable cluster of interlocking problems. I would suggest, however, that if we adopt the neo-Wittgensteinian use-theoretic perspective outlined in section 10, a coherent network of plausible solutions to them may be found. My hope for the following chapters is to vindicate this conjecture.[79]

[77] Brandom, R. (1996), "The Significance of Complex Numbers for Frege's Philosophy of Mathematics', *Proceedings of the Aristotelian Society* 293–315.
[78] Field, H. (1998), 'Some Thoughts on Radical Indeterminacy', *The Monist* 81: 253–73.
[79] I am grateful to Ned Block, Tim Crane, Michael Devitt, Stephen Schiffer, and Barry C. Smith for their comments on a draft of this chapter.

2

A Use Theory of Meaning

How should we go about trying to identify which particular non-semantic property of a given word is responsible for its meaning? And what sort of property will that turn out to be? The use theory, as I want to develop it (UTM), offers answers to these questions. It begins by contending that the meaning of a word is the common factor in the explanations of its numerous occurrences, and proceeds to argue that the underlying basis of each word's meaning is the (idealized) law governing its usage— a law that dictates the 'acceptance conditions' of certain specified sentences containing it.

For the sake of concreteness (but only to a first approximation) here are some examples of the sort of meaning-constitution claim that issues from UTM:

> "true" means what it does to us in virtue of the fact that the law governing its use is that we are prepared to provisionally accept any instance of the schema, "<p> is true ↔ p".

> "bachelor"'s meaning is engendered by the fact that its basic regularity of use is our acceptance of the sentence, "The bachelors are the unmarried men."

> "red"'s meaning stems from the fact that its law of use is a propensity to accept "That is red" in response to the sort of visual experience normally provoked by observing a clearly red surface.

The meaning of "water" is constituted by the fact that the law explaining its overall use is that we accept, "x is water ↔ x has the underlying nature of the stuff in *our* seas, rivers, lakes and rain."

"neutrino" means what it does in virtue of our unsupported acceptance of the conditional, "$\exists\phi T(\phi) \Rightarrow T(\text{neutrino})$", where "$T(\text{neutrino})$" is a formulation of neutrino theory.

"and" means what it does because the fundamental regularity in its use is our acceptance of the two-way argument schema, "p, q // p and q".[1]

These illustrations may strike some critics as too varied in structure to be part of a simple, attractive theory. And it is true that most accounts of meaning in the literature are more uniform. But I will be suggesting that the proper place for uniformity is that every word's meaning-constituting property be the 'law of use' for that word; and that it is a dangerous misconception to presuppose that all such laws must have the same shape.[2]

In light of the particular constitution claims that it directs us towards, UTM shows how semantic phenomena arise within a fundamentally non-semantic world. In earlier work I have sketched such a theory, together with arguments in favour of it

---

[1] Note that a prima facie reasonable objection to some of these particular proposals is that they fail to accommodate the possibility of speakers who, while fully understanding the word in question, do not conform to the specified acceptance-law because they don't think that there exists any property (or entity) that could make it correct to accept the designated sentences. (For example, someone might understand the word "true" yet deny that there is a single property, f-ness, which any proposition, <p>, possesses if and only if p). The force of this objection is assessed in Chapter 6. When it is valid—and I shall argue that it nearly always is—the remedy is to *conditionalize* the proposal (as has already been done in the "neutrino" case). The meaning-constituting property—instead of taking the form 'being governed by the acceptance-law, L('f')'—will then be something like this: 'having the disposition, conditional on there being *some* term w for which L(w) is the governing law, for that law to be L("f")'.

[2] For further discussion of this point see chap. 3.

and defences against a broad variety of objections.[3] The purpose of the present chapter is to improve that account and to respond to some of the criticism it has provoked.

I will start with a short crude statement of UTM's two-pronged central thesis. Then I will go one by one through the elements of this initial formulation, explaining how each of them is supposed to be understood.

(a) **The meaning of a word, w,** is engendered by the non-semantic feature of w that explains w's overall deployment. And this will be an acceptance-property of the following form:— 'that such-and-such w-sentences are regularly accepted in such-and-such circumstances' is the idealized law governing w's use is (by the relevant 'experts', given certain meanings attached to various other words).

The focus here is on the *literal semantic* meaning of a word-type[4] within a given language. This is the sense of meaning in which "I" has a *single* meaning in English, the same one that "Ich" has in German; in which "and" and "but" possess a common meaning, whilst diverging in pragmatic import; in which "everyone" covers *all* people, although a speaker may use it to 'mean', in a different sense, "everyone present", or "everyone in Boston", etc.; in which "She's a genius" does *not* mean either "She's incompetent" or "Let's give her the job", although there certainly are other brands of meaning relative to which it can 'mean' one or the other of these things.

Of course one would wish, eventually, to be able to treat all those additional forms of meaning too, i.e. propositional content, truth conditions, reference, speaker's intended meaning, conventional pragmatic import, conversational implicature, metaphor, irony, etc. But UTM does not itself supply theories of them. The most that can be plausibly claimed is that insofar we find

---

[3] See *Meaning*, particularly chap. 3, "Meaning as Use".

[4] Including prefixes and other morphemes. Note that the types to which I am referring are individuated non-semantically, e.g. in terms of their sounds or shapes.

ourselves in possession of an adequate account of literal semantic meaning we will be well placed to devise theories of these further interrelated phenomena. For one might well suppose that the propositional contents (hence, satisfaction conditions) of our thoughts, including our intentions, are determined by the literal semantic meanings of the sentences formulating them (plus a contextual fixing of the referents of demonstratives and indexicals); that the other brands of meaning apply to public expressions alone; and that they do so in virtue of our *intentions* concerning what thoughts to communicate and how best to do it. Thus all forms of meaning would rest on literal semantic meaning.[5]

Note that UTM deals, in the first instance, with *unambiguous* word types—with sounds (and marks and gestures and mental symbols) that possess a single literal semantic meaning. But the theory is easily broadened. A word type's having more than one meaning will consist in the need for more than one non-semantic ground, i.e. more than one basic acceptance property, in the explanations of when and why tokens of that type occur. And the meaning of an individual token is fixed by the particular basic acceptance property to which its occurrence is linked. Such a link may be *explanatory*, as when I accept "John is at the bank" *because* I accept "John went for a swim in the river" and "A side of a river is a bank" (whose acceptance is meaning-constituting). Or the link may be a matter of *inferential association*, as when I continue my train of thought with "If John is at the bank, then either he is at the bank or in a café", "Therefore he is either at the bank or in a café", where I fix the

---

[5] The various forms of meaning were distinguished in section 11 of chap. 1. And the relationship between literal semantic meaning and truth conditions (including reference conditions) is addressed in chap. 3.

For accounts of some of the other notions, see *Meaning*, chap. 3. There is a discussion in section 12 of that chapter of how the literal semantic meaning of a given sentence, given the context in which it is produced, determines which propositions (*de dicto*, *de re*, and *de se*) are expressed by the sentence. And the distinction between semantic meaning and conventional pragmatic import is treated in section 22.

meaning of the two tokens of "bank" which occur in the logical truth by combining them in inference with another token (of the same type) whose meaning has been fixed independently, via its explanatory link with a certain basic acceptance property.

If a language of thought is assumed, we can suppose that a token of an ambiguous *public* expression-type means what it does in virtue of the particular expression *in thought* with which it is associated. As for how we should deal with ambiguity *within* the language of thought, one option is to invoke the strategy just sketched. Another is to suppose that there couldn't be any ambiguous *mental* expressions. After all, when the mind encounters two tokens of the same mental symbol, how would it be able to 'tell' whether or not they can be connected in inference? Thus we might suppose, for example, that the sound "bank" is associated with two terms in thought, perhaps "bank1" and "bank2".[6]

There is no reason not to allow (as just indicated) that the word-types whose meanings are explained by UTM may be in *any* language, including languages of thought. For in order that a word, w, be meaningful (according to UTM) it suffices that there be *basic* regularities governing the acceptance of sentences containing it (which will presumably exist whenever there is an acceptance practice involving w). And, in order for a sentence, u, to be *accepted* by a person, it suffices that the mental sentence that u expresses (i.e. the mental sentence that is correlated with u by his 'language faculty') be in his belief box—i.e. be *relied upon*, be deployed as a premises in theoretical and practical inferences.[7]

Thus I am against certain 'two stage' accounts—most prominently, the approach that would take the meanings of *mental*

---

[6] For further discussion see chap. 7, fn 14.

[7] Note the important degenerate case in which a *mental* sentence, m, is accepted—where the 'correlated' sentence in the belief box is m *itself*. Stephen Schiffer has expressed a concern that this feature makes my account of acceptance—and hence of meaning—unattractively *disjunctive*; giving it the form, "x is accepted ↔ either x or R(x) is in the belief box". But notice that we are often quite contented with theories possessing an analogous disjunctive character, e.g. "x is a number ↔ x is 0, or x is the successor of a number". Moreover, as unwelcome as this feature may be it nonetheless yields a theory that is simpler and better than

terms to be relatively fundamental, that would somehow explain (e.g. informationally, teleologically, or use-theoretically) how these facts arise, and that would then add, following Grice, that a *public* term's having a certain literal meaning consists in there being an intention or convention to use it to communicate a certain concept, i.e. to express a mental term with that meaning.[8] Instead, I favour a *uniform* account, which will deal in the same way with both overt and mental terms. My reasons, in a nutshell, are: (i) that insofar as a public expression and its mental correlate have exactly the same meaning, then their having that meaning must be constituted in exactly the same way; (ii) that conventional agreements about how concepts are to be expressed could be reached only with the help of meaningful public language, and so cannot constitute it; (iii) that automatic causal correlations between public words and their mental correlates are established in infancy, as a result of training rather than agreement; (iv) that such connections are especially intimate (and obviously non-intentional) if, as is likely, a person's language of thought is predominantly the same (but in mental form) as his public language; (v) that the central Gricean principle (which associates the meaning of a sentence with the belief it expresses) can be acknowledged as *correct* without being

the Gricean model that we are about to consider, according to which literal semantic meaning in a public language and literal semantic meaning in a language of thought are two separate phenomena.

The characterization of 'acceptance' with which I am working presupposes that a person's *thinking* takes place in a language—either in a mental version of his public idiolect, or in a universal Mentalese. But this assumption, though convenient and highly plausible, is not strictly required by UTM. We might say instead (roughly) that a public sentence is *accepted* by a person if his disposition to utter it is correlated with his being in a mental/neural state that grounds one of his premises in theoretical and practical reasoning.

8 This sort of two-stage, neo-Gricean picture may be found in the work of Jerry Fodor (e.g. "Language, Thought and Compositionality"), Stephen Schiffer (e.g. *The Things We Mean*), Brian Loar (1981), Stephen Neale (e.g. "This, That, and the Other"), Dan Sperber and Deidre Wilson (e.g. *Relevance*). The *locus classicus* is Paul Grice's "Meaning", although Grice himself does not subscribe to a language-of-thought account of mental states.

regarded as an articulation of the *nature* of public language meaning; and (vi) that on those atypical occasions in which meanings *are* instituted by agreement, this is because the agreement establishes a meaning-constituting use.

These considerations are elaborated in an Appendix to this chapter. I think they provide a strong case against the two-level approach. But notice that even if I am wrong here, this would scarcely diminish the potential importance of UTM. For the more puzzling of the two levels would surely be the realm of facts about mental content; and these, I would suggest, are to be explained in terms of the use theory of meaning.

(b) The meaning of a word, w, **is engendered by** the non-semantic feature of w that explains w's overall deployment. And this will be an acceptance-property of the following form:— 'that such-and-such w-sentences are regularly accepted in such-and-such circumstances' is the idealized law governing w's use is (by the relevant 'experts', given certain meanings attached to various other words).

A word means what it does, according to UTM, *in virtue of* its basic use; a word's use is *responsible* for its meaning what it does. Thus, not only does a meaning-property *supervene* on a basic acceptance property, but possession of the former is *immediately explained* by possession of the latter.

Are we to suppose, moreover, that meaning-properties *reduce to*, i.e. *are constituted from*, use-properties? Or perhaps even that these properties are *identical*? A look at how such notions are deployed outside the domain of semantics, suggests that we may well say these further things. In general, when properties U and S are co-extensive, the main import of claiming that S reduces to U is that features of S are explained by their co-extensivity. So, we judge that 'being a sample of water' *reduces* to 'being made of H_2O molecules', not merely because we find that they are possessed by the same bodies of stuff, but because that fact explains why water is transparent, boils at 100 degrees Centigrade, etc. And in a similar way we can, for example, conclude that the property of 'meaning TRUE' reduces to (or is constituted from) a given use-property: we observe that the same words have them and we find that this fact explains the circumstances in which sentences containing "true", "vrai", etc., are accepted.

Moreover, we are at perfect liberty to deploy, as well, a more coarse-grained ('thicker') conception of PROPERTY—one whose *identity* conditions resemble the above-mentioned *constitution* conditions of fine-grained properties:

> S-ness and U-ness are the same PROPERTY
> IF
>
> (1) S-ness and U-ness are exemplified by the same things; and
> (2) The correlations between S-ness and the various properties that are symptomatic of it are explained by (1).

Accordingly, just as we sometimes say that being water *is* being made of H_2O, we might, in the same sense, *identify* thick meaning-PROPERTIES with certain use-PROPERTIES.

But now consider facts of the form

> w means k to S,

where w is a word, k is a meaning, and S is a person (or a community). One might wish to know not merely how such *facts* are constituted, which is the question we have just addressed. In addition one might well wonder how the *components* of these facts are constituted. Specifically, (Q1) what kinds of things are the meaning-*entities*, k? And (Q2) what is the nature of the triadic meaning-*relation*, "w means k to S"?

The answers that I would suggest to these two further questions are

> (A1) Meaning-entities are universals—in particular, they are *use*-properties.
> (A2) w means k to S ≡ S's w exemplifies k.

Thus UTM's claim, that to have a certain meaning is to exemplify a certain use-property, might be factored into an analysis of 'means' as 'exemplifies', and an analysis of meanings as use-properties. The idea is that just as a flower has a colour and a stick has a length, so a sound has a meaning; just as colours and lengths are properties, meanings are also properties. Therefore the logical form of a simple meaning-fact is '$M(w_s)$', which entails 'S's w has (or exemplifies) the property of M-ness'. And each such property, M-ness, reduces to a use-property.

These answers are better, I think, than the ones I gave in *Meaning* (pp. 19–20). There I suggested that the meaning-entities might be ordinary properties (e.g. that the meaning of "dog" is the property of *being a dog*) and that 'w means k to S' might be analysed as 'w indicates the presence in S's thought of k'. But that proposal suffers from the following pair of difficulties. First, what could be the import of saying that a certain *mental* term of S's *indicates the presence in his thought* of a certain property, except to say that the term *means* that property? So the account is circular. And, second, the identification of meanings with ordinary properties has a certain prima facie plausibility only in the case of *predicates* (indeed, only those that are context-insensitive), and it is far from clear how to extend it to terms that do not fall into that rather narrow category.[9]

Although I think it is wrong to be constantly insisting on reductive analysis, I do not believe—in light of (A1) and (A2)—that

---

[9] Schiffer ("Horwich on *Meaning*") has objected that since meaning-properties of the form 'S's w means k' are relations to abstract entities and a use-properties are not, they cannot be identical. But my present proposal, in (A1) and (A2), is to identify meaning-properties with *exemplifications of use properties*, which *are* relations to abstract entities. Moreover, his objection does not succeed against my earlier proposal either. For, relative to the coarse-grained notion of PROPERTY, it is not obvious what would make such a thing relational; we might well decide to say that a PROPERTY is relational whenever *some* concept that stands for it is relational. But in that case Schiffer's second premiss (to the effect that the use-PROPERTY is not relational) would be false. Or we might decide that whether a PROPERTY is to qualify as relational depends on the structure of the *most fundamental* concept that stands for it. But in that case we can't accept Schiffer's other premiss (to the effect that meaning-PROPERTIES *are* relational).

meaning-properties provide illustrations of that error. Nonetheless, there are some genuine and important illustrations of it in the offing—namely, the urge to analyze truth-theoretic properties (such as "w is true of dogs"). Knee-jerk reductionism would lead us to expect that these will be analyzed via a reduction of the common component, 'w is true of x' (to 'wCx'). And since 'w means F' entails '(x)(w is true of x ↔ fx)', we would then be led to expect (in order to square with that entailment) that what constitutes 'w means F' must take the form 'Pw & (x)(wCx ↔ fx)'—e.g. a word would mean DOG in virtue of standing in this relation to *dogs*.[10] Moreover, if that were so, then any predicate's extension could be *read-off* its meaning-constituting property, and we would be in a position to *explain* why any given meaning-constituting property engenders the particular extension it does. However, as Kripke first made plausible, we will not in fact be able to find meaning-constituting properties of that particular relational form! So we won't be able to find meaning-constituting properties on the basis of which we can read off and explain the meanings of the words that possess those properties. That result led him to doubt the possibility of non-semantic analyses of meaning-properties. But this conclusion is unwarranted, since the reasoning that leads up it goes wrong at the outset in presupposing that there is some naturalistic analysis of 'w is true of x'. Instead, the proper morals to draw are to beware of that mistake ('inflationism') and hence of the alleged requirement that meaning-constituting properties need to take the form that would permit the meanings they constitute to be read off and explained. A distinctive feature of UTM is its incorporation of these important morals.[11]

[10] The conjunct "Pw" is needed in order to capture the fact that co-extensional predicates may differ in meaning—that what constitutes w's meaning entails, but is not entailed by, what constitutes its truth-condition.

[11] See S. Kripke, *Wittgenstein on Rules and Private Language*. The above paragraph compresses a complex line of thought. For a proper presentation of it see chap. 3, "The Pseudo-Problem of Error". See also chaps. 4 and 10 of *Meaning*.

(c) The meaning of a word, w, is engendered by **the non-semantic feature of w** that explains w's overall deployment. And this will be an acceptance-property of the following form:—'that such-and-such w-sentences are regularly accepted in such-and-such circumstances' is the idealized law governing w's use is (by the relevant 'experts', given certain meanings attached to various other words).

For each meaning-property, UTM tells us how to find a particular non-semantic use-property such that anything's possession of the former is grounded in its possession of the latter. Thus UTM is a form of reductionism. However, the reason for being attracted to this feature of the theory need not be some gut metaphysical conviction that *all* facts *must* be grounded in physical (or 'naturalistic') phenomena. Rather, what motivates the search for a theory like UTM is that it promises certain explanatory advantages over wholly non-reductionist accounts. Specifically, it has the potential to explain why it is that meaning a certain thing by a word is manifested in characteristic ways of using the word[12]; and it will also be able to show how a fundamentally material world gives rise to semantic phenomena. And these are desirable results, even if one is not a diehard physicalist or naturalist. Of course, the benefits that might be derived from a particular reductionist theory can be genuine only if the theory is correct. So the real test of whether meanings can and should be reduced to non-semantic phenomena lies in the assessment of specific proposals of that form, such as UTM.

---

[12] If there were no such explanation, we would have to conclude, surprisingly, either (a) that some of our linguistic activity—our acceptance of sentences—has no complete non-semantic cause (so the realm of non-semantic phenomena would not be explanatorily autonomous); or (b) that this activity is weirdly over-determined (—caused independently both by what we mean and by certain non-semantic states); or (c) that our uses of words do not, contrary to what we naively think, result in part from what we mean by them.

Note, by the way, that 'non-semantic' does not amount to 'physical', or even 'behavioral'. It is intended to preclude accounts of meaning based on concepts like:

> w is used to *refer* to dogs
>
> w is used to express the *belief* about something that it is a dog
>
> w is used with the *intention* of getting the listener to recognize that the speaker believes of something that it is a dog
>
> . . . and so on

That is, it is intended to avoid circularity by excluding from the analyzing-properties anything that would itself require analysis in terms of meaning. But this leaves open accounts of meaning in *psychological* terms (as long as they are not semantic), including the crucial notion of 'accepting a sentence.'[13]

(d) The meaning of a word, w, is engendered by the non-semantic feature of w **that explains w's overall deployment**. And this will be an acceptance-property of the following form:—'that such-and-such w-sentences are regularly accepted in such-and-such circumstances' is the idealized law governing w's use is (by the relevant 'experts', given certain meanings attached to various other words).

By "the overall deployment of w", I have in mind the multitude of facts of the following sort:

(A) that S accepts certain sentences containing w (or would counterfactually accept them in certain circumstances);

(B) that certain w-sentences (or their mentalese correlates) articulate S's desires (i.e. appear in S's "want-box") in certain circumstances;

---

[13] For more on what justifies the assumption, vital to UTM's reductive aspirations, that *acceptance* (in my technical sense) is not a semantic notion, see *Meaning*, 94–6, where I sketch an account of theoretical and practical reasoning, which implicitly defines acceptance in terms of its role in these activities.

(C) that those of S's decisions that are articulated using w
(i.e. that are constituted by appearances in S's "decision-
box" of the mental correlates of sentences containing w)
have a characteristic behavioral import.

According to UTM, there is a unique non-semantic property of
w that figures in the best explanations of these facts about w;
and this property is what provides the word with its meaning.[14]

Thus UTM's answer to the rhetorical Quinean question,
"How can we possibly draw an objective line around which particular facts about a word engender its meaning?" is simply this.
Our project is to associate with each word a single non-semantic
characteristic such that when these characteristics of the various
words in a language are taken together, and when they are combined with other *non-semantic* facts that do not concern specific
words, e.g. facts about the environment and about human psychology, we are able to explain all the various phenomena of the
form (A), (B), and (C). And there is no reason to expect that the
results of such an investigation will typically be indeterminate,
although they might sometimes be.[15]

The term "holism" is sometimes used for the radical doctrine
that *any* variation in the overall use of a word—the *slightest* change
in which sentences containing it are accepted—makes *some* difference to its meaning. This doctrine is certainly contrary to ordinary
talk about meaning, and is embraced only by those who see no

---

[14] The need for meaning-constitution properties to explain, not merely the
acceptance-facts of type (A), but also desire-facts and action-facts of types (B)
and (C), was impressed on me by Michael Devitt. However, this observation,
though correct and important, does not necessarily provide an *additional*
constraint on the identification of meaning-constituting properties, since (as
I argue in section (e)) it may well be that the desire-facts and action-facts will be
explained by whatever explains the acceptance-facts.

[15] Quine's sceptical point (from "Two Dogmas of Empiricism", in *From a
Logical Point of View*) is pressed by Allan Gibbard in his "Horwich on Meaning"
(unpublished manuscript, 2002). How are we to identify the basic acceptance
property of Jonah's word "dag", and thereby to find out whether it means FISH,
or SWIMBEAST, or nothing determinate? Well the plausible alternatives for which

prospect of a decent response to Quine's sceptical challenge. A virtue of UTM is that it enables us to avoid this particular form of holism. (Although, as we will see in section (i), there is a different type of 'holism', namely, 'meaning-interdependence', which, to a limited degree, is required by UTM.)

Why should we think that the property of a word that accounts, for its overall usage is what constitutes its meaning? Because, in general, questions about the underlying nature of a phenomenon are answered by finding out what explains general facts about that phenomenon, including the ways in which it is typically manifested. And the meaning of a word issues in, and is revealed by, a certain overall use. More specifically, support for the first part of UTM—the thesis that

> the meaning of a word is engendered by the non-semantic property that explains its overall deployment.

derives from the simple way in which it accounts for a range of prominent facts about meaning, namely,

(1) the role of attributions of meaning in the explanation of sentence-acceptance, inference, and non-linguistic behaviour;

sentence is the one whose acceptance provides the meaning of "dag" would seem to be (Hebrew translations of) something like either

(1) "x is a dag ↔ x has the internal structure and reproductive power of most animals streamlined for underwater swimming"

or

(2) "x is a dag ↔ x is an animal streamlined for underwater swimming."

In order to decide between them, we must consider what Jonah would have said if he had come to believe that there are creatures (e.g. whales) that, while being animals streamlined for underwater swimming, do not have the internal structure and reproductive power that is common to the great majority of such animals. If he would have abandoned (2) and continued to accept (1), then that would indicate that (1) provides the meaning of "dag"; but (1), once we have replaced "dag" with "fish", is plausibly what provides "fish" with its meaning; so "dag" means FISH. If, on the other hand, he would have abandoned (1) and continued to accept (2), that would indicate that (2) provides the meaning of "dag"; so it means SWIMBEAST. And if it is indeterminate what he would have done, that would indicate that it is indeterminate which of these two meanings "dag" has.

(2) the epistemological import of these phenomena for the confirmation of attributions of meaning;

(3) the fact that acceptance is preserved under inter-substitution of terms with the same meaning;[16]

(4) the utility of translation manuals, i.e. of knowing the meanings of another person's words.

These phenomena are explained along the following lines. Fact (1) stems trivially from the first part of UTM. Fact (2) is then to be expected, since we can reasonably infer to the best explanation of overall usage. Regarding fact (3): given that words v and w have the same overall-use-explainer, if the sentence #(v) is accepted in certain circumstances, then whatever explains that will also determine that #(w) is accepted in those circumstances. And as for fact (4): if translations were not based on preserving overall-use-explainers, then we could not, as we in fact do, give a foreign utterance the very same behavioural and environmental import that we would give, at home, to the translation of that utterance.

The most telling of these explanations is the fourth one, since it concerns the most obvious characteristic of meaning—the property that provides the raison d'etre of our concept—namely, that our beliefs about the meanings of a foreigner's expressions function in a specific way in our interactions with him, and that the correctness of such beliefs facilitates the success of those interactions. UTM accounts for these phenomena; it does so in virtue of explaining fact (3); and it is able to do that, and also to account for fact (2), because it (trivially) yields fact (1).

But what is it to *accept* a sentence? As already indicated I have in mind something like Quine's 'disposition to assent' and Davidson's 'holding true' (but minus their behaviourism!): namely, the psychological (but non-semantic) relation to a

---

[16] For a discussion of apparent counter-examples due to Mates and Kripke, see *Meaning* 100–1.

sentence that is manifested in our relying on it as a premise in theoretical and practical inference. A picturesque way of explicating this idea is to say that S accepts a sentence just in case that sentence, or its mental correlate, is in S's belief box.[17]

Insofar as we can explain which sentences containing w are *accepted*, we should then be well poised to explain which sentences are *uttered*; for linguistic behaviour results in part from what is accepted. However, there are various further causal factors involved in utterance, including what the speaker wishes to express, how he wishes to express it, and the distinctive pragmatic characters of words that render their use appropriate on particular occasions given the speaker's desires. Therefore, since UTM merely aims to specify how the *literal semantic* meanings of words are constituted, and not their pragmatic meanings, the explanatory scope of the meaning-constituting properties it postulates does not include overt linguistic behaviour, but merely the phenomenon of sentence-acceptance and its import for action.

Anil Gupta has suggested that what engenders our understanding of a word should *not* be identified with the thing that explains the word's overall use.[18] For we accept many things on the basis of *testimony*: we might accept "p" because we accept "S accepts 'p'" and "S is reliable". And in such a case nothing that we could plausibly take to be constituting our understanding of "p" is involved in our acceptance of it. In response, however, it should be noted that UTM does not demand of a word's

---

[17] Note that in the normal case, when we are dealing with a person who thinks, speaks, and writes all in the same natural language, it may be convenient to regard a correlated sound, inscription, and mental symbol, as versions of a single expression, and to speak of a sentence (in whatever form) as being in the belief box just in case the mental form of it is there.

Gibbard ("Horwich on Meaning") rightly observes that our basic use of a word might also involve the *rejection* of certain sentences containing it, where rejection goes beyond mere non-acceptance. For example, I suspect that the meaning of "not" is engendered in part by our underived practice of rejecting "not p" to the extent that we accept "p". See my *Truth*, 71–3, and Ian Rumfitt's "Yes and No", *Mind*, vol. 109.436.

[18] A. Gupta, "Deflationism, the Problem of Representation, and Horwich's Use Theory of Meaning", *Philosophy and Phenomenological Research*.

meaning-constituting property that it be a cause of *every* acceptance fact regarding that word. Rather, the requirement (to account for overall use) is holistic: the totality of meaning-constituting properties, together with other facts that do not concern particular words, should permit the explanation of all the acceptance phenomena. (For example, our acceptance of "It's either red or not" is explained in part by the meanings of "or" and "not", but not at all by the meaning of "red"). Therefore it is not required by UTM that someone's acceptance of "p" on the basis of testimony be derived from what provides her understanding of it. Nonetheless, it is worth noting that in normal cases of testimony those meaning-constituting properties *will* play an explanatory role. For normally the listener does not blindly and permanently accept what she hears. Rather, she makes some independent assessment of how plausible the statement is, including, how her informant might have acquired evidence for it. And she is continually prepared to revise her initial acceptance in light of her own observations. Both these normal concomitants of acceptance-on-hearsay will typically depend on her understanding of the words involved.

(e)   The meaning of a word, w, is engendered by the non-semantic feature of w that explains w's overall deployment. **And this will be an acceptance-property** of the following form:—'that such-and-such w-sentences are regularly accepted in such-and-such circumstances' is the idealized law governing w's use is (by the relevant 'experts', given certain meanings attached to various other words).

Having specified, in its first part, how to go about identifying the meaning-constituting property of a word, the second part of UTM proceeds to take a stand on what sort of property that will turn out to be. The proposal is that the *overall* use of a word is best explained by a certain *core* use, by the acceptance of a certain narrow set of sentences containing it. This proposal owes its plausibility to the availability of a familiar *inferential model* that enables us to see very easily how such explanations would go. For it is clear how a basic propensity to accept certain sentences in certain conditions might, given environmental circumstances and the deployment of rules of inference, naturally bring about the acceptance of other sentences.[19]

Michael Devitt has alleged that this second component of UTM is not in fact well supported, because there is an equally plausible alternative view of which properties best explain the overall uses of words. He is thinking of his own so-called 'truth-referential' account of meaning-constitution, an account whereby each meaning-property, e.g. 'w means DOG', is taken to be constituted from a truth theoretic-property, e.g. '(x)(w is

---

[19] One might object that there is a certain inconsistency between, on the one hand, our supposing the meaning-constituting property of a word to be whichever of its features explains the word's overall use, but, on the other hand, our identifying that feature with a specific fact about the word's use. For since nothing can conceivably explain itself, that fact will not be able to explain *all* the facts concerning the word's use. The moral to be drawn from this tension, it seems to me, is that our initial intuition—that (subject to the 'holism' proviso mentioned at the end of section (d)) *all* the use-facts concerning a word are explained by its meaning—should be given up. The truth of the matter is that *almost* all of w's use-facts are explained, in part, by w's meaning—all but one. So it is hardly surprising that the more general intuition should have seemed compelling.

In addition it might be objected that insofar as someone's accepting a public sentence p_k consists in the presence in her belief box of a correlated mental sentence m_k, then the acceptance of one public sentence can never explain the acceptance of another. For, although m_1's presence in Mary's belief box might bring about m_2's presence there, thereby constituting her acceptance of p_2, her accepting p_1 would play no role in explaining these events. And one might then conclude that UTM cannot work as a theory of meaning for *public* language terms, but only (at best) as a theory of meaning for *mental* terms. But consider an analogous case. Surely, the fact that Mary has whatever kind of DNA engenders blonde hair is *explained* (in some sense) by the fact that her parents have that sort of DNA. And, in the same sense, the fact that Mary has in her belief box whichever mental sentence correlates with p_1 *explains* the fact that she also has there whichever mental sentence correlates with p_2. But Mary's acceptance of a public sentence is nothing other that the state of there being in her belief box a correlated mental sentence. Therefore her acceptance of p_1 does explain her acceptance of p_2.

true of x ↔ x is a dog)', which is in turn reduced to something non-semantic, e.g. '(x)(w Cx ↔ w is a dog)'.[20]

However, there are two things to be said against Devitt's allegation. In the first place, a good case can be made that any adequate version of truth-referentialism would itself qualify as a use-theory of meaning and so would not necessarily be in conflict with the sort of account offered by UTM. But, in the second place, the special form of use-theory that is characteristic of truth-referentialism presupposes commitments that we have no reason to make.

To elaborate: if the basic meaning-constituting properties postulated by truth-referentialism are to account for overall usage (as Devitt acknowledges they must), they are likely to have to be articulated in terms of 'sentence acceptance'. For only then can the above-mentioned inferential model be exploited, and no other model has been suggested for how we might explain what needs to be explained. Moreover, a truth-referential theory *can* be so articulated, i.e. a theory in which the naturalistic analysis of each meaning-property emerges from a preliminary analysis of it in terms of truth/referential characteristics and then a further reduction of those in terms of acceptance-conditions. The result will be something like this:

> *For substantive primitive predicates:*
> w is a colour term $\Rightarrow$
>> [w means F $\equiv$ P^{j}w & (x) (We would, in condition
>> I^1, accept the application of w to x ↔ fx)].
>
> w is an animal term $\Rightarrow$
>> [w means F $\equiv$ P^{k}w & (x) (We would, in condition
>> I^2, accept the application of w to x ↔ fx)]
>
> . . . and so on.

---

[20] See Devitt's "Meaning and Use", *Philosophy and Phenomenological Research*. For a fuller exposition and defense of truth-referentialism see his *Coming to Our Senses*.

For logical and mathematical terms:
> w means AND $\equiv$ we accept "p, q// p w q"
> w means TRUE $\equiv$ we accept instances of "w ($<$p$>$)
> $\leftrightarrow$ p"
> . . . and so on.

For theoretical terms:
> If "f" is introduced via the theory "#f", then it means
> what it does in virtue of our underived acceptance of
> $$fx \leftrightarrow (\exists\phi)\,(\#\phi\ \&\ \phi x).$$

. . . etc.

Thus the dialectical situation is that a truth-referentialist needs not only to embrace UTM, but to defend a further claim, namely, that the concrete meaning-constitution theory that issues from UTM will take the specific shape exemplified above. And in order to do that he must justify the assumption that the various naturalistic relations involved in the meanings of primitive predicates—e.g. "We would, in condition I^1, apply w to x", "We would, in condition I^2, apply w to x", . . . and so on—each constitutes the "is true of" relation for the range of predicates with which it is associated.

But there is no reason to think that this assumption is correct. The only conceivable rationale for it rests on presupposing that the truth-theoretic notions *must* be reducible to non-semantic terms. But no such theory of truth (or satisfaction, or reference) has ever been made plausible. Moreover the availability of deflationary accounts of the truth-theoretic concepts—accounts that emphasize their role in anaphora and generalization—reinforce the suspicion that the search for a traditional-looking reductive account of truth is misconceived.[21] Thus, truth-referentialism is not really an *alternative* to UTM. It is a *form* of use-theory, and not an especially plausible one.

---

[21] See chap. 1 (section 9), chap. 2 (section (b)), chap. 3 (sections 4 and 5), and chap. 5 (section 3).

In support of the second component of UTM I have emphasized that we have an attractive inferential model of how the meaning-constituting acceptance of a certain restricted class of sentences can help to account for all further acceptance-facts. But what about the additional things that meaning-constituting properties are supposed to explain: specifically, those use-facts, mentioned at the start of section (d), that relate to desire, deliberation, and action? Is there any good reason to hold that basic acceptance-properties can be adequate in these further respects? I think that the answer is yes. Indeed I would go further, though this need not be considered part of UTM. I would argue that the very same core use-properties that explain the overall acceptance of sentences, i.e. the presence of beliefs, will equally explain the other ways in which sentences are deployed in thought, and will also do justice to the behavioural implications of these forms of deployment.

Here is a crude sketch of the argument. First, consider the use of a term, w, within formulations of someone's *desires*, i.e. within sentences that appear in his want-box (through being correlated with mental sentences that do). I am claiming that such uses of w are explained by the very same basic acceptance-properties that account for w's appearance in S's belief-box. And this can be supported by exploiting the rough equivalence of a person's *wanting* something to happen and his *believing* that its happening would make him happy. Insofar as desires tend to be correlated with beliefs in this way, then the use of w in articulations of what is desired will be explained by whatever property explains w's deployment in accepted sentences.[22]

---

[22] To amplify a little, we might take it to be in the very nature of the desire-box that certain sentences (including "I am happy") are necessarily in it. Moreover (and very roughly speaking) any further sentence, "p", will be added to S's desire-box if and when there is a "q", already in it, such that S accepts "p → q". Consequently, if certain core use-properties of the words in "p" help explain S's acceptance of sentences of the form "p → q", they will also help explain the presence of "p" is S's desire-box.

Second, consider the use of w within sentences that formulate S's *decisions* about what immediately to do, i.e. sentences that appear in his 'decide-to-do-now' box. To a first approximation, we decide to perform an action when, and only when, we believe that it will bring about something that we want. In other words there is, very roughly speaking, a psychological law

[S belief-boxes "a→q" and S want-boxes "q"]
IFF
S decide-boxes "a"

where "a" means something of the form I DO x*, and where x* is an action under the agent's control, e.g. a simple bodily movement. Thus, insofar as w's deployment in formulations of belief, and hence desire, can be explained, then its appearances in the decide-box can also be explained.

Finally, consider the fact that a word's meaning-constituting property must help to account for the correlation between, on the one hand, the occurrence in someone's decide-box of certain sentences containing it and, on the other hand, his performance of certain characteristic *actions*. For example, the meaning-constituting property of "I raise my left hand" must explain why the presence of that sentence in my decide-box results in my raising my left hand. Here's how this can be done. Suppose the decide-box operates in the following manner. Given the appearance in it of "I do x*", it causes the bodily movement that will bring about the subject's acceptance of that sentence. In that case, whatever properties of the words in "I do x*" explain its acceptance-behaviour (including, that it is accepted if and only if S does x*) will also explain the relationship between the appearance of the sentence in S's decide-box and his subsequent action.

This line of thought obviously makes a great number of highly simplifying assumptions. But there is no reason to think that a more accurate version would undermine its conclusion: namely, that whatever basic acceptance property of w suffices to help account for its appearance in the belief-box (i.e. its deployment in accepted sentences) will also explain its *overall* usage.

(f) The meaning of a word, w, is engendered by the non-semantic feature of w that explains w's overall deployment. And this will be an acceptance-property **of the following form:— 'that such-and-such w-sentences are regularly accepted in such-and-such circumstances'** is the idealized law governing w's use is (by the relevant 'experts', given certain meanings attached to various other words).

The precise acceptance-relation to sentences that is required here varies, depending on the particular meaning-property with which we are concerned. In some cases what is involved is the acceptance of a specific sentence (or finite set of sentences). For example, it may well be that we mean what we do by "neutrino" in virtue of accepting a certain theory formulation—or, more plausibly, a *conditional* whose consequent is a theory formulation and whose antecedent is specified in terms of the 'old' vocabulary (including observation terms).[23] In other cases what is involved is the acceptance of a *schema*—something manifested in a tendency to accept its instances. For example, arguably, our meaning TRUE by "true" derives from our acceptance of the schema, "<p> is true ↔ p".[24] In yet other cases what is involved is the acceptance of a principle of inference, manifested in the propensity to accept certain sentences as a result of having accepted certain related sentences. Thus it may

[23] The view (mentioned at the outset) that what is meaning-constituting is merely our acceptance of this *conditional* (rather than our acceptance of the full theory-formulation), accommodates the possibility of not believing in neutrinos while nonetheless understanding the word "neutrino". For similar reasons, it may be that some (perhaps all) of the other sample basic acceptance properties that are proposed here need to be conditionalized in this way. For more on this point, and its negative import for the explanation of interesting epistemic norms, see chap. 6.

[24] In light of the liar paradoxes, we can see that the type of acceptance involved in this case must be *provisional*. Certain instances of the schema will be initially accepted, but subsequently retracted in order to avoid contradiction.

be that what provides the word "and" with its meaning is that its law of use is acceptance of the two-way argument schema, "p, q // p and q". A further possible form for a meaning-constituting fact is that it be a propensity to accept a certain type of sentence in certain conditions. For example, it may be that what provides the word "red" with its meaning is (to a first approximation) our tendency to accept "That is red" in response to the sort of visual experience normally provoked by a clearly red surface.[25]

(g) The meaning of a word, w, is engendered by the non-semantic feature of w that explains w's overall deployment. And this will be an acceptance-property of the following form:—'that such-and-such w-sentences are regularly accepted in such-and-such circumstances' **is the idealized law governing w's use** is (by the relevant 'experts', given certain meanings attached to various other words).

Let me stress that each of the above cases invokes a purely factual *law-like regularity* of usage, not a *norm* concerning what usage *ought* to be displayed. However, this does not prevent us from supposing, if we want, that meaning is a matter of *implicit rule-following*. For the laws governing a word's use are not *strictly* obeyed; they are not like 'conservation of energy' or 'F = ma'. Rather, they dictate what happens in the absence of a variety of distorting circumstances. For example, our activity with "or" is the joint product of our following idealized laws of use (e.g. to accept everything of the form, "pv-p") and further

---

[25] UTM *leaves room* for 'physical' externalism, insofar as it does not preclude the possibility that the conditions of acceptance involved in certain meaning-constituting properties will include aspects of the environment. But it is not *committed* to externalism, insofar as it allows that the best explanations of overall use may turn out never to call for that kind of basic acceptance property. For example, perhaps we mean what we do by "water" in virtue of accepting as basic, "x is water ↔ x has the underlying nature of the stuff in *our* seas, rivers, lakes and rain." In that case the concept would have a certain indexical character. So the Twin-Earth word would mean the same as ours. Nonetheless (in conformity with Putnam's intuitions) these words would have different extensions.

('distorting') factors, e.g. the length and complexity of "p". Thus they resemble the ideal gas laws and the laws of ideally rigid bodies. Moreover, the idealized laws governing word use operate within a person as a result, in part, of corrective reinforcement by the community. Therefore it is not untoward to speak of them as "implicitly followed rules".

However, although the terminology of 'rule following' may be fairly natural here, it is not compulsory. For the case at hand differs considerably from paradigm cases of rule following, which involve a *formulation* of the rule, an *understanding* of that formulation, and a *conscious decision* to do what it says. In virtue of these differences, it seems plausible to suppose that there is no determinate fact as to whether *so-called* "implicit rule-following" (and hence meaning) is really a matter of rule following.

But even if we do choose to liberalize the normal notion, and to allow that meaning *does* involve rule following, we cannot infer that meaning-attributions, such as 'w means DOG', are *constitutionally evaluative* (or normative). On the contrary, in judging that S *is* following rule R, one is certainly not contending that S *ought* to follow R. Nor is one even claiming that S ought to *conform* with R. Granted, the latter conclusion may normally be drawn (since following a rule involved *desiring* to conform to it); but only by relying on a further premiss—a normative premiss—namely, that one ought to conform with the rule one is following. Thus, rule-following is not *constitutionally* normative, so neither is meaning.[26]

What engenders the meaning of a word is not merely our *acceptance* of certain sentences; nor is it that this pattern of activity with the word is *law*-like. Rather, the meaning-constituting fact is that some such specified regularity is *the causal-explanatory basis of the word's overall use*, the law (or conjunction of laws) that governs our activity with it.

---

[26] For further discussion, see chap. 5, esp. sections 5, 6, and 7. Note that the evaluative *import* of meaning, e.g. "w means DOG → one ought to aim to apply w only to dogs", is perfectly consistent with "w means DOG" being *constitutively* non-evaluative. (Compare, "x is a killing → x is wrong".)

Nothing weaker can accommodate our sense that a meaning-constituter must be the sort of property such that, whenever two terms have the same one, then the sentences containing them that we are prepared to accept will be the same. So, for example, it cannot be that the meaning of "true" is fixed simply by our *acceptance* of "<p> is true ↔ p". For, it were fixed in that way, and if we introduced a new word, "glub", to abbreviate "true and not red", then—since we would be equally inclined to accept "<p> is glub ↔ p"—"glub" would possess the property that constitutes the meaning of "true". But, in fact, the meanings and overall uses of these two words are clearly *not* the same, e.g. "glub" logically entails "not red", whereas "true" doesn't.[27]

The solution—as I've indicated—resides in the fact that our acceptance of the *truth*-schema is the law explaining our overall use of "true". But our acceptance of the *glub*-schema is *not*, analogously, the basis of our usage of "glub". Rather, that usage results from a combination of

 (i) "glub"'s actual law of use (namely, our acceptance of "x is glub ↔ x is true and not red"),
 (ii) "true"'s law of use
(iii) our acceptance of "No proposition is red"

So "glub" does not really have the property that constitutes the meaning of "true".

Thus we must suppose, in general, that a word's meaning-constituter is a property to the effect that a certain acceptance practice with it is the explanatory basis of its overall usage.

(h) The meaning of a word, w, is engendered by the non-semantic feature of w that explains w's overall deployment. And this will be an acceptance-property of the following form: 'that such-and-such w-sentences are regularly accepted in such-and-such circumstances'

---

[27] The problem addressed here was put to me by Gupta in October 1992, and appears in fn. 17 of his "Deflationism, the Problem of Representation, and Horwich's Use Theory of Meaning".

is the idealized law governing w's use is (**by the relevant 'experts'**, given certain meanings attached to various other words).

Presumably, each individual's overall use of a word is explained by his particular basic use of it—which will vary somewhat from person to person. Thus UTM applies in the first instance to *idiolects*. However, we can still accommodate the 'social externalist', 'anti-individualist' observations of Kripke, Putnam, and Burge: namely, that very often the meanings we attribute to someone's utterances (and the beliefs we take to be expressed by them) depend not merely on how that person uses his words, but also on their usage by others within his linguistic community.[28] For example, people whose applications of the predicates "elm" and "arthritis" reveal considerable ignorance of their proper use, may still be taken to have ascribed the properties of being an elm and having arthritis, i.e. the properties designated by those individuals whose usage is not deficient. Thus we recognize that there is such a thing as the meaning of a word within a group of speakers, where many of the members of the group do not fully grasp that meaning.

As for how, according to UTM, this meaning is constituted, we can exploit Putnam's distinction between those individuals who, in the case of a given word, qualify as 'expert' in its use, and those who do not; and we can suppose that the word's communal meaning derives from the basic acceptance property governing 'expert' usage. Spelling this out a bit further: for each word w there is a group of people whose members share the following characteristics: (i) their use of w is governed by the same basic acceptance property; and (ii) they are deferred to (either directly or indirectly) by other members of the community—i.e. other people are disposed to alter their basic acceptance properties so as to conform with that of the 'experts'. (Note that in some cases, e.g.

[28] See Kripke's *Naming and Necessity*, Putnam's "The Meaning of 'Meaning' ", and Burge's "Individualism and the Mental".

"red" and "dog", the group of 'experts' will more-or-less coincide with the whole community).

Needless to say, these few remarks leave many questions unanswered. What exactly is the phenomenon of deference? Can't the 'experts' disagree amongst themselves? Exactly how far from expert can someone's usage of a word be in order for him still to qualify as meaning by it what the 'experts' do? If his use happens not to be close enough—or it is just close enough but he refuses to defer—what communal meaning can be attributed to the word? Or does it not have one? Of course, such questions are not necessarily objections. Nor is it at all clear that determinate answers should be expected. Moreover *any* account of meaning-constitution will have to confront them, and none is peculiarly well placed to respond. So they leave no particular reason to suspect that UTM is on the wrong track.

(i) The meaning of a word, w, is engendered by the non-semantic feature of w that explains w's overall deployment. And this will be an acceptance-property of the following form:—'that such-and-such w-sentences are regularly accepted in such-and-such circumstances' is the idealized law governing w's use is (by the relevant 'experts', **given certain meanings attached to various other words**).

Obviously our acceptance of "Bachelors are unmarried men" can help constitute what we mean by "bachelor" only insofar as the rest of the sentence, "are unmarried men", is given its standard meaning. And, in general, the acceptance of specific sentences containing a word provides it with a definite meaning only relative to particular construals of the remaining words in those sentences. Consequently, each word can mean what it does only given the presence of other words with other meanings. Therefore, on pain of infinite regress, it must be that there are sets of basic terms whose meanings are mutually dependent on one another.

In these cases—sometimes referred to as instances of "limited holism"[29]—the single underlying non-semantic fact that is responsible for all the words in the set having the meanings they do will take the form of a use-relation between them

$$UR(word_1, word_2, word_3 \ldots, word_N)$$

However, although the meaning of each of those words depends on there being other words used in specific ways in relation to it, it clearly does not matter exactly what those other words (i.e. sounds) are, as long as they are used appropriately. For example, "bachelor" would mean exactly what it now means, even if its meaning derived from the acceptance of "Bachelors are unwashed dishes", provided that "wash" and "dish" were used just as "marry" and "man" are actually used. Therefore, the meaning-constituting property, $MC_1(w)$, of $word_1$ will be

$$(\exists x_2) \, (\exists x_3) \ldots (\exists x_N) \, UR \, (w, x_2, x_3, \ldots, x_N)$$

and similarly for the others. Thus meaning interdependence (aka "holism") *per se* does not prevent each meaning-property from being constituted in a distinctive non-semantic way.

However, in certain special circumstances, a problematic situation of this sort *will* arise. And this is the basis for Quine's *second* critique of meaning.[30] The first one—the alleged impossibility of carving out those uses of a word that are to qualify as meaning-constituting—was addressed in section (d) above). The difficulty is that there are (or may be) cases in which the relation UR is *fully symmetric*: cases in which

$$UR^*(word_1, word_2) \equiv UR^*(word_2, word_1)$$

But then, despite the fact that these terms do not have the same meaning as one another, the above technique for identifying

---

[29] See Dummett, M. (1991) *The Logical Basis of Metaphysics*.
[30] See W. V. Quine, *Word and Object*, chap. 2.

their individual basic use-properties would arrive at the same thing for both of them, namely

$$(\exists x)\, UR^*(w, x)$$

Therefore, we are forced to concede that, in the case of these words, there are no individual non-semantic properties that constitute their meanings. And this would imply—since it would be bizarre for some meaning-properties to be analyzable and others not—that such terms don't have meaning-properties.

For example, consider a language whose symbols for the two square roots of -1 are "$/$" and "$\backslash$".[31] It seems clear that the only fact available to constitute their meaning what they do is the explanatory role of our acceptance of

$$\backslash^2 = /^2 = -1 \text{ and } \sim(/ = \backslash)$$

So here we have an instance of the above problem. For although the two symbols are not synonymous, we cannot extract from this acceptance-fact any plausible meaning-constituting property for "$/$" that isn't also possessed by "$\backslash$".

Because of such examples, UTM must be modified. We have to acknowledge the possibility of meaningful words that do not possess individual meanings; for there may be no non-semantic characteristics that could constitute those meanings. What remains true, however, is something slightly more complicated: namely, that the *collection* of symmetrically-used terms possesses a certain meaning, and this meaning fact is constituted by some non-semantic use-relation between them. For example, the fact that

$$S\text{'s set of words } \{\text{"v"}, \text{"w"}\} \text{ means } / + \backslash$$

[31] This is Hartry Field's improved version (from "Some Thoughts on Radical Indeterminacy"), of an example due to Robert Brandom (in "The Significance of Complex Numbers for Frege's Philosophy of Mathematics"). A further example is given in *Meaning*, chap. 9, whereby a theory of fundamental particles deploys terms, "A" and "B", symmetrically but non-synonymously. For an early articulation of the problem (based on a different hypothetical example) see Ned Block's "Troubles With Functionalism", in C. W. Savage (ed.), *Minnesota Studies in the Philosophy of Science*, 9: 261–325.

(where "/ + \" is the name of a 'collective meaning') is engendered by the non-semantic fact that

> The law governing S's use of "v" and "w" is that S accepts "$w^2 = v^2 = -1$ and $\sim(w = v)$".

Thus, understood holistically, we can continue to suppose that meaning-properties are founded on non-semantic use-properties.[32]

My aim here has been to give a clear statement of a plausible use-theoretic account of meaning. I have not spelled out supporting arguments, although in sections (b), (d), and (e) there are indications of how such arguments would go. Nor have I attempted to deal thoroughly with certain widely held objections to this sort of theory—doubts, for example, as to whether it could be extended to deal with *complex* expressions,

---

[32] Thus I am endorsing Quine's denial that terms such as "/" and "\" have individual meanings, while disagreeing with him—see chap. 1, section 2—about how widespread the phenomenon of fully symmetric meaning interdependence can be. This diverges from the line I took in *Meaning* (62–3, and 211) where, because of the attractiveness of the general schema, " 'e' means E", I wanted to hang on to the idea that every meaningful term has its own individual meaning.

Hartry Field ("Meaning Attributions" in his *Truth and the Absence of Fact*) suggests that insofar as we insist on countenancing meanings at all, we should postulate merely *local* (language-dependent) ones, so that, for example, the meanings of "dog" and "chien" would be distinct things, 'correlated' with one another but not identical. An advantage of this policy, he argues, is that we won't have to admit (as I did in *Meaning*) that although "/" means the same as either "i" or "−i", we can never know which; we can say rather that the meaning of "/" correlates equally well with both the meaning of "i" and with the meaning of "−i". However, the ontological cost of Field's alternative is high: meanings would have to be multiplied by the number of languages. Moreover the position sketched in the text, which I now favour, would no longer leave us with unanswerable questions about sameness of meaning. For, in denying that either "\" or "/" or "i" or "−i" have individual meanings, I am saying that "\" definitely does *not* have the same individual meaning as either "i" or "−i". This doesn't imply that we couldn't obtain a decent translation of "/" and "\". On the contrary, either of the two pairings with "i" and "−i" would be perfect. For we should not require of an "exact translation" that it match *individual* meaning: preservation of *collective* meaning will be good enough.

as to whether meaning is really given by regularities rather than "oughts", as to whether the theory would enable the rationality of fundamental epistemic rules to be explained, and as to whether Kripke's famous meaning-sceptical considerations can be deflected. Those issues are taken up in subsequent chapters.

APPENDIX

The purpose of this appendix is to set out the reasons, mentioned in section (a) above, for rejecting a two-level picture of meaning—a picture in which *mental* terms somehow mean what they do (i.e. embody the concepts they do), perhaps in the way described by UTM; whilst *public* terms derive their meanings, à la Grice, from the concepts that it is intended and agreed they are to express.[33]

It is certainly possible for meaning *sometimes* to be given in the way that Grice describes: namely, by our agreeing that certain sentences are to express certain beliefs. One might, for example, coin a new term, "autofanticide", and obtain agreement with the members of one's community that it be used when speakers wish to communicate thoughts involving the concept, KILLING BY A TIME-TRAVELLER OF HIS INFANT SELF. Or a man may tell his wife, before going to a dinner party, that he will give his left ear a little tug when he wants to leave. So instances of meaning investment á la Grice clearly do occur. We may question however (a) whether this can be the way that the meanings of *all* public language expressions are constituted, and (b) whether,

---

[33] I must thank Stephen Schiffer for pressing me to clarify my resistance to the Gricean picture, and for mounting a stronger case for it than I had thought was possible. Some of his arguments are in "Horwich on Meaning: Critical Study of Paul Horwich's *Meaning*", *Philosophical Quarterly*, 2000.

even where Grice's model does apply, it precludes the sort of account offered by UTM.

One reason for thinking that his account of meaning-constitution cannot handle *all* public expression is that a certain amount of communication in public language is needed to make the agreements that must be in place in order that a speaker have any right to think that his utterances will be taken to manifest the beliefs that they do.

Another ground for scepticism is the sheer implausibility of supposing that our everyday literal use of familiar words is backed by Gricean intentions. The idea reeks of over-intellectualization. Surely the intimate correlation between a public sound and a language-of-thought term is normally fixed during early child-hood, so the adult's production of the sound to express a concept is not mediated by processes of deliberation and intention. And this non-Gricean view of the matter becomes virtually compul-sory if we suppose—as will be argued in Chapter 7—that each person's language of thought is simply a mental version of his public language, i.e. English, Chinese, etc.

To see this—to see that the relation between a person's mental terms and their verbal expression is non-intentional—consider (for simplicity) a person S who speaks and understands just one language, and suppose that none of its words is ambiguous. In that case there will be a certain causal correlation between these words and the terms of S's language of thought. More specifically, whenever a sentence—a sequence of sounds—is heard, that causes S to have a thought roughly of the form 'So-and-so said that such-and-such'; and the 'such-and-such' is articulated in the corresponding mental terms. I.e. there is a one-one correspond-ence, f, between S's public word-types, w, and his mental term-types, m $[= f(w)]$ such that, whenever a sound sequence includes a token of w, the mental sequence that S uses to specify what was said includes a token of $f(w)$. Conversely, if S has decided to say a certain thing and articulates what he has decided to say using a mental sentence containing term, m, this will bring it about that S utters a sequence of sounds containing $f^{-1}(m)$. (See Chapter 7 for further discussion).

There is, of course, always the possibility of intentionally *changing* the literal meaning of a public expression. But to conclude, on that account, that its earlier meaning was a product of our intentions would be on a par with supposing that, since we could conceivably agree to cut down all the trees, their present existence derives from our intentions.

Moreover, we can press a further point against Grice. It is not implausible that any *awareness* that a person has of one of his own beliefs depends on his being aware of a disposition to overtly express that belief. But one may intend to express a belief in a certain way only if one is aware of having it. Thus such an intention rests on being aware of an utterance-disposition. Therefore it cannot be that all public language meaning is constituted by that kind of intention. For any such case of meaning-constitution presupposes the existence of some public sentence which already has that meaning.

This is not to deny that intentions play an important role in communication. Suppose someone thinks "Everyone at my party yesterday was drunk" and expresses that thought to his friend by saying "Everyone was happy". No doubt various intentions are involved: he intends to speak; he intends to drop the "at my party yesterday", given what he takes his friend to know and to be able to figure out; and he intends to employ a playful euphemism. But no decision was made, and no intention was formed, about the literal meanings of the word-types that were used. Those facts were fixed when the language was learned.

It is maintained, on the contrary, by some philosophers of language (e.g. Charles Travis[34]) that most predicates do not have extensions *absolutely*, but only relative to a context of the speakers' local intentions. For example, whether a given apple qualifies as "green" depends on whether it has been decided,

---

[34] See his *Unshadowed Thought*, Harvard University Press, 2000.

given the conversation's purpose, to include red ones that have been painted green, or ones that are green on the outside but not on the inside, etc. However, it is hard to see how this extreme context-sensitivity could be right vis-à-vis a language of thought—a language in which any temporary reference-fixing intentions would have to be articulated. And most of a person's public language is intimately, automatically, and non-intentionally linked to his language of thought. So a more plausible picture, it seems to me, is that each predicate has a context-independent, 'default', literal, reference-fixing meaning—but that its public, verbal form may sometimes be meant non-literally; the speaker may decide to use the word to express some term of his language of thought other than the one with which it is automatically correlated.

One way of trying to rescue something like a Gricean picture from these criticisms would be acknowledge that *explicit* intentions and agreements are not normally involved in meaning-constitution, but to say that Griceans should be read as invoking *implicit* intentions and agreements. Of course, in that case the question arises as to what it is to be in such states merely *implicitly*. And a natural answer is that they are constituted by law like regularities. In particular (and roughly speaking) the implicit intention (agreement, convention) to utter u only in certain circumstances would be constituted by the tendency to utter u only in those circumstances. Thus the Gricean account would amount to something like this:

(G) u means *that p* within community C ↔
There is an implicitly respected convention (i.e. law-like regularity) within C to the effect that a speaker utters u only when he believes *that p*, and wants his audience to recognize that he does, and . . . etc.

Now, from the perspective of UTM, the *correctness* of some such principle is not at all objectionable. What is objectionable, however, is the idea that it tells us *what it is* for an utterance to have a certain meaning. We should, instead, take the correlation articulated by (G) to be the product of two more fundamental facts: one to the effect—very roughly speaking—that members of a linguistic community tend to produce a sentence only when they intend to manifest their acceptance of it:

(A) There is an implicitly respected convention (i.e. law like regularity, within C) to the effect that a speaker utters u only when he accepts it, and wants his listeners to recognize that he does, and . . . etc.

and the other to the effect that *believing* a given proposition is nothing more than *accepting* some sentence that expresses it:

(B) (u means *that p* within community C and S is a member of C) → (S accepts u ↔ S believes *that p*)

Now (A) and (B) together entails (G). Moreover, neither of these explanatory premises takes a stand on what meaning *is*. So we see that the (purified) Gricean biconditional, though true enough, can be reconciled with any account whatsoever of how facts of the form 'u means *that p*' are constituted; so it gives absolutely no information about the nature of meaning.

These various considerations give us good reason to reject the suggestion that public meaning is *always* established as Grice says it is. His model does not articulate the essence of public language meaning. There remains, however, the possibility of claiming that it does at least accurately account for *certain* cases of literal meaning, e.g. ear-tuggings, and consequently that UTM cannot be generally correct either.

Actually, it would not detract greatly from the scope of UTM if we were to concede this point. For the cases in which Grice's story applies are extremely few and far between. Moreover, one might mitigate the concession by distinguishing between the *primary* literal meanings possessed by 99 per cent of public expressions, which are constituted by fact of usage (as specified by UTM), and the *secondary* literal meanings of those few

terms, gestures, and other ad hoc signals, which are established
à la Grice by means of communication that relies on primary
meanings.

However, there is no need for even this minor concession.
For even when decisions and intentions and agreements *are*
involved in the investment of a meaning, we can suppose that
what is created by them, in the first instance, is a certain use-
propensity (a certain basic acceptance property) and that it is
this result—rather than the intentions, etc. that helped bring
it about—which constitutes the meaning. For example, if "autofanticide" is introduced through the explicit communal decision
to use it to manifest the concept, KILLING BY A TIME-TRAVELLER
OF HIS INFANT SELF, what happens is the institution of a certain
law like regularity, namely, the tendency to accept the sentence,
"autofanticide = killing by a time traveller of his infant self".
And we can take it to be that use-fact which gives the word its
meaning. Similarly, if Fred tells his wife that he will tug his ear
when he wants to leave, he is instigating a certain meaning-
constituting rule of use: namely, to accept "Fred wants to leave"
when Fred tugs his ear. Thus, even in the rare cases when explicit
decisions, intentions, and agreements are involved in establishing
a meaning, there is no need to suppose that their occurrence is
essential to something's having that meaning. We can and
should say, rather, that those phenomena are merely the causal
antecedents of what really underlies that meaning, which, in
every case, is a certain use-propensity.[35]

[35] I am indebted to participants in the 2001 colloquium on Language and
Mind at New York University, and especially to Ned Block, Paul Boghossian,
Michael Devitt, Hartry Field, and Stephen Schiffer, for their helpful reactions to
an early version of this chapter.

3

The Pseudo-Problem of Error

1. INTRODUCTION

The theory I have just been elaborating presupposes that word-types have meanings—Pierre's "chien" means DOG, Paola's "vero" means TRUE, etc.—and addresses the question of how this sort of thing comes about. In other words, it assumes that there are meaning-properties such as

> w means DOG
> w means TRUE
> ...and so on,

which terms may possess and sometimes share with others, and it aims to specify how they are reducible to, or derived from, or engendered by, underlying non-semantic phenomena: it aims to say precisely what are the non-intentional characteristics, U1, U2, ..., such that

> w means DOG $\Leftarrow$ U1(w)
> w means TRUE $\Leftarrow$ U2(w)
> ...and so on?[1]

---

[1] I shall be using the "$\Leftarrow$" sign to stand for the relation of "constitution" between properties, leaving it open whether this gives rise to an identity. Thus, when Sx $\Leftarrow$ Ux, one may hold either that "Sx" and "Ux" express different concepts of the same "thick" PROPERTY, or that these predicates stand for different properties of which one engenders the other. As outlined in chap. 2, section (b), these alternatives are terminological, reflecting the decision to use the jargon-term, "property", in either a relatively course-grained sense or a relatively fine-grained sense.

The answer that I have been urging is that each word's meaning derives from a certain aspect of its *use*. However, there is a familiar, influential objection to any such proposal: namely, that it will not be able to accommodate the *truth*-theoretic features of word-meanings. And my goal in the present chapter is to rebut that charge.

I will be focusing on a particular conception of this alleged adequacy condition, a particular assumption about *how* a decent reductive account is required to accommodate the truth-conditional import of meaning (and hence some of its *normative* import). Many philosophers have imposed this form of the requirement, at least implicitly; but my main point will be to suggest that it should *not* be imposed. If I am right, then—since it has been no easy matter to find a non-semantic analysis of meaning that could satisfy this requirement, and arguably *no* such account could satisfy it—the prospects for a naturalistic reduction of meaning are much brighter than many people these days are inclined to think.

2. THE EXPLANATION REQUIREMENT

The adequacy condition on meaning-constitution that I want to scrutinize can be articulated schematically as the following *explanation requirement*:

ER w means F $\Leftarrow$ U(w)
   only if it is possible to explain
   (a) why this is so
   (b) why words with U(w) are true of fs and only fs
   (c) why words with U(w) should ideally be applied
     only to fs,[2]

---

[2] In the case of *non*-predicative simple concepts, parts (b) and (c) of the explanation requirement would have to be formulated somewhat differently. In order for "U(w)" to constitute "w means K", ER would require explanations of why it is (b) that if U(w), then "#w" is true if and only if #*k; and (c) that if U(w), then "#w"

where "f" is to be replaced by an arbitrary English predicate, e.g. "dog" and "F" by a name of the concept expressed by that predicate, e.g. "DOG". To begin with, I shall concentrate on part (a) of this requirement; for, as we shall see, it is more fundamental than parts (b) or (c).

There are three alternative ways of putting ER(a). First, there is the formulation just given, namely, that the facts of meaning-property constitution be *explicable*. For example, if a specific nomological correlation between a certain word-type and a certain object-type is to be responsible for the word's meaning DOG, then one must be able to say *why* the correlation gives the word *that* meaning rather than a different one or none at all.

Second, this condition is equivalent to the requirement that there be a general reductive schema (or a *set* of reductive schemata) of the *relational* form

$$w \text{ means } F \Leftarrow R(w, f).$$

For if there is a set of such general theories—perhaps invoking different relations, R^1, R^2, ..., R^k, for different kinds of predicate, e.g. colour terms, species terms, theoretical terms, etc.—then we will be in a position, as required by the first formulation of ER(a), to *explain* any particular fact of meaning-constitution, say

$$w \text{ means } DOG \Leftarrow R^1(w, dog),$$

as an instance of one of these theories; and no other form of explanation seems feasible. For example, the general schematic theory

$$w \text{ means } F \Leftarrow (y) \text{ (There is a disposition, in ideal conditions, to apply } w \text{ to } y \leftrightarrow y \text{ is an } f)$$

ought to be accepted only if #*k, where "#w" is an arbitrary (non-indexical) sentence containing w, and "#*_" is the English translation of "#_". In order to avoid these complexities, the present discussion is restricted to predicate meanings.

has the required relational structure. Therefore it puts us in a position to explain the particular fact that

w means DOG $\Leftarrow$ (y) (There is a disposition, in ideal conditions, to apply w to y $\leftrightarrow$ y is a dog).[3]

A third variant of the requirement under discussion is that, in order for 'w means F' to reduce to 'U(w)', it must be possible, given the information that a certain word possesses the property U(w), for us to *read off* from this information exactly what that word means. Such reading off—such inferring in a rule-governed way—can take place if and only if 'U(w)' takes the form 'R(w, f)', where R remains constant over a range of cases. In other words, there must be a general *relational* theory (or set of theories) fitting the schema, 'w means F $\Leftarrow$ R(w, f)'. And this, as we have just seen, is necessary and sufficient for there to be *explanations* of why particular meaning-constituting properties constitute the particular meanings that they do.

Thus, part (a) of what I am calling "the explanation requirement" has three equivalent formulations. The first is that the facts of meaning-constitution be *explicable*. The second is that they exhibit the *relational* form 'w means F $\Leftarrow$ R(w, f)'. And the third is that any meaning-constituting property be something from which the meaning-property it induces can be *read off*.

However, two complications are worth noting. First, the requirement is, in a certain sense, a matter of *degree*. At one extreme it may be construed as insisting that there be a *single* relation R, covering all predicates "f", such that

w means F $\Leftarrow$ R(w, f),

---

[3] As this example illustrates, the two-place relational expression "R" applies to a singular term (referring to a word) and a predicate (whose extension is a set of things). Thus "R('chien', dog)" schematizes a sentence containing the terms "'chien'" and "dog".

—a *constant* way of reading off, and accounting for, the meaning engendered by any given non-semantic ground. At the other extreme, one might want to say that, even if the neatest account we could find invoked a separate item for each meaning, viz:

$$w \text{ means DOG} \iff R^1(w, \text{dog})$$
$$w \text{ means CAT} \iff R^2(w, \text{cat})$$
$$\ldots \text{and so on,}$$

we could nonetheless use it to read off, and to explain, which meaning is constituted.

Second, we must distinguish between the question of whether an explanation requirement should be imposed as a *filter* and the question of whether some such requirement simply *happens to be satisfied*. It is one thing to maintain that ER(a) provides a condition of adequacy—that in assessing any given proposal for how meaning is constituted one must first check to see whether that condition is met. And it is quite a different thing to observe, on the basis of having already found a theory that meets all the appropriate adequacy conditions, that relationality turns out to be satisfied (to a certain degree), so reading off and explanation may (to a certain degree) be carried out. The aim of this chapter is to criticize merely the former sentiment, namely, that the explanation requirement should be used to weed out inadequate theories.

3. ILLUSTRATIONS

Although the requirement ER(a) is rarely spelled out (in any of its three versions), most reductive theories of meaning to be found in the philosophical literature appear to be designed to meet it. For example, there is the so-called 'informational' approach, favoured by Fodor and Stampe,[4] whereby roughly speaking

---

[4] See Fodor's *Psychosemantics*, and Stampe's "Toward a Causal Theory of Linguistic Representation".

> w means F ⇐ Occurrences of w (in the mind) are nomologically correlated with the presence of things that are f.

There is also the 'teleological' approach, advanced by Dretske, Millikan, Papineau, Jacob, and Neander,[5] whereby roughly speaking

> w means F ⇐ The (evolutionary) function of w is to indicate the presence of fs.

And there is the Peacockean[6] conceptual-role-cum-determination-theory approach, whereby

> w means F ⇐ The primitively compelling sentences (or rules) containing w are true (or truth-preserving) ↔ w is true of fs and only fs.

Despite the great differences between these theories, each of them satisfies ER(a): each takes the relational form

> w means F ⇐ R(w, f)

enabling particular cases of meaning-constitution to be explained, and enabling the meaning-property of a word to be read off its meaning-constituting property.

An explicit statement of our third version of ER(a)—the 'reading off' formulation—is to be found in Kripke's *Wittgenstein on Rules and Private Language*. In the course of his critique of the theory that meaning-properties may be analysed as dispositions to verbal behaviour, he says

> The criterion, i.e. the reductive theory under consideration, is meant to enable us to "read off" which function I mean by a given function symbol, from my disposition (p. 26).

---

[5] See Dretske's "Misrepresentation", Millikan's *Language, Thought and Other Biological Categories*, Papineau's *Reality and Representation*, Jacob's *What Minds Can Do*, and Neander's "Misrepresenting and Malfunctioning".

[6] See Peacocke's *A Study of Concepts*. He presents his account as a theory of concept identity. Here I have reformulated it as a theory of meaning.

Switching to our first version of the requirement, one of his main objections to all proposed candidates for the particular dispositional property that constitutes 'w means PLUS' is that for none of these candidates can we *explain* why it should engender precisely *this* meaning-property rather than a slightly different one, e.g. 'w means QUUS'.

Moreover, the only dispositional account that Kripke seems to consider worth criticizing is that

$$\text{w means F} \Leftarrow (y)(\text{We would, in ideal conditions, apply w to } y \leftrightarrow y \text{ is f})$$

a glaringly *relational* account, on the basis of which the meaning of a word could easily be *read off* from, and *explained* in terms of, the pertinent dispositions for its use.

Thus it is fair to conclude that part (a) of the explanation requirement, in one form or another, is widely presupposed.[7]

4. MOTIVATIONS

But why should it seem reasonable, indeed, overwhelmingly natural, to impose the condition ER(a) on reductive analyses of meaning-properties? Certainly not because we are inclined to impose some such condition on the reductive analysis of *any*

---

[7] Further implicit endorsements of the requirement come flooding in from Kripke's many commentators who take issue with one or another point in his argument but do not question his imposition of that adequacy condition. See, for example, essays by Simon Blackburn, "The Individual Strikes Back", Crispin Wright, "Kripke's Account of the Argument against Private Language", *Journal of Philosophy*, 1984, 759–78, and Paul Boghossian, "The Rule Following Considerations" *Mind* 98: 507–50.

See also Robert Brandom who argues, in his *Making It Explicit*, that a word's meaning-property cannot reduce to a *non-normative* regularity in its use because no such regularity could *explain* why the word ends up meaning what it does. It's worth noting that if this argument against non-normative regularity analyses were correct, it would tell equally well against Brandom's own positive view: namely that meanings are engendered by *norms* of use. For one can read off a meaning from a *norm* of use no more easily than one can read it off a *regularity*. See chap. 5, section 7, for further discussion.

sort of property. In order to establish that 'being a sample of water' is constituted by 'being made of H_2O molecules', what we need to show is that the underlying property, 'being made of H_2O', can explain the *symptoms* of the superficial property, 'being water'. But we are *not* required to *explain* why being a quantity of water reduces to being made of H_2O. Indeed, one might well regard such constitution facts, like facts of identity, as not susceptible to explanation. No doubt one can explain why *we believe* that to be water is to be made of H_2O and why *we believe* that Hesperus is Phosphorus; but the facts themselves would seem to be explanatorily fundamental.[8]

So why does the meaning case look different? Why require explanations of the constitution facts here, but not elsewhere? I think there are two tempting lines of thought that could motivate the imposition of ER(a).

In the first place, meaning-properties such as

> w means DOG

and

> w means TRUE

appear to be *complex*: they would seem to contain the meaning-relation, 'w means x', and they would also seem to contain the things meant, i.e. *concepts* such as DOG and TRUE. But one might well think that any analysis of a complex property must derive from analyses of some or all of its parts. Therefore, the fact that a given underlying property constitutes a given complex property will always be something we can *explain*. It will be explicable on the basis of how some or all of the constituents of the complex property are analysed. In particular

> w means DOG

---

[8] Note that the argument:– (1) Water is what has superficial properties M; (2) H_2O has M; ∴ (3) Water is H_2O—is not an *explanation* of (3) in terms of (1). Rather, (1), even if it is a priori, is explained by the conjunction of (2) and (3).

must reduce, in the first instance, to something of the form

R*(w, DOG),

where we have begun by analysing the 'w means x' component of the meaning-property. And then, in order to facilitate dealing with the concept DOG, it is tempting to suppose that the constituent

R*(w, x)

will have to take the more specific form

R(w, thing that falls under x).

This is tempting because if R* does take that form, then

R*(w, DOG)

will be

R(w, thing that falls under DOG)

reducing to

R(w, dog),

from which reference to the meaning-entity, DOG, has been eliminated. Thus, any decent naturalistic reduction of 'w means DOG' will have to take the form, 'R(w, dog)'. To summarize: the idea is that we need to explain the constitution of each meaning-property in terms of analyses of its parts, and that this will require a relational theory of the form 'w means $F \Leftarrow R(w, f)$'. This line of thought offers one possible motivation for ER(a).

An alternative (and I suspect more influential) route to the same conclusion rests on the truth-theoretic import of meaning. In general, any word that means F is true of precisely the fs: that is

w means $F \rightarrow (x)(w$ is true of $x \leftrightarrow fx)$.

And in particular

> w means DOG $\rightarrow$ (x)(w is true of x $\leftrightarrow$ x is a dog).

Moreover one might think that the extensional relation 'w is true of x' is surely reducible to some (as yet unknown) naturalistic (causal?) relation or other—call it 'wCx'. Therefore the non-semantic property that constitutes 'w means DOG' must entail '(x)(wCx $\leftrightarrow$ x is a dog)', which has the form, 'R(w, dog)'. Thus the meaning-constituting property must take that form too. So it would seem that the truth-conditional import of meaning can be accommodated only if there is some relational theory

> w means F $\Leftarrow$ R(w, f),

where R is fairly independent of which meaning-property is being analysed.[9] And, as we have seen, such a theory will enable *explanations* of particular facts of meaning-constitution, and will enable us to *read off*, from a given non-semantic property of a word, which meaning (if any) it engenders.[10]

Thus we appear to have two distinct reasons for imposing part (a) of the explanation requirement.

---

[9] Here is an epistemological variant of this motivating argument. Since 'meaning DOG' has a certain truth-theoretic import, 'U(w)' can be taken to constitute that meaning only if it can be shown to have the same truth-theoretic import; so one must be able to show that

> U(w) $\rightarrow$ w is true of dogs.

But that could be done only if 'w is true of x' is assumed to have some non-semantic analysis (as, say, 'wCx'), in which case 'U(w)' will have to be given the form, 'R(w, dog)'.

[10] The truth-theoretic import of meaning would appear to be what lies behind Kripke's imposition of the requirement. For this motivation would explain why the only reductive analysis that he seriously entertains is:

> w means F $\Leftarrow$ (y)(We would, in ideal conditions, apply w to y $\leftrightarrow$ y is f).

It presumably is the only account that he feels can meet the requirement. For only it can be combined with a prima facie plausible analysis of 'w is true of x' (as 'We would, in ideal conditions, apply w to x') to enable any predicate's truth-condition (and hence its meaning) to be derived and explained. Where the account fails, according to Kripke, is in its reliance on the notion of "ideal conditions" which, he argues, cannot be satisfactorily explicated.

5. CRITIQUE OF MOTIVATIONS

However, neither of these motivating considerations stands up to scrutiny. Consider the first one, which rests on the principle that the analysis of a complex property must involve the analysis of at least one of its components. One objection is that fairly plausible counter-examples to this principle are not hard to find:

x exemplifies doggyness $\Leftarrow$ x is a dog.

The concept DOG is true of x $\Leftarrow$ x is a dog.

The dogs owned by x number 2 $\Leftarrow$ $(\exists a)(\exists b)(aDx \,\&\, bDx \,\&\, a \neq b \,\&\, (t)[tDx \rightarrow (t=a \,\lor\, t=b)])$.

Thus it seems not to be *always* the case that the analysis of a complex property involves the analysis of a constituent. Perhaps this is *often* the case. Perhaps the underlying property that best explains the symptoms of a complex superficial property is *normally* the product of analyses of the constituents of the property. For example, what best accounts for the symptoms of 'x is harder than glass' seems likely to be some property of the form 'x bears H to G', where 'xHy' underlies the "harder than" relation and "Gy" specifies what it is to be glass. But perhaps this sort of thing need not generally be so, as suggested by the three above examples. Moreover, the fundamental criterion of property U constituting property S, namely, that U explain the symptoms of S, does not appear to *entail* that it be so. Therefore it might not be so for meaning-properties.

A second objection is that even if, despite these grounds for doubt, the analysis of a complex *must* in fact proceed via analyses of its components, one may well question the coherence of the above rationale, based on that principle, for analysing meaning-properties relationally. For the rationale was that 'w means F' ought to be reduced initially to 'R(w, thing that falls under F)', and thereby to 'R(w, f)'. However the last step violates the very principle of analysis that is being insisted on: one cannot, by analyses of the *components* of 'thing that falls under the concept DOG', reduce it to 'dog'.

And there is a third objection, even more telling than these. It was suggested, in order to facilitate the eventual elimination of our reference to concepts in

w means F

i.e. in

$R^*(w, F)$,

that we are going to have to reduce the meaning-fact to something of the form

R(w, thing that falls under F).

But this suggestion is easy to resist. For a simple alternative, proposed in the previous chapter, is to analyse "w means x" as "w exemplifies x", and to identify the concept F, with whatever non-semantic property, U-ness, of a word is responsible for its meaning F. In that case

w means F

reduces to

w exemplifies U-ness

which is no more semantic than

U(w).

Thus the principle that complexes be analysed via analyses of their constituents, which can easily be accommodated in along these lines, has no tendency to suggest either a relational theory (taking the form 'x means F $\Leftarrow$ R(w, f)') or any other way of satisfying part (a) of the explanation requirement.

Turning to the second potential motivation for ER(a), namely, that it is needed in order to accommodate the truth-conditional import of meaning, the reasoning behind that idea presupposed that the relation 'w is true of x' has some naturalistic *reductive analysis*. For only given that presupposition does the entailment of 'w is true of dogs' by 'w means DOG' put any constraint whatsoever on what can constitute the meaning-property. But this presupposition might well be false. Indeed, from the perspective of *deflationary* views of truth, it definitely *is* false. The central idea of deflationism is to challenge the traditional assumption that our truth predicate is governed by some explicit definition (of the form 'y is true ≡ y is Q'). And the same considerations undermine the idea that 'w is true of x' is explicitly definable. Moreover, on this basis it can be argued that we have no reason to expect *any* sort of reductive analysis of the truth-theoretic properties and relations, and that the truth-theoretic equivalence schemata are not susceptible to explanation.[11] But if this is right, then we have no reason to suspect that (for example) '(x)(w is true of x ↔ x is a dog)' is reducible to something of the form '(x)(wCx ↔ x is a dog)'. Consequently, even though a word's meaning DOG surely does trivially entail that it is true of dogs, we have no reason to infer that whatever constitutes that meaning-property must take the form, 'R(w, dog)'.[12]

But what about the argument: if 'U(w)' is to constitute 'meaning DOG' it must have the same truth-theoretic import; and so we must be able to show 'U(w) → w is true of dogs'; but this can only be done via a non-semantic analysis of truth, together with an analysis of 'w means DOG' which takes the form 'R(w, dog)'? This

---

[11] See my *Truth* (25–31, 50–1) for a defence of this deflationary ("minimalist") position.

[12] Let me emphasize that the present suggestion is certainly *not* that predicates aren't really true of things and that sentences don't really have truth conditions. The suggestion is, rather, that the truth-theoretic characteristics of expressions flow trivially from their meanings and do not constrain how those meanings are constituted.

One might think that a more plausible motivation for ER(a)—accommodating the deflationary thesis that there is no *general* analysis of "w is true of x"— would be based on the idea that there is a *variety* of analyses of it for different kinds of predicate. But that idea is no less incompatible with the deflationary view that the truth schemata are *explanatorily basic*. See fn. 16 for further discussion.

line of thought overlooks the possibility that 'U(w)' *derives* its truth-theoretic import from the fact that it constitutes 'meaning DOG'. Consider, by analogy, the fact that if something is a sample of water then it is either water or ammonia. Proponents of the theory that water reduces to H_2O do not (and cannot) arrive at their theory by *first* accommodating that conditional, i.e. by first showing that if something is H_2O then it has the property of being either water or ammonia. Rather, they are entitled to infer and explain the conditional on the basis of their theory— independently motivated—that water is H_2O. Similarly, the conclusion that 'U(w)' constitutes 'w means DOG' does not *rest upon* some prior reason for thinking that it implies 'w is true of dogs'. The proper order of justification, rather, is first to motivate the constitution thesis (by reference to the capacity of U("dog") to explain the overall use of "dog") and thereby to arrive at U(w)'s truth-theoretic import.[13]

Thus both of the considerations that motivate part (a) of the explanation requirement on a theory of meaning-constitution are defective; so there is no reason to respect that requirement. And if we are not bound by it, then the chances of being able to devise a decent theory are much improved.

6. VIOLATING THE REQUIREMENT

What sort of theory might we give if we *don't* impose the explanation requirement? Let me summarize the answer that I elaborated in the previous chapter. An underlying property U constitutes a

---

[13] Anil Gupta, in "Deflationism, the Problem of Representation, and Horwich's Use Theory of Meaning", criticizes this strategy on the grounds (a) that it would be correct only if the *sense* of "w is true of x" were given by our stipulative acceptance of the schema "w means F → (w is true of x ↔ fx)"; and (b) that this is implausible, since it implies that someone could fully understand "w is true of x" only if he understood *every* predicate of English. However, it is vital to distinguish "stipulative acceptance of each instance of the schema" from "following the *rule*: to stipulatively accept those instances that concern the predicates that one already understands". An understanding of every English predicate is implied by the former; but a full grasp of

relatively superficial property S if and only if the co-extensiveness of U and S explains why S is manifested in the characteristic ways that it is. For example, we judge that 'being made of H_2O molecules' constitutes 'being a sample of water' because, on the basis of the assumption that water is made of H_2O, we can explain why water is a colourless, tasteless liquid that boils at 100 °C. In the same way, in order to identify how meaning-properties are constituted, we should look for underlying non-semantic properties that can explain the symptoms of those meaning-properties. But the symptom of a word's meaning is its overall use, principally, the collection of sentences containing it that are accepted and the circumstances in which this is done. Moreover, it is not unreasonable to conjecture that each word has a fundamental law of use, which explains, in conjunction with other facts (including the laws of use of other words), its overall deployment. Thus we naturally arrive at the idea that each word's meaning-property is constituted by some such law of use.[14] That is

> w means DOG $\Leftarrow$ L1(w)
> w means TRUE $\Leftarrow$ L2(w)
> ... and so on,

the truth predicate requires merely the latter. For further discussion see my "The Minimalist Conception of Truth", in *Truth: Oxford Readings in Philosophy*, eds. S. Blackburn and K. Simmons, 239–63.

[14] Or, more accurately (see chap. 2, section (g)) by the fact that a certain regularity is *the* law governing, hence explaining, the words usage.

Note that a *law* of use need not be considered a *rule* of use. So even if (as seems plausible) some suitably modified form of "explanation requirement" should be imposed on an account of what constitutes 'implicitly following rule R', the picture of meaning proposed here need not confront the further problem of showing how *that* requirement might be satisfied.

However, as suggested in other parts of this book (esp. chap. 5, section 6), it seems to me that a solution to this further problem is within fairly easy reach. We can suppose (very roughly) that S implicitly follows R if and only if (1) there is an *ideal law* to the effect that S conforms with R, i.e. S conforms with R is the absence of distorting factors; and (2) this law was inculcated by means of communal "correction", i.e. by processes of reinforcement. Note that the concept of 'ideal' deployed here is fully naturalistic and commonly relied on in scientific explanations (n.b. ideal gases, ideally flat planes, ideally rigid bodies, etc.). Therefore, although it is neater and cleaner to avoid entanglement with the contentious notion of where L1("dog") is a fact concerning the explanatory basis of our deployment of the word "dog", L2("true") is a fact concerning the explanatory basis of our deployment of the word "true", etc. For example, a strong case can be made for the thesis that

$$w \text{ means TRUE} \Leftarrow \text{The law governing our use of } w \text{ is that} \\ \text{we accept the schema "} <p> \text{ is } w \leftrightarrow p\text{"}$$

on the grounds that this use-property of the truth-predicate, in conjunction with other factors that have nothing specifically to do with that word, suffices to account for its overall use.

Notice that there is no need for such reductive facts to take the relational form

$$w \text{ means } F \Leftarrow L(w, f).$$

There is no need for a word's law of use to relate occurrences of that word to members of its extension. Thus there is no reason to expect, given some alleged meaning-constituting law of use, $L(w)$, that we will be able to read off, and hence explain, which particular meaning any word possessing it would have to have.[15]

'implicit rule following' and to reduce meaning-properties *directly* to laws of use (as suggested in the text) one can, by reference to the analysis just proposed, easily accommodate the idea of an *intermediate* level of implicit rule-following.

It is worth stressing that the present, respectable notion of 'ideal law' will not dispel the Kripkean difficulty (mentioned in fn.10) of specifying 'ideal conditions' in which our range of application of each predicate would coincide with its extension. For there is little plausibility to the idea that there is a lawlike tendency for us to accept what is true.

[15] A further objection sometimes levelled against use theories of meaning (and arguably to be found in Kripke's discussion) is that one can imagine a community of speakers whose use of (say) "plus" is *exactly* like ours although they mean something very slightly different by it.

Of course, their *overall* use of "plus" could exactly parallel ours and yet be the product of a different *law* of use, because of compensating variations in other explanatory factors, and this prospect would be no threat to the present version of the use theory of meaning. But suppose that what is allegedly imagined are people whose *law* of use for "plus" is the same as ours though they give the word a slightly different meaning. To this suggestion we can respond (turning the author of *Naming and Necessity* against his later self!) that it is just like trying to imagine a sample of H_2O that is not water. There is indeed such an *epistemological* possibility, but, in entertaining it, the *metaphysical* possibility we would have in mind is *not* one in which the H_2O isn't water, but rather one in which H_2O (i.e. water) fails to be a colourless, tasteless liquid, etc. Similarly, we can imagine that our law of use for

7. TRUTH

Affiliated with part (a) of the explanation requirement is the further idea—part (b)—that one must be able to explain why any meaning-constituting property engenders the particular *extension* that it does. That is

ER(b)   w means F $\Leftarrow$ L(w) only if it is possible to explain **(without assuming 'w means F$\Leftarrow$L(w)')** why words with L(w) are true of fs and only of fs.

Here I have emphasized something that is merely implicit in my earlier formulation—implicit in the fact that ER(b) appears just after ER(a)—namely, that the required explanation *not* go via an unexplained premiss specifying which meaning-property is engendered by L(w).

As far as I can see, the only way to make sure that this requirement is satisfied would be, first, to assume that there is some reductive theory of the form

$$w \text{ is true of } x \Leftarrow wCx$$

second, to show that

$$L(w) \rightarrow (x)(wCx \leftrightarrow fx)$$

and third to conclude that

$$L(w) \rightarrow (x)(w \text{ is true of } x \leftrightarrow fx),$$

thereby explaining why the extension of any word that possesses L(w) will be the set of fs. But this strategy presupposes that the "is true of" relation has some reductive analysis, which, in light of deflationism, cannot be taken for granted. Thus ER(b) is

---

"plus" might yield the acceptance of a somewhat different range of sentences from those we actually tend to accept, because that law might be combined with different circumstantial factors. And similarly, the correct characterization of this hypothetical situation is that it is one in which the property of 'meaning PLUS' is not manifested in the familiar way.

misconceived. We cannot be expected to explain, without an independently justified assumption regarding which meaning-property is engendered by a given law of use, why any word governed by that law has the particular truth-conditional import that it does.[16]

Notice, however, that if we *are* allowed to make such an assumption then things are quite different. For in that case the following explanatory argument schema is entirely adequate.

Word k is governed by L(w).

Moreover, in light of the fact that our predicate "f" is governed by L(w):

w means F $\Leftarrow$ L(w).

Therefore: k has the property, 'w means F'.

---

[16] As already mentioned in fn. 12, it might be objected (see, for example, Anil Gupta's "Deflationism, the Problem of Representation, and Horwich's Use Theory of Meaning") that, though the deflationist may be right that there is no *general* analysis of the "is true of" relation, there could nonetheless be various *restricted* analyses, applying to various types of term, i.e. it could be that

w is a predicate of type $T^1 \to (x)(w$ is true of $x \leftrightarrow wC^1x)$
w is a predicate of type $T^2 \to (x)(w$ is true of $x \leftrightarrow wC^2x)$
... and so on.

And, in that case, we *should* be expected to be able to show *directly*, for any term belonging to one of these types, how its meaning-constituting law of use engenders its extension. Thus ER(b) would appear to have some bite after all.

But this is an illusion. In the first place, the existence of restricted analyses would equally go against the deflationary view of truth, according to which the trivial truth-theoretic schemata are explanatorily fundamental. And, in the second place, the only *ground* we might have for being tempted to accept some such restricted analysis for a range of predicates, "f", "g", ... (of type T^k), would be the *prior* discovery that their various laws of use entail

$(x)(wC^kx \leftrightarrow fx)$
$(x)(wC^kx \leftrightarrow gx)$
... and so on,

i.e. the discovery that such laws are what best explain the words' overall uses. Thus the requirement to satisfy ER(b) could not provide a substantive constraint on our search for the correct meaning-constituting properties, since the legitimacy of imposing that requirement would be epistemologically *posterior* to our having identified those properties.

But: w means F $\rightarrow$ (x)(w is true of x $\leftrightarrow$ fx).

Therefore: (x)(k is true of x $\leftrightarrow$ fx).

Thus we *can* explain, on the basis of a word's law of use, why it has the extension it does. True, we must be allowed to employ, as an unexplained explanatory premiss, an assumption regarding which meaning-property is constituted by that law of use. But, as we saw in our discussion of ER(a), such an assumption may be entirely justified.[17]

8. NORMATIVITY

How is it possible, within the framework just sketched, to account for the *evaluative* import of meaning? How can it come about that a given non-semantic and non-evaluative meaning-constituting law of use determines the way in which any word conforming to that law ought and ought not to be applied (or, at least, what we ought and ought not be *aiming* to apply it to)? Why should it be, for example, that

$$L1(w) \rightarrow (x) \text{ (It is desirable that w be applied to x,}$$
$$\text{only if x is a dog)}$$

The *wrong* approach to this problem—the approach implicit in ER(c)—is to think that we can explain such implications of a

---

[17] One might say that the use of a predicate 'determines' its extension (i.e. same use implies same extension) but does not 'DETERMINE' it (i.e. enable it to be read-off). This is how I put the matter in "Meaning, Use, and Truth", *Mind*, 1995.

As we shall see in the next chapter, renunciation of ER(b) has important implications for the proper treatment of *vagueness*. For it is widely held that vague predicates cannot have sharp boundaries. And the main rationale for this conviction is that there would be no way of *explaining*, on the basis of our use of a vague predicate, why any exact boundary it might have would be located just where it is, rather than somewhere slightly different. But if the explanation requirement is misguided, then this argument is undermined. And so the apparent conflict (embodied in the sorites paradox) between vagueness and sharp boundaries is dissolved.

given law of use without making any assumption as to which meaning that law constitutes. One way of *trying* to implement this wrong approach would be by first trying to explain the truth-conditional import of the meaning-constituting property. But this falls foul of deflationism, as we have just seen. Alternatively, if there were a reductive analysis, 'wC*x', of the relation 'It is desirable that w be applied to x', then one might hope to show, for example, that

$$L1(w) \rightarrow (x)(wC^*x \rightarrow x \text{ is a dog})$$

and thereby to explain the normative import of L1(w). But from a deflationary perspective such a reduction is no less implausible than an analysis of truth.

The *right* approach, rather, is to begin by explaining why we should aim to believe only what is true. Or, what comes to the same thing, to explain why, if a predicate means F, we should aim to accept applications of it only to fs. And it is plausible that the basis for such an account is either pragmatic, or moral, or both. For it is uncontroversial that deliberating on the basis of true belief tends to facilitate successful action. And it is also fairly uncontroversial that a commitment to truth 'for its own sake' is a basic virtue. Therefore we might develop the following explanatory sequence. The non-semantic facts about w's use would constitute its having a certain meaning; that would enable us to see (as shown in the previous section) why w is true of certain things and not others; and that, given the pragmatic and moral norms of truth, would in turn account for how we should wish the word to be deployed.[18]

9. THE 'PROBLEM OF ERROR'

It is often suggested that a fundamental constraint on a decent theory of meaning-constitution is that it solve the so-called

---

[18] For further discussion, see chap. 5.

'problem of error': the account must provide a criterion by which we can distinguish which deployments of a term are correct and which are erroneous.

But we are now in a position to see that there are two quite different ways of construing this proposed constraint: one way making it illegitimate and the other making it trivial.

If we take it to require that the correct-application condition for a word must be derivable from its meaning-constituting property *without any assumption about which particular meaning that property constitutes*, then the problem of error presupposes an inflationary view of truth; so it is a pseudo-problem.

If, on the other hand, we require that derivation, but we allow that some independently established meaning-constitution thesis can be a premiss of it, then the problem of error will place no constraint at all on a theory of meaning-constitution. For a given underlying property will enable us to solve the problem *because* it is meaning-constituting, not the other way round.

10. CONCLUSION

My aim in this chapter has been to focus attention on a certain alleged adequacy condition on reductive accounts of meaning-properties: roughly, that each constitution fact itself be explicable. I have tried, first, to articulate this 'explanation requirement' in various forms; second, to show that it is widely assumed; third, to lay out the reasons for assuming it; fourth, to criticize those reasons; fifth, to indicate the attractiveness of theories that violate it; and sixth, to show how the representational and normative import of meaning might nevertheless be accommodated.

The main moral of this story is simple. Kripke, Boghossian, Brandom, and others have made a good case for thinking that the explanation requirement cannot be satisfied by a purely naturalistic account of meaning. But instead of concluding, as they do, that no such 'pure facts' can underlie what words mean, we ought to appreciate that the explanation requirement need not and should not be respected. This would open the door to a more flexible and viable view of the matter: meanings are engendered by non-semantic and non-evaluative laws of use.[19]

---

[19] It seems to me that this was Wittgenstein's picture. It explicates the 'definition' that he offers in para. 43 of the *Philosophical Investigations*: "the meaning of a word is its use in the language." Thus I don't agree with Kripke's reading of him as being *opposed* to accounts that seek to analyse meanings in terms of dispositions of use, and as denying that there are any 'naturalistic' facts as to what words mean.

4

The Sharpness of Vague Terms

1. THE SORITES PARADOX AND HOW BEST TO APPROACH IT

The sorites paradox may be articulated as a classically correct argument for the conclusion that every predicate has a sharp boundary—a conclusion which might appear to rule out the existence of phenomena that obviously do exist, namely, 'borderline cases' and vagueness. In other words, given a long sequence of gradually more and more f-like objects—a sequence which begins with things that are unquestionably *not* f and ends with things that unquestionably *are*—we can prove by means of the sorites reasoning (which is valid in classical logic) that one of these objects is the *first* f in the sequence: nothing before it, and everything after it, is f.

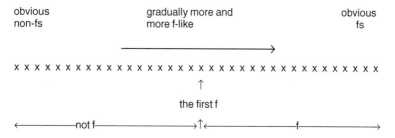

We can prove, for example, that there is a particular number of dollars, such that having assets worth that amount is enough to make you rich, but having assets worth just one dollar less than that is not enough.[1]

To this surprising result there are only two prima facie reasonable responses; but both seem initially unattractive, which is what gives us a paradox. One is to suspend or revise or abandon classical logic. This would mean, at the very least, not relying on it in certain contexts where vague terms are deployed. But perhaps, more radically, it would mean replacing classical principles with a quite different logic. The other possible solution to show that the conclusion of the sorites argument is, on reflection, not really counter-intuitive after all—to show that there is, on reflection, no genuine tension between a predicate"s being vague and its having a sharp boundary.

---

[1] The argument may be formulated as follows. Let 'Rn' be short for 'Net assets worth n dollars suffice for being rich'. Now it is obvious that $R10^9$ and that $-R3$. And we can add various instances of the law of excluded middle, to get

$$R10^9 \ \& \ (R10^9-1 \ v \ -R10^9-1) \ \& \ldots \& \ (R5 \ v \ -R5) \ \& \ (R4 \ v \ -R4) \ \& \ -R3.$$

Now, given the law of distribution of conjunction over disjunction (and given that if n will suffice then anything more than n will suffice, and that if n won't suffice then anything less than n won't suffice), we can infer

$$[R10^9 \ \& \ -R10^9-1 \ \& \ -R10^9-2 \ \& \ \ldots \ \& \ -R5 \ \& \ -R4 \ \& \ -R3]$$
$$\vee [R10^9 \ \& \ \ \ R10^9-1 \ \& \ -R10^9-2 \ \& \ \ldots \ \& \ -R5 \ \& \ -R4 \ \& \ -R3]$$
$$\vee [R10^9 \ \& \ \ \ R10^9-1 \ \& \ \ \ R10^9-2 \ \& \ \ldots \ \& \ -R5 \ \& \ -R4 \ \& \ -R3]$$
$$\vdots$$
$$\vdots$$
$$\vee [R10^9 \ \& \ R10^9-1 \ \& \ R10^9-2 \ \& \ \ldots \ \& \ R5 \ \& \ -R4 \ \& \ -R3]$$
$$\vee [R10^9 \ \& \ R10^9-1 \ \& \ R10^9-2 \ \& \ \ldots \ \& \ R5 \ \& \ R4 \ \& \ -R3]$$

This proves that there is a precise cut-off point—a minimum number of dollars needed to be rich—which is either 10^9 or $10^9 - 1$ or...or 5 or 4. We have not thereby determined what that point is; but we have nonetheless shown that there exists such a point.

Note a couple of convenient (but inessential) idealizations: (1) that "rich" is a proper predicate, i.e. that there is an absolute property of *being rich*, simpliciter, and not merely *being rich, relative to group G* or *being rich, relative to standard S*; and (2) that the only richness-determining underlying parameter is 'cash value of net assets'. Anyone who doesn't like assumption (1) can substitute something that they *will* accept as a genuine predicate (perhaps "man", or "table", or "heap". And we can dispense with assumption (2) by taking the underlying parameter to be some function of the several relevant f-making characteristics.

The second of these options ought to be thoroughly explored before we resign ourselves to the first one. For classical logic is deeply entrenched, instrumentally reliable, and appealingly simple. And no decent alternative, more friendly to the intuition of 'fuzzy boundaries', has ever been devised.[2] So it can be sensible to give up classical logic in response to vagueness only if the classically derivable sorites conclusion really is intolerable. Therefore, if one could show that it *isn't* intolerable, that there is in fact no cogent reasoning behind the conviction that vagueness precludes sharp boundaries, then the pressure to suspend classical logic would be relieved.

In what follows I will attempt to do just this. I will describe and criticize three distinct lines of thought that, individually and jointly, have brought so many philosophers to that conviction. The sense of there being a conflict between vagueness and sharp boundaries—i.e. the sense of there being no fact of the matter as to which is the cut-off point between rich and not rich, bald and not bald, etc.—will thereby be exposed as a misconception, a product of confusion, an 'intuition' not worth respecting.

Before proceeding let me quickly mention a couple of alleged solutions that I will not be considering in detail. (1) There's the idea promoted by Peter Unger[3] that vague terms are not true of anything (e.g. that nobody is rich). However, not only is this highly counter-intuitive, but it threatens to make vague terms (i.e. nearly *all* terms) unusable. Moreover, the sorites proof of it could equally well be turned on its head to show that each vague predicate is true of *everything*, e.g. that since a billionaire is

---

[2] In light of the argument given in fn. 1, the paradoxical conclusion can be avoided only by rejecting either the classical law of excluded middle, 'pv-p', or the classical law of distribution of conjunction over disjunction, 'p & (qvr) → (p & q)v(p & r)'. But see Timothy Williamson's *Vagueness*, 1994 for an account of the extreme difficulties facing various attempts to develop a vagueness-oriented non-classical logic. Amongst the philosophers who have, nonetheless, gone in that direction are Stephen Schiffer ("Vagueness and Partial Belief", *Philosophical Issues, 10: Skepticism*, 2000) and Hartry Field ("No Fact of the Matter", *American Journal of Philosophy*, Dec. 2003).

[3] P. Unger "There are no ordinary things," *Synthese* 1979 pp. 117–154.

obviously rich, then someone with no assets at all must also be rich. (2) There's the idea that the specification of a *context of utterance* eliminates vagueness. However, as mentioned in fn. 1, I shall be focused here on extensions that are determined, independently of contextual considerations, by the literal semantic meanings of predicates. I am assuming that there exist such predicates (if not "rich", then perhaps "man", etc.), i.e. that *speaker meaning*—an occasional intentional decision to mean by an expression something beyond that literal semantic meaning, e.g. to mean "tall man" by "tall"—is not *inevitably* involved in extension fixing. (Note, to repeat a point from chap. 1, section (a), that without such an assumption it is hard to see how a language of thought could operate. For, given different instances of the same mental term, how could the mind "know" whether or not they are meant in the same way and, hence, whether or not they are inferentially relatable?). Anyway, and independently of that assumption of mine, it seems pretty clear that contextual speaker meaning will not *eliminate* vagueness. The alternative more specific meanings that may be given to a vague term in a particular context will *continue* to be vague (although, perhaps, *less* vague).

2. THE LEGITIMACY OF INEXPLICABLE EXTENSIONS

The most potent of the various considerations suggesting a conflict between vagueness and sharp boundaries goes like this:

(1) There must be some 'direct' explanation of why it is that the non-semantic facts about our use of the word "rich" engender whichever extensional characteristics it has, i.e. that it is true of certain things and not others—where a 'direct' explanation is one that does not proceed via an unexplained premise about what meaning derives from those facts of use.

(2) There could be no such explanation of why, given our use of "rich", it is true of all and only those people who have at least $400,404 (rather than, at least $400,405). It is absurd to think that there is anything in our patterns of deployment of this term that could single out that particular extension.

(3) Therefore, "rich" is not true of just those people.

(4) Therefore, by parallel arguments "rich" has *no* precise extension.[4]

But premiss (1), I would suggest, is simply wrong. It is closely affiliated with what I have called the 'Explanation Requirement'—the condition that any adequate theory of meaning-constitution must allegedly satisfy that I criticized at length in Chapter 3. Thus, even if the predicate "rich" *does* apply to exactly those individuals with $400,404 or more, we should *not* expect any 'direct' explanation of why our use of "rich" implies that it does. Note that this is not to deny that there is any explanation *at all* of the word's extension in terms of its use. For if we assume, as unexplained explanatory premisses, (a) that a certain use of w is what constitutes the semantic property 'w means RICH', and (b) that 'being rich' is constituted by 'having at least $400,404', then it is a very simple matter to explain the relationship between the word's extension and its use.[5] But premiss (1) states that an explanation must be possible without assumptions (a) and (b), and this claim is a mistake.

---

[4] This sort of reasoning is widely endorsed. See, e.g., Stephen Schiffer, "Vagueness and Partial Belief"; and Crispin Wright, "The Epistemic Conception of Vagueness", *Southern Journal of Philosophy* 33, 133–59.

[5] The explanation goes as follows:

w has use-property U-ness
U(w) → w means RICH [premiss (a)]
w means RICH → w is true of, and only of, rich people.
x is rich ↔ x has at least $400,404 [premiss (b)]
∴ w is true of, and only of, people with at least $400,404.

Note that this explanation goes through, even if the extension of "rich" is context-dependent, as long as it is issued from within a context in which premiss (b) holds.

To see why, consider the reason that one might be tempted to demand the more stringent explanation. Suppose the extension of "rich" really is the set of people with at least $400,404. Now it is uncontroversial that the meaning of a 'proper' predicate determines its extension. Therefore

$$w \text{ means } \text{RICH} \;\rightarrow\; (x)(w \text{ is true of } x \leftrightarrow \$400,404x).$$

That is, if any word w means what the English word "rich" does, then it must be true of just those people who have $400,404 or more. From this conditional we may infer that whatever constitutes its antecedent must determine the presence of whatever constitutes its consequent. But the antecedent—that w means RICH—is constituted by something in our use of w. And, insofar as the relation 'w is true of x' reduces to some non-semantic relation 'wCx', the consequent (that w is true of people with at least $400,404) is constituted by '$(x)(wCx \leftrightarrow \$400,404x)$'. Therefore, from non-semantic facts about the use of "rich", it must be possible to deduce that $(x)(wCx \leftrightarrow \$400,404x)$ and thereby to explain why it is that $(x)(w \text{ is true of } x \leftrightarrow \$400,404x)$.

But, as emphasized in the previous chapter, the possibility of this sort of explanation depends on there being some reductive analysis of the "true of" relation. Thus the demand for a *direct* explanation of a word's extension on the basis of its use—which leads to the conclusion that a vague predicate can have no precise extension—is founded on an *inflationary* view of truth. However, insofar as one takes the view that our understanding of the truth predicate is constituted by our acceptance of instances of the schema "<p> is true $\leftrightarrow$ p", then we have no reason to expect either a reductive analysis of truth or a reductive analysis of the 'true of' relation. Thus the rationale for demanding a direct explanation of a word's extension in terms of its use is fallacious.[6] Hence the argument, based on that

---

[6] Even when the predicate under consideration is context-sensitive, even if the extension of "rich", contrary to my simplifying assumption, does vary from

demand, for supposing that vague terms cannot have sharp boundaries, is also fallacious. Exposing this fallacy should help to undermine and remove such sentiments. Thus we might solve the sorites paradox without having to sacrifice classical logic.[7]

3. EXPLAINING THE UNLOCATABILITY OF BOUNDARIES

Let me turn now to a second influential consideration underlying the intuition that if "f" is vague, then there is no line such that everything on one side of it is f and everything on the other side is not f. Everyone agrees that it is impossible to *find out* exactly where the boundaries of the extensions of such predicates lie. For example, we cannot conceivably come to know

one conversational setting to another, my line of argument, slightly modified, nonetheless applies. The questionable claim will then be that:

> The predicate, "rich", cannot have, relative to context C, a precise extension, because there could be no explanation of how our meaning-constituting use of "rich" would, relative to that context, engender any precise extension.

And my basis for questioning it will be that, unless one presupposes the existence of some inflationary analysis of "word w is true of object x", then one has no right to expect that the condition

$$w \text{ means RICH} \rightarrow (x) \ (w \text{ is true, in C, of } x \leftrightarrow x \text{ has at least } \$400{,}404)$$

will have to be grounded in an entailment, by the meaning-constituting use of w together with a characterization of context C, of the set of things of which w is true in C.

[7] The preceding discussion (of what I think is the principal basis for imagining that vague predicates can't have sharp boundaries) is an improved version of some passages in my "Stephen Schiffer's Theory of Vagueness" (*Philosophical Issues 10: Skepticism*, 2000).

By the way: it would be illegitimate to complain that since deflationism has a highly counter-intuitive consequence, namely, that vague terms are sharp, then there is good reason to embrace inflationism. For we have just seen that the *source* of the intuition that vague terms cannot have sharp boundaries is the prior tacit assumption that inflationism is correct. Therefore a legitimate criticism of the position advanced in the text would have to take the form of an *independent* argument in favour of inflationism and against deflationism. There is no space to review that debate here. But for articulation and defence of the deflationary perspective see my *Truth*, 2nd edn.

precisely how little money would suffice to make a person rich. But does this not suggest that there are no such facts to be known—in particular, that there is no specific number of dollars that marks the cut-off between those who are rich from those who aren't?

This reasoning comes in two forms. The more ambitious variant involves the verificationist thesis that it is *impossible* for there to be a fact that cannot, at least 'in principle' be discovered. But what could motivate this form of verificationism? How might one be seduced into feeling that if a word is true of a thing then that's being so will always be possible for us to verify, given sufficiently favourable epistemic conditions? I suspect that the source of this idea is the fallacious line of thought we have just examined: the inclination to think that there must be some direct explanation of a word's extension in terms of its use. Certainly, if the existence of such explanations could be counted on, then since explanations are derivations, we could in principle find out what every predicate is true of; and so there would indeed to be no room for undiscoverable facts of the sort in question. But if some such inflationism-inspired line of thought is in fact what lies behind verificationism, then the deflationist criticisms presented in section 2, should help to undermine its appeal.

However, there is a second way of arguing from the unlocatability of sharp boundaries to their non-existence: namely, by inference to the best explanation. If there really were facts about the exact locations of the boundaries of vague predicates, then why on earth would they be undiscoverable? Surely, one might feel, the best way of accounting for the unknowability of such facts is to suppose that there just aren't any. Surely, the best explanation of our inability to give the precise locations of the boundaries of vague concepts is that these boundaries don't have precise locations.

But what calls for explanation here is not merely that we can't *know* exactly where the boundary of a vague term is located, but, and more fundamentally, that we can't even have a stable *belief* about where it is. Once we have accounted for our inability to settle on precisely where we *think* the boundary is between the f's and the non-f's, the impossibility of *knowing* where it is follows trivially. Moreover, it is not at all clear how the difficulty we have in reaching a firm conclusion about its exact whereabouts would result from there being no such fact. What is needed, rather, is some explanation of that difficulty in terms of the fundamental rules or practices that govern our use of vague predicates.

And such an explanation is not hard to find. We can suppose that the basic conceptual role of a vague predicate consists (to a first approximation) in our inclination to apply the predicate to certain things, and to apply its negation to certain other things, leaving unspecified what to say about things in the middle (the obviously borderline cases). Somewhat more realistically, we might suppose that the meaning-constituting basic

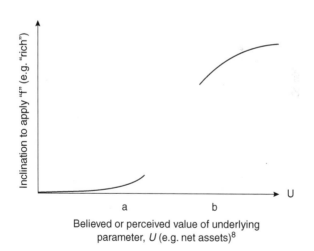

Believed or perceived value of underlying
parameter, U (e.g. net assets)[8]

FIGURE 1

[8] In the case of observation terms, such as "red", which are applied as a result of the mental registering of some unarticulated underlying property, e.g. a precise hue, it may be inappropriate to speak of there being any *belief* about, or *knowledge* of, that property. Perhaps "perceived" or "sensed" would be more accurate in such cases.

acceptance-property of a vague predicate "f" is given by the sort of regularity depicted in Figure 1, which specifies the degree of inclination to apply the predicate to an object as a function of the perceived or believed value of some underlying parameter, U.

And to be even more realistic, we should appreciate that the exact shape of the function will vary somewhat from person to person and time to time.[9] Insofar as this is the *fundamental* fact about our use of "f", i.e. the fact on the basis of which all other facts about its use are to be explained, we can see that no one who has a full grasp of "f"'s meaning will confidently apply it to things that are identified as being in the middle range. For if someone's basic law for the use of "f" is to apply it when U is held to be greater than b and to reject its application (i.e. to apply "not f") when U is held to be less than a, then he can acquire no information that would incline him to begin applying either predicate to things whose value of U is held to be between a and b. To make this especially obvious, consider—by analogy—an artificial 'gappy' predicate, "glub", introduced by the rule to apply it to any number greater than 20 and to apply its negation to any number less than 10. Clearly this basic law of use will, whatever happens, never engender the attribution of either of "glub" or of "not glub" to numbers in the middle, such as 14. Similarly, the basic laws of use of vague predicates explain why there is no stable inclination to apply them to their so-called 'borderline cases'.[10] Therefore, given our introspective capacity

---

[9] This variation is consistent with there being a constant *communal* acceptance-property (hence a constant *communal* meaning and extension) determined by some form of 'averaging' over individual acceptance-properties.

Imagine a series of communities exemplifying a series of gradually (monatonically) varying acceptance properties for "rich". Plausibly, the extensions of their terms will vary accordingly. And certainly, each community, A, will assign a high probability, for certain values of x and B to the proposition *that object x is within the extension of its own term and is not within the extension of community B's term.* So it will be generally agreed that there is variation in the extension of "rich". But there need be no explanation of *why* this occurs, and no knowledge of exactly *how* extension varies as a function of acceptance property.

[10] In further support of this claim see my "The Nature of Vagueness" *Philosophy and Phenomenological Research* LVII: 4. And see also the discussion at

to become aware of such inclinations, anyone confronted with an object in that middle range can appreciate that no further investigation could help him decide which of "f" or "not f" applies.[11]

These considerations explain why someone who possesses certain information about an object, k—namely, that its value of the parameter U (determining degree of f-ness) is in the middle range—will experience the peculiar paralysis of judgement that is symptomatic of vagueness: he will feel that neither "f" nor "not f" applies and that nothing he might discover could settle the matter. In order to explain, in addition, why no one can *know* whether k is f, note that a *belief* that k is (or is not) f could qualify as knowledge only if it were inferred, perhaps unconsciously, from k's value of U.[12] But (as we have just seen) whenever something's value of U is in the middle range, then anyone who recognizes this, and who fully understands "f", will *not* infer that "f" (or "not f") applies. Consequently, even if "f" really does apply to k, knowledge of that fact is conceptually impossible: it is precluded by the particular property of k that happens to be responsible for its f-ness, in conjunction with the

---

end of this section. But even if the claim is mistaken, more-or-less the same account of vagueness-induced ignorance can be given. It will suffice to suppose that the meaning-constituting conceptual role of a vague predicate "f" is not merely to apply it to certain things and to apply "not f" to certain other things, but, in addition, to apply neither predicate to things in the middle range. Thus instead of trying to *explain* our response to the middle range in terms of the *basic* conceptual role of the predicate, we can retreat to the option of building that feature in to the basic conceptual role.

[11] Imagine a person who starts out using a certain vague term just as we do, but who then begins to have definite, stable, intuitive opinions about its application to objects that were previously regarded as borderline. Since this individual has no inclination to defer to us, and since his new opinions are *underived*, we can only suppose that he has come to give the term a somewhat new basic acceptance-property, hence a somewhat new meaning.

[12] Someone may be told, and thereby *know*, that something is f, without *himself* inferring it from any view about, or sense of, the thing's underlying nature; but this process provides knowledge only if whoever is the source of the information *has* carried out such an inference.

particular property of "f" that is responsible for its meaning.[13] Thus a sharp boundary between the f's and the non-f's may exist, and yet its undrawability—and hence unknowability—be perfectly well explained.

One might be tempted to think that a supersmart Martian, fully aware of each detail of our practice with "rich", could conceivably figure out where its boundaries lie. But what method of discovering this could the Martian employ? To suppose that he knows of a general rule associating an extension with any given use-practice is simply to assume the falsity of what has just been argued, which is that certain meaning-constituting conceptual roles preclude knowledge of the associated extensions. And it's wrong to respond that the Martian need not himself be governed by a given conceptual role in order to report on the extensional properties of predicates possessing it. For deflationism entails that the only route to a judgement to the effect that foreign term, α, is true of object, k, is by inferring it from a combination of

(i) α means the same (i.e. has the same conceptual role) as my term "h"

(ii) α means the same as my term "h" $\rightarrow$ (x) [α is true of $x \leftrightarrow h(x)$],

(iii) $h(k)$.

Thus the Martian can report on the extension of our term "rich" only via a term of his own that has the same conceptual role, and which, therefore, he will not know how to apply in a variety of borderline cases.

---

[13] Another way of explaining why it cannot be known that k is f is to invoke the principle that genuine knowledge cannot be undermined by the acquisition of further knowledge. For, if someone were to come to know k's value of U, then any earlier conviction he might have had that k is f (or that k is not f) would be undermined.

It is perhaps worth noting a certain potentially anti-theistic implication of the present perspective on vagueness. Since there are facts that cannot be known, omniscience is impossible.

Before leaving this account of the epistemological import of vagueness, let me address a couple of objections to it that have been raised by Tim Williamson.[14]

First, he denies that the vagueness of "f" depends on there being a range of cases in which neither "f" nor its negation is confidently applied. For he imagines an *opinionated* society where, whatever object is presented to someone, either "f" or "not f" is applied with great conviction, but where, in the case of certain objects, these judgements exhibit no inter- or intra-personal consistency. It seems to me, however, that the use of "f" by members of that society is sufficiently bizarre from our point of view, that one may well doubt whether they could mean exactly what we do by it and doubt whether, in their meaning, it is strictly speaking *vague*. But even if it is, the explanation of our irremediable ignorance about the location of its boundary will be similar to what I am suggesting. For the basic use-property of their "f" will be specified by a graph very like the one I propose in Figure 1, but where the y-axis registers *relative frequency* of application, rather than degree of belief. And the explanation of their inability to *know* exactly where the boundary of "f" is located would hinge on the fact that the basic use-property of "f" would, for those cases, preclude any *stable* judgement about it.

Second, Williamson questions whether it is in fact possible to explain, on the basis of the meaning-constituting basic use-properties that I postulate for vague predicates, why they will not be (consistently) applied in a certain range of 'obviously

---

[14] The present approach to vagueness and the sorites paradox (emphasizing the retention of classical logic and the sharpness of vague terms) is sketched in my *Truth* (1st edn., 1990). Similar ideas, but combined with a very different explanation of the irremediable ignorance caused by vagueness, are developed by Williamson in *Vagueness*. This alternative is criticized in my "The Nature of Vagueness", where an elaborated version of my initial account is offered in its place. Williamson's response to my criticism and his objections to my positive account may be found in his "Reply to Commentators", in the same issue of *Philosophy and Phenomenological Research*.

borderline' cases. Surely, he says, I would first have to explain why it is impossible to discover the particular U-property that suffices for f-ness. I agree; but I think it is pretty clear why that prior discovery cannot be made. In the case of a so-called 'natural kind term' (e.g. "water"), its meaning-constituting rule of use licenses the predicate's tentative application on the basis of specified symptoms (e.g. 'colourless liquid', 'coming from one of our lakes') but then identifies its extension as whichever underlying property, if any, explains those symptoms (e.g. being made of H_2O molecules). But the vague predicates on which we are focused are not used in this way. In the case of "rich", "bald", etc., there is an underlying parameter, U; the rule of use tells us that the fundamental basis for whether or not "f" may be applied to a thing is its U-value; and it tells us, more specifically, that it *is* to be applied within a certain range of U-values and that its negation is to be applied within a certain different range. We are not allowed, without changing the meaning of "f", to override or supplement these dictates by supposing that if some relatively sharp 'joint in nature' happens to be discovered somewhere near or within the middle range, then it is to be regarded as the boundary between the f's and the non-f's. Thus there appears to be no way of discovering, given the basic rule of use for a vague predicate "f", the precise underlying property that constitutes f-ness. Moreover, see fn. 10, where I contemplate modifying my proposal—as a fall-back position—so as to *build in* to the basic conceptual roles of vague predicates that neither the predicate nor its negation is applied in the middle range.

4. TRUTH VERSUS DETERMINATE TRUTH

So much for the second rationale for the common conviction (amongst philosophers) that the extensions of vague predicates cannot have sharp boundaries. There is, as far as I can see, just one more source of that conviction. This is our practice of judging, with respect to certain applications of any vague predicate, that there is simply no clear (or definite, or objective, or determinate) fact of the matter as to whether it holds: we recognize 'borderline cases' of which neither "f" nor "not f" is true without qualification. Indeed, many speakers will be prepared to drop the hedging term, e.g. "clearly", and to assert simply that there are things of which neither the predicate nor its negation is true. Thus it can seem that if "f" is vague, then our conceptual/linguistic practice acknowledges a range of things in between those that are really f and those that are really not: our practice appears to reject any sudden transition from f's to non-f's.

The mistake here is a failure to keep clearly in mind the distinction we can and do draw between *truth* and *determinate truth*. Anyone who makes this distinction, however he articulates it, can happily acknowledge a space between the determinately true and the determinately not true (i.e. the determinately false) without thereby allowing any gap between the true and the false. And, as for those speakers who seem to be *explicitly* endorsing such a gap, we can suppose that they are using "true" and "false" to mean "determinately true" and "determinately false". Thus sharp boundaries are quite reconcilable with borderline cases.[15]

In order to sustain this diagnosis it is necessary to elaborate the meaning of "determinately" in such a way as to show that the needed distinction between truth and determinate truth indeed exists.[16] But there is no particular difficulty in doing so.

[15] Throughout this chapter, when I speak of there being a *sharp* boundary between the f's and the non-f's, I mean simply that in the series of more-and-more f-like objects there is something such that everything on one side of it is an f and everything on the other side is a non-f. That is the alleged phenomenon that is often claimed to be inconsistent with vagueness. But clearly my critique of this claim is independent of my use of the word "sharp" to describe the phenomenon. We could equally well employ a different terminology for it, i.e. for there being a particular cut-off point, and we could instead reserve "*sharp* boundary" for one such that everything on one side is *determinately* f and everything on the other side is *determinately* non-f.

[16] It is of *some* help to identify *determinate truth* with *truth relative to every legitimate precisification of the vague terms*. (See Kit Fine, "Vagueness, Truth, and Logic", *Synthese* 30: 265–300, 1975.) For this "super-valuationist" formula provides

We might suppose, to begin with, that the concepts of mere truth and mere falsity are captured by the equivalence schemata

> \<p\> is true ↔ p
> \<p\> is false ↔ not p.

And we can go on to say that an object x is *determinately* f if and only if

> (1)   x is f

and (in a certain sense)

> (2)   It is 'conceptually possible' to know that x is f

—where the intended import of (2) is to deny that the facts about x in virtue of which it is f (i.e. its U-value) and the facts about "f" in virtue of which it means what it does, together entail that "f" is not stably applied to x and hence imply that that "f" is not known to be true of x.[17]

The present account covers other cases of indeterminacy besides those due to vagueness. Consider, for example, Wittgenstein's example of the chair-like entity that keeps on disappearing and reappearing.[18] Does the word "chair" truly apply? The answer would seem to be that it is indeterminate: given the nature of this entity, the basic regularities responsible for our overall use of the word will not, and cannot, engender an answer one way or the other. On the other hand, there are

something of a constraint on the notion—sufficient to imply that every logical truth is determinately true, e.g. "John is rich or not rich". But it does not constitute a full enough account. For, in the absence of any deeper analysis of "legitimacy", "a *legitimate* precisification" can only be understood as "a precisification that is consistent with the *determinate* facts"—which takes us in a circle.

[17] For example, if having $400,404 does in fact suffice for being rich, even though the rule of use for "rich" dictates that it is not to be attributed in such a case, then this fact about someone's net assets, together with that rule of use, will entail that "rich" is not stably applied to him, and hence (for the reasons discussed above) that its applicability cannot be known.

[18] See his *Philosophical Investigations*, para. 80.

alleged examples of indeterminacy that would not, on the present account, be genuine ones. For example, Hartry Field has suggested[19] that the truth value of Newton's statement, "The mass of the moon is invariant", is indeterminate: because it is true if "mass" is taken to mean the same as our "rest mass" and false if it is taken to mean "inertial mass"—and because there is no determinate fact as to which of these things Newton meant. But I can see no reason for doubting that there are determinate facts as to what the ideal law was that governed Newton's use of his term "mass", and as to whether or not it coincides with either of the laws governing our uses of our two terms. Even if there turned out to be more than one equally simple hypothesis about the identities of these ideal laws, we would then have a case of under-determination of theory by data, rather than a case of indeterminacy.

Notice that our account of determinacy does not assimilate it to *knowability*. It says, rather, that if something is determinate then there is no *conceptual* bar to our discovering it: more specifically, our coming to know it is not precluded by the facts in virtue of which it obtains and the facts in virtue of which our words mean what they do. In contrast, it may be in *some* sense 'impossible' for us to find out what Julius Caesar had for breakfast on a given day. But we are not inclined to say that there is no determinate fact of the matter there. For the cause of our ignorance is not simply the intrinsic nature of this fact and the meanings of our words. In this case, the temporal *remoteness* of the fact plays a crucial role in explaining why we will never know it.

It might be feared that this account would obliterate the distinction between *indeterminacy* and *under-determination of theory by data*. For the latter arises when competing theories have the same observational import, when the empirical evidence in favour of them is, and must always be, equally good, so that (arguably) it will always be unreasonable to believe either one

---

[19] See his "Theory Change and the Indeterminacy of Reference" (1973), reprinted in his *Truth and the Absence of Fact*, Oxford University Press, 2001.

of them—i.e. always unreasonable, given their meanings, to accept either theory-formulation. Thus we have facts that are conceptually impossible to know, which is roughly how I have been identifying cases of indeterminacy.

But this assimilation rests on not reading the fine print. In cases of indeterminacy (on my account of it), the meaning-constituting rules of use for certain terms, together with the facts concerning the underlying parameters to which these rules make reference, entail that certain true sentences are not stably accepted, and that is why their truth cannot be known. Whereas, in a case of underdetermination, the meanings of the terms in a given theory-formulation do not preclude *accepting* it; what is precluded rather, is its *rational* acceptance; thus our norms of justification enter the story.

To be a little more specific, note (as we shall see in chap. 6, section 7) that a scientific theory, "T(f, g, ..)", where "f", "g", . . . are its theoretical terms, can be factored into two components: a Ramsey sentence, "$\exists\Phi\exists\Theta\ldots T(\Phi,\Theta,\ldots)$"; and a Carnap conditional, "$\exists\Phi\exists\Theta\ldots T(\Phi,\Theta,\ldots)\to T(f, g,\ldots)$". Acceptance of the latter is explanatorily basic with respect to the use of the theoretical terms—hence it constitutes their meanings. And acceptance of the former—assuming that it is empirically adequate—will be consistent with, but not required by, the meanings of the observation terms and logical terms from which it is composed. What tells us not to accept it—given an empirically equivalent and equally simple competitor—are norms of rationality, not rules of meaning-constitution. Thus underdetermination and indeterminacy are distinct sources of irremediable ignorance.

Thus we may indeed distinguish bare *truth*—even various kinds of *knowable* truth—from *determinate* truth. And this puts us in a position to reconcile the sharpness of vague terms with our characteristic way of responding to their borderline cases.[20]

---

[20] Both Stephen Schiffer ('Vagueness and Partial Belief') and Hartry Field ('Indeterminacy, Degree of Belief, and Excluded Middle', *Nous*, 2000) claim that the mark of indeterminacy (and, in particular, vagueness) is the adoption of

5. CONCLUSION

I have considered and criticized the three considerations lying behind the widespread conviction that if "f" is vague then the transition from the f's to the non-f's must be gradual and fuzzy. Since these lines of thought are defective we are left with no good reason to accept their conclusion. So there's no need to think that classical logic, which tells us, via the sorites argument, to *reject* that conclusion, will have to be ignored and replaced. On the contrary, classical logic is incomparably simple, familiar, and useful. Therefore the eminently rational stance is to retain a full-blown commitment to it, unperturbed by its allegedly 'counter-intuitive' implication that vague terms are, in a certain sense, *precise*. For the supposed oddness of that implication is nothing but a philosophical theory based on bad arguments.[21]

non-probabilistic degrees of belief (whereby one might, quite rationally, have a very low degree of confidence that a certain person is rich, and also have a low degree of confidence that he is not rich). I would argue, however (a) that there is no *direct* evidence for that claim; and (b) that the present account shows that there is no *theoretical* reason to make it either: there is no need to get embroiled in the undesirable complexities of non-probabilistic credibility functions in order to obtain an adequate account of indeterminacy.

[21] Thanks to Ned Block and Tim Williamson for their comments on an early draft of this chapter. And thanks especially to Hartry Field whose insightful, through questioning of the penultimate version forced me to spell out my position in gory detail.

5

Norms of Truth and Meaning

1. HOW DOES THE NORMATIVE CHARACTER OF TRUTH AND MEANING BEAR ON THE ACCOUNTS WE SHOULD GIVE OF THEIR UNDERLYING NATURE?

There can be no doubt that our notions of 'truth' and 'meaning' have a certain normative flavour. After all, true belief is *valuable*. And the meaning of a predicate (e.g. "chien") determines the things (e.g. the dogs) to which one *should* aim to apply it. However, a further thesis of 'the normativity of truth and meaning' is often maintained. It is often supposed, in light of their obvious normative significance, that an adequate account of these notions cannot be entirely 'naturalistic' or 'factual'. In particular, it is alleged that the *deflationary* view of truth and the *use-regularity* conception of meaning, insofar as they are articulated in entirely non-evaluative terms, must for that reason be defective.[1]

In advocating UTM, I am of course opposing this point of view. It can't be denied that there are correct norms concerning truth and meaning—requirements and prohibitions that flow from what an expression means and from whether or not a sentence is

---

[1] Besides the meanings associated with sounds and marks in public languages, this chapter also concerns the meanings of terms *in thought*. Thus the discussion that follows covers the normativity of *mental* content.

true. But it has been suggested in earlier chapters, and will now be argued in detail, that these evaluative implications can easily be reconciled with fully adequate conceptions of truth and meaning that are wholly *non*-evaluative. If this is right then, although truth and meaning do indeed have evaluative *import*, they are not *constitutively* evaluative—they are not themselves evaluative notions. So those of us who are attracted to the deflationary view of truth and to naturalistic analyses of meaning (in terms of 'law-like regularities of use', for example) have nothing to worry about, at least as far as normativity is concerned.[2]

In denying that truth and meaning are constitutionally, i.e. intrinsically evaluative, what I mean, very roughly, is that although these notions no doubt figure in evaluate principles (such as those mentioned at the outset), they are not to be analysed conceptually in terms of uncontroversially evaluative notions such as 'ought', 'rational', or 'good'. A more general definition—one making room for the fact that a notion might be unanalysible and yet still be constitutively evaluative—would have it that a concept is constitutively evaluative if and only if its possession requires possession of 'ought', or, 'rational', or some other uncontroversially evaluative concept.[3] But neither of these attempts to demarcate the set of constitutively evaluative notions is free of difficulties. In the first place, they don't square with the fact that the concepts of *'regarded* as rational', *'believed* to be good', etc. are *not* themselves

---

[2] It might be thought that proponents of non-evaluative theories of truth or meaning would have nothing to worry about even if these phenomena *were* constitutionally evaluative. For, it might be thought that the uncontroversially evaluative ideas (i.e. 'ought') in terms of which truth and meaning would, in the first instance, be analysed could then be reduced to non-evaluative ideas, leaving us, after these two stages of analysis, with non-evaluative accounts of truth and meaning. However, there is no plausible *conceptual*, i.e. definitional, analysis of 'ought' in terms of 'is'; and a weaker (non-conceptual) reduction could not help those, such as deflationists and use-regularity theorists such as myself, who advocate non-evaluative accounts of our *concepts* of truth and meaning. Moreover, it is extremely hard to see how any such two-stage analysis would result in the *particular* accounts of truth and meaning that are championed in this book.

[3] The latter formulation is given by Paul Boghossian in his "The Normativity of Content", *Philosophical Issues*, 13:1, 2005, 33–45.

evaluative concepts, although their possession clearly depends on the possession of such concepts. In the second place, those accounts presuppose, perhaps wrongly, that all evaluative notions are in some way based on some specified stock of uncontroversially evaluative concepts. And in the third place, even if that presupposition is correct, it is undesirable for the evaluative character of the fundamentally evaluative concepts to remain unexplained, i.e. for there to be nothing more than a list of them.

Thus it is far from clear what it is to be a constitutively evaluative concept. However, we can articulate the central issue of this chapter without adverting to any such problematic notion. The central issue is simply whether or not deflationism about truth and the use-regularity theory of meaning can, or cannot, accommodate the value of truth and the relationship between a word's meaning and how it should be applied.

2. DUMMETT AND KRIPKE

Many philosophers have urged the point of view that I will be criticizing in this chapter, but let me single out Michael Dummett and Saul Kripke as especially influential examples. Dummett has argued that the redundancy picture of truth is incomplete, since it misses out the *value* of our having true beliefs and of our making true assertions. And his point applies with equal force to other versions of deflationism.[4] In his 1959 paper, "Truth", he draws an analogy between making true statements and winning a game.[5] Take chess, for example. We might tell someone all

---

[4] The redundancy theory says that 'The proposition *that p* is true' means the same as simply 'p'; whereas certain more recent forms of deflationism about truth, whilst agreeing that our concept is fixed by the intimate relation between 'The proposition *that p* is true' and 'p', take that relation to be *weaker* than synonymy. For example, according to the 'minimalism' defended in my *Truth*, the truth predicate is implicitly defined by means of our commitment to the *material biconditional*, 'The proposition *that p* is true ↔ p'.

[5] M. Dummett, 'Truth', *Proceedings of the Aristotelian Society* n.s. 59: 141–62 (1958).

the rules for how to move the various pieces, what counts as a winning position, etc. But we still wouldn't have fully communicated our concept of 'winning at chess', for we would not yet have mentioned the vital fact that that the players must *try* to win. And similarly, he says, deflationary theories merely identify the different circumstances in which different beliefs and statements are true; they tell us, for example, that the proposition *that killing is wrong* is true if and only if killing is wrong; but they leave out the vital fact that we *want* our beliefs to be true; this is how they are *supposed* to be.[6]

Another philosopher who has laid great stress on the 'evaluative' nature of semantic notions is Saul Kripke. He points out that, for example,

$$\text{``}+\text{'' means PLUS} \;\rightarrow\; \text{one } \textit{ought} \text{ to apply ``}+\text{'' to the triple} <68, 57, 125>$$

and maintains that any adequate analysis of the antecedent meaning-fact

$$\text{``}+\text{'' means PLUS} \;\Leftarrow\; L(\text{``}+\text{''})$$

would have to do justice to such evaluative implications.[7] But he goes on to argue that no reductive account could possibly

---

[6] Something like this position has been reiterated by Crispin Wright in his book *Truth and Objectivity*. He maintains that deflationism is wrong on the grounds that truth is a *goal*, hence a genuine property, not merely a device of generalization. See the Postscript of my *Truth*, 2nd edn., for discussion of Wright's argument. Robert Brandom repeats and endorses Dummett's line of thought in his *Making It Explicit* Surprisingly, he goes on (in chap. 5) to advocate a form of deflationism, namely, his 'anaphoric' form of the prosentential theory of truth. See section 7 of the present chapter for further discussion of Brandom's views. Bernard Williams has also claimed that redundancy-style accounts of truth cannot do justice to its value. See his "Truth in Ethics", *Ratio* 8: 227–42. For similar anti-deflationary ideas see Hilary Putnam's "Does The Disquotational Theory of Truth Solve All Philosophical Problems?" and "On Truth", both repr. in his *Words and Life*.

[7] See Kripke's *Wittgenstein: On Rules and Private Language*, esp. pp. 11, 21, 24, and 87. Strictly speaking, the implication of "+" meaning what it does is, "It is desirable that one apply "+" to the triple $< x, y, z > \leftrightarrow x + y = z$", as in formulation (M) below.

meet this constraint and, consequently, that no such account can be correct. So, for example, one might find it plausible to suppose that when a person means PLUS by the "+" symbol, he does so in virtue of being disposed to assent to certain sums, e.g. "1 + 2 = 3" and not others, e.g. "1 + 2 = 4". But surely no such *factual* dispositions could possibly explain what the person *ought* to accept![8]

In one form or another Dummett's and/or Kripke's sentiments have been endorsed and elaborated by many philosophers (I have just cited Simon Blackburn, Paul Boghossian, Robert Brandom, Allan Gibbard, John Hawthorne, Mark Lance, John McDowell, Hilary Putnam, Bernard Williams, and Crispin Wright)[9]; but I want to suggest that these sentiments are incorrect. As I said at the outset, I don't wish to deny the evaluative *import* of truth and meaning: there certainly are norms that govern them. More specifically, I agree with the following principles:

> (T) It is desirable (i.e. our aim ought to be) to believe only what is true

and

> (M) If a sentence means *that dogs bark*, then it is desirable for us to accept it only if dogs bark; and if a sentence means *that killing is wrong*, then our aim ought to be that we accept it only if killing is wrong, . . . , and so on

But it remains to be seen whether these commitments should lead us to the conclusion that truth and meaning cannot be analysed in non-evaluative terms.

---

[8] Some others who have expressed sympathy for the evaluative character of meaning are John McDowell ("Wittgenstein on Following a Rule"), Allan Gibbard ("Meaning and Normativity"), Robert Brandom (*Making It Explicit*), Paul Boghossian ("The Rule Following Considerations" and "The Normativity of Content"), Simon Blackburn ("The Individual Strikes Back"), and Mark Lance and John Hawthorne (*The Grammar of Meaning*).

[9] For references, see fns. 6 and 8.

After all, it is fairly clear that something can perfectly well have evaluative import *without* being constitutionally evaluative. Surely, infection with smallpox is a bad thing—something one ought to try to prevent—even if (as is plausible) our concept of it is characterizable in purely biological terms. Similarly, there would seem to be no incoherence in fundamentally valuing the preservation of giant pandas, even though the existence of these animals is in itself a non-evaluative state of affairs. These examples illustrate what is surely a common propositional structure: the subject identifies something in 'descriptive' (entirely non-evaluative) terms; and the predicate proceeds to appraise it, to assess it, and to evaluate the identified phenomenon. Thus it is evident that the issue of whether truth and meaning are constitutionally evaluative is not settled simply by calling attention to their evaluative implications: that is, to principles (T) and (M).

Indeed, one might well think that something's figuring in evaluative principles provides no reason *at all* to suspect that it is intrinsically evaluative. And this might be regarded as a decent defence of non-evaluative accounts of truth and meaning against the critique under consideration: namely, that (T) and (M) can hold, and can be recognized as holding, only if truth and meaning are evaluative notions. However, it is one thing to show that this critique is not well founded, and another thing to argue that it is wrong. The latter can be done only through a detailed investigation of precisely how the evaluative implications of truth and meaning really are to be accommodated. Do the best explanations of (T) and (M), and of our commitment to them, require that the notions of truth and meaning be cashed out in terms of explicitly evaluative concepts (such as 'ought'); or is it better to work with wholly non-evaluative theories of truth and meaning?

I will proceed (in sections 3 and 4) to present a case in favour of the latter perspective: I will argue that (T) and (M) are easily squared with the deflationary theory of truth and the use-regularity theory of meaning. Then (in sections 5, 6, and 7) I'll go on to consider whether certain *other* norms might create difficulties for those theories. I will examine three proposals for the analysis of meaning in normative terms: one, due to Bob Brandom and Allan Gibbard, whereby the underlying facts are norms of epistemic justification; another, due to Mark Lance and John Hawthorne, whereby the underlying facts are norms of translation; and a third whereby the underlying facts are cases of irreducible rule-following.

Note that I am simplifying matters in certain respects. First, I am focusing on its being desirable, if one has a certain belief, for that belief to be true rather than false; and I am not explicitly considering the desirability of believing something because it is true. I allow myself this simplification because the two norms, though logically distinct from one another, seem likely to be explicable along similar lines.

Second, belief is not an all-or-nothing matter: rather, we experience a variety of *degrees* of conviction, including 'absolute certainty', 'pretty sure', 'no idea one way or the other', 'fairly unlikely', etc. Therefore, since (T) is concerned merely with full belief, it is incomplete. An adequate version of it would specify, not merely the value of all complete certainties being true, but also the relative desirability of a person's degree of belief (between 0 and 1) in a given proposition being relatively close to the actual truth value (0 or 1) of that proposition. However, given the focus of this chapter, there is nothing to be gained from working with the more complex formulation; on the contrary, its additional complexity would obscure the central issues.

Third, I am writing as though what we *ought* to do, strictly speaking, is not *actually* to avoid false belief, but rather to *aim* to avoid it, presumably, by conforming to certain canons of epistemic justification. In other words, I take it that, insofar as we have no *direct* control over our conformity with the norm of truth, it should not be thought to tell us what we *ought* to believe but rather to specify epistemic situations that are *desirable* or *valuable*. Perhaps this squeamishness on my part is unnecessary, and there *is* a sense of 'ought' in which we ought to believe only what is true. However, I shall ignore this possibility in what follows. Its correctness would call for some reformulations, but would not effect the substance of my argument.[10]

3. REDUCING THE NORM OF TRUTH TO THE NORMS OF MEANING

To begin with, we can simplify the problem considerably by recognizing that (T) and (M) are more intimately related to one another than they might at first appear to be. It might seem that we are confronted with two distinct norms: one regarding truth and the other regarding meaning, one emphasized by Dummett and the other by Kripke. But in reality they are basically the same: the norm (T) is nothing more than a generalization whose particular instances are trivially equivalent to the various elements of (M). More specifically, (T) generalizes the particular norms of belief:

> (B)　It is desirable to believe that dogs bark, only if dogs bark
> 　　　It is desirable to believe that killing is wrong, only if killing is wrong
> 　　　. . . and so on

which, modulo the schematic linking principle

> (L)　We believe *that p* if and only if there exists a sentence, u, such that
> 　　　(i)　u means (to us) *that p*, and
> 　　　(ii)　we accept u[11]

[10] For further discussion of the issues raised in the previous three paragraphs see my 'The Value of Truth', *Nous*, 2006.

[11] Accepting a sentence u is, to a very first approximation, a matter of uttering it to oneself. More accurately, it is a psychological (non-semantic) relation to u that involves relying on it in theoretical and practical reasoning, i.e. putting it (or a mental correlate) into one's 'belief box'. For further discussion, see chap. 2 and see *Meaning* 94–6.

is equivalent to (M). Thus the concept of truth, as it appears in (T), is serving merely as a device of generalization. Since this is precisely the role that is stressed by deflationism, it would be surprising if principle (T) could yield an objection to that point of view.

To confirm these claims let me first review the deflationary account of the *function* of our concept of truth.[12] Generalization normally proceeds according to a simple rule: given some statement about a particular object, we replace the term referring to the object with a (possibly restricted) universal quantifier. For instance

> This raven is black

might become

> Every raven is black.

However, not all generalizations can be constructed in this way: for example, the one whose instances include

> Either snow is white or it is not the case that snow is white

and

> Either there are infinitely many stars or it is not the case that there are infinitely many stars.

Here, and in various others cases, the usual rule seems not to be applicable. How then can the generalization be obtained? What is the single statement that captures all these particular disjunctions?

The deflationist's thesis is that it is merely in order to solve this sort of problem that we have the concept of truth. More specifically, what we need is the schema

> The proposition *that p* is true $\leftrightarrow$ p.

---

[12] Readers who already find these claims plausible enough might well skip straight to section 4.

For by means of it we can convert our original pair of propositions into an obviously equivalent pair

> The proposition *that either snow is white or it is not the case that snow is white* is true

and

> The proposition *that either there are infinitely many stars or it is not the case that there are infinitely many stars* is true

in which the same property, namely, "x is true", is attributed to objects of a certain type, namely, to propositions of the form, <Either p or it is not the case that p>; that is, <pv-p>. So this second pair of claims can be generalized in the standard way, as

> Every proposition of the form, <pv-p>, is true.

Thus our concept of truth is acting as an instrument of generalization. Indeed, wherever it is deployed (in its predominant sense) this would appear to be its function. And what is necessary and sufficient for it to be able to carry out this function is the above truth-schema. Thus it is our acceptance of that schema, rather than any traditional-looking explicit definition, that constitutes what we mean by the word "true".

Let us now return to the main line of thought. Remember that the agenda is to account for (T) and (M), and for our acceptance of these evaluative principles, without assuming that truth and meaning are constitutionally evaluative. And what I said I wanted to do first was to simplify this problem by showing (in light of what we have just seen about the generalizing function of truth) that (T) and (M), despite their superficial difference in topic, really amount to the same thing. Or, more precisely, that the truth norm (T) is just the generalization whose instances are the belief norms (B), which are themselves equivalent, modulo the linking principle (L), to the meaning norms (M). To verify that this is so, consider the belief norms again

> (B)   It is desirable to believe that dogs bark, only if dogs bark
> It is desirable to believe that killing is wrong, only if killing is wrong
> ... and so on

or a little more formally,

> D [Bel *that dogs bark* $\rightarrow$ dogs bark]
> D [Bel *that killing is wrong* $\rightarrow$ killing is wrong]
> ... and so on,

where "D" means "It is desirable that", and 'Bel *that p*' means "We believe that p". What is the general principle of which these claims are instances? Well this is just one of those problematic cases in which the normal method of arriving at a generalization doesn't immediately work. As explained above, the solution is provided by our conception of truth, in virtue of the fact that it is governed by the equivalence schema

> The proposition *that p* is true $\leftrightarrow$ p.

For this enables us to recast each component of (B) into a form that *is* susceptible to generalization in the normal way. Given its instances, namely,

> (The proposition) *that dogs bark* is true $\leftrightarrow$ dogs bark
> (The proposition) *that killing is wrong* is true $\leftrightarrow$ killing is wrong
> ... and so on,

the components of (B) are equivalent to

> D [Bel *that dogs bark* $\rightarrow$ *that dogs bark* is true]

D [Bel *that killing is wrong* → *that killing is wrong* is true]
... and so on,[13]

which generalizes in the standard way to

(x) D [Bel x → x is true],

or, in English

(T) It is desirable to believe only what is true.

This is the generalization of (B)'s components that we were try-ing to find. For, modulo the truth schema, every one of them is entailed by it.

Moreover, relative to the above-mentioned linking schema

(L) (∃u)(u means *that p* & Acc u) ↔ Bel *that p*,

(where 'Acc u' means 'We accept utterance u'), our belief norms (B) entail our meaning norms (M). For example, the component of (B)

D [Bel *that dogs bark* → dogs bark]

together with the necessary and a priori truth of what follows from (L)

u means *that dogs bark* → (Acc u → Bel *that dogs bark*)

yields

D [u means *that dogs bark* → (Acc u → dogs bark)],

which, given that we *know* what we mean by u, entails

u means *that dogs bark* → D (Acc u → dogs bark).

And in a parallel way we are able to explain *every* component of (M).[14]

---

[13] Substitution within the scope of the 'Desirable'-operator of 'the proposi-tion *that p* is true' for 'p' is licensed by the fact that these expressions are *known a priori* to be materially equivalent.

[14] It is also a simple matter to show that [(M) & (L)] → (B). (M) yields "D[(u means *that p* & Acc u) → p]"; (L) yields (as a priori) "Bel *that p* → (∃v)(v means *that p* & Acc v)"; and from these conclusions we can infer "D[Bel *that p* → p]".

Thus we may conclude that there is indeed a single norm here, an instance of which is

> It is desirable to believe that dogs bark, only if dogs bark

or

> If a sentence means that dogs bark, then it is desirable that we accept it only if dogs bark

and that the concept of truth enters the picture only as a way of generalizing such examples. Therefore Dummett could not be more mistaken: not only does the norm of truth reveal no inadequacy in the deflationary conception; on the contrary, that norm provides a paradigm for the deflationist's view that truth is merely a device of generalization.

4. THE SIMILARITY OF 'MEANING' TO NOTIONS THAT ARE NOT INTRINSICALLY NORMATIVE

So far so good. But we have still not arrived at our destination. We have seen that there is, in substance, just one norm here— namely, (M)—rather than two or three different ones. And the argument for this point amounts to a defence of the deflationary view of truth. But it remains to rationalize that single norm. For I still need to motivate my contention that it will hold, and will be respected, even if meaning-properties (such as, 'w means DOG' and 'u means that dogs bark') are analysed in wholly factual, naturalistic, non-evaluative terms—in the way proposed by, for example, certain versions of the use theory of meaning, such as the one developed in Chapter 2.

To that end, my strategy will be to show that our meaning/ truth norm is analogous in character and content to the norms that recommend characteristics, such as courage and perseverance, characteristics which are clearly not constitutionally evaluative.

In each of these cases there might *appear* to be a simple *prudential* explanation of the evaluative fact. For example, an individual will usually benefit from possessing the fortitude to overcome fears and from the ability to pursue goals with determination. And similarly, since the decisions we make that are based on *true* beliefs can be expected to promote the satisfaction of our desires, anyone will tend to benefit from a certain dedication to the truth.

Here is an explicit reconstruction of the elementary reasoning that vindicates this claim. Suppose I want X, and suppose I believe that if I do A, then I will get X. In that case, assuming that A is a possible action under my control, it is likely that

> I do A

Moreover, *if my belief is true* then

> If I do A, then I will get X.

Therefore, by modus ponens,

> I will get X.

Thus

> I will get what I wanted.

So it is clear why I should, in this case, wish for my belief to be true. And it is, for similar reasons, clear why, in general, I should try to ensure that all of my beliefs of the form, 'If I do A, then I will get X', are true. But such beliefs result from inferences that I reasonably take to be truth-preserving. Therefore, I should try to ensure, that all premisses of such inferences are true. But I have no belief that might not at some point be employed as a premiss in such an inference. Therefore I should try to ensure that *all* my beliefs are true.[15]

---

[15] For a more elaborate version of this explanation, taking into account degrees of belief and more realistic decision procedures, see, *Truth*, chap. 3, and Barry Loewer's "The Value of Truth" in E. Villanueva, ed., *Philosophical Issues* 4, Atascadero, Cal.: Ridgeview Publishing Company, 1993.

Thus a concern for truth can be beneficial in the same self-interested way that perseverance and courage can. However, in none of these examples do such prudential considerations fully explain why the traits are good; for it is clear, on reflection, that the norms concerning them remain in full force even when self-interest is unlikely to be served. For example, self-interest is not typically promoted by acts of great courage in battle; and the desirability of knowledge 'for its own sake' in abstruse areas of set theory does not derive from its role in prudential deliberations. Thus these norms are not in the end pragmatic; they do not hold in virtue of the self-centred utility of the traits that they recommend. Rather, they would each appear to be *moral* truths—indeed, they may well be explanatorily fundamental moral truths.

Nonetheless, turning from the question why they hold to the question of why they are *taken* to hold, it *is* quite plausibly the *social* utility of courage, perseverance, and concern for truth, that explains why the norms recommending them are inculcated and widely embraced. We do all benefit from living in a community whose other members are brave in battle; and similarly, we stand to gain valuable knowledge from interacting with people who try to make sure that their beliefs and communications are true. Such considerations cannot *justify* our normative convictions, but might nonetheless *explain* why we have them.

Thus the nature of our meaning/truth norm—its structure, its relation to self-interest, its explanatory status, and the causes of our respect for it—exactly parallels the nature of the norms that recommend bravery and perseverance. Therefore, insofar as it is plausible that those features have moral import without being constitutionally evaluative, it is equally plausible that 'speaking truly' and, more specifically, 'applying words meaning DOG, only to dogs', 'applying words meaning ELECTRON only to electrons', etc. are desirable qualities, but not themselves evaluative.

A distinctive route to the contrary conclusion—namely, that meaning *is* intrinsically evaluative—has been proposed by Paul Boghossian.[16] He begins with the contention that unless someone appreciates that false belief *should* be avoided, she cannot be credited with the notion of belief. But, assuming that every concept's possession conditions include its deployment in certain specific beliefs (or specific types of inference amongst beliefs), then one can understand and assert, "S has concept C", only if one has the concept of *belief.* Therefore, any attribution of concepts (and of meanings) requires possession of a normative concept.

I can see little to quarrel with is this reasoning; but its initial premise—the constitutive normativity of belief—may well be challenged. For consider, in general, how we can tell whether, in order to possess the concept F, it is required that one believe a certain proposition, #F. We must find out what basic rules for use of the concept are necessary and sufficient (given extraneous factors) for explaining the concept's overall deployment. If these rules include 'Believe #F', then that belief is indeed required for possession of F. However if that belief is itself explained on the basis of some more fundamental, more economical rule, then it is not required.

Now applying these principles to the present case, we find that there does exist a plausible explanation—on the basis of a non-normative conception of belief—of why we regard false belief as undesirable. It suffices to assume that believing a proposition is a matter of relying on it in theoretical and practical inference. We can then understand—as we have just seen—why it is that, if a belief's content is the proposition, *that p*, then it tends to be advantageous to have that belief only if p. And we can go on to explain why it should come to be regarded as valuable 'for its own sake' to believe only what is true. Thus there would appear to be no good reason to suppose that our notion of belief (and hence of meaning) is constitutionally evaluative.

---

[16] "The Normativity of Content".

5. FURTHER NORMS OF LANGUAGE

My primary concern so far in this chapter has been to argue that the norms, (T), (B), and (M), provide no basis for supposing that truth or meaning are constitutionally evaluative, and therefore no basis for suspecting that either deflationism or the regularity-of-use theory of meaning must be rejected. And this argument has been completed. However, there are various *other* language-related norms in light of which such suspicions might be harboured. Let me briefly indicate why none of these further normative phenomena in fact justifies concluding that either truth or belief or meaning are constitutionally evaluative.

To begin with, consider:

(A)   Norms of epistemic justification, specifying what it is reasonable for us to accept, either a priori or in light of available empirical evidence.

Certain norms of justification dictate how one ought to use words, given what they mean. For example: if a word means RED, then it would be desirable to apply it to red surfaces observed in good light; if a sentence operator, 'O', means NOT, then one ought not simultaneously to accept both 'p' and 'Op'. On this basis we might be tempted to think that a word means RED *because* it would be desirable to apply it to observed red things, and that 'O' means NOT partly *in virtue* of the fact that one ought to refrain from accepting both 'p' and 'Op'. Thus it may seem that meaning is constitutionally evaluative.[17]

However, this position confronts a pair of related difficulties. To begin with, the question arises of how it could possibly be that the right (i.e. justified) use of a given word (i.e. sound) varies from one linguistic community to another. The only

---

[17] This view is advanced by Robert Brandom in his *Making It Explicit*. See section 7 for a more thorough discussion of his position. The idea is also explored by Allan Gibbard in his "Meaning and Normativity".

plausible answer is that such a variation would have to derive from some variation in how the word is *in fact* used. Thus it must be conceded that there are conditional norms of the form

> Within community C, w's use *actually* accords with regularity R(w) $\rightarrow$ Within C, w's use *ought* to accord with EN(w).

But it would then seem preferable to identify w's meaning property with the 'factual' antecedent of this conditional, rather than with its normative consequent. For, in the first place, we think of a word's meaning as helping to *explain* various non-evaluative facts. For example, my meaning what I do by "rain" helps to explain why and when I sometimes accept "It's raining". But, *what ought to be the case* doesn't have *causal* consequences; it's my *taking* some claim to be justified—not its actually *being* justified—that explains why I make it. Therefore, the causal import of meaning would be hard to understand if meaning were constitutionally evaluative. And this leads to a second point. How are we to establish that certain specific norms of use are the ones that engender a given meaning? The usual basis for a claim of property constitution, i.e. reduction, is that the claimed underlying property explains features of the superficial one, including the symptoms on the basis of which the superficial property is recognized. But the symptoms of a word's possessing a given meaning-property are the ways in which it is used—the circumstances in which sentences containing it are accepted. And, as just noted, it is hard to see how a word's *norms* of use could account for such *factual* phenomena.

These puzzles are dissolved if we invert the imagined explanatory order of meanings and norms, that is, if we take it that a tendency to conform with regularity R(w) engenders the fact that w means what it does; and if we maintain that it is in virtue of this fact that epistemic rationality requires it to be deployed in accordance with EN(w).[18]

---

[18] The origin of epistemic norms is the topic of chap. 6.

Let us turn to a second class of norms that might be alleged to engender meanings namely:

(B)   Norms concerning the desirability of using w in the same way that one of our current expressions,"f", is actually used.

In attributing a meaning to a word by saying "w means F", we refer to the meaning of one of our familiar terms, "f", and we assert that w has that meaning too. The point of such a claim is often to communicate that w *ought* to be used in just the way that "f" is actually used. For example, in the case of a foreign word, w, the idea would be that we are well advised, when abroad, to come out with w in just the circumstances in which, were we at home, we would come out with "f". And one might be tempted to go further:—one might be tempted to suppose that this sort of normative information *exhausts* the content of the meaning attribution, to suppose that a word's meaning F is *constituted* by the fact that it ought to be used as "f" is. In which case meaning is constitutively normative.[19]

It seems clear, however, that the normative fact in view here is a consequence of the non-normative fact that w's basic (expert) usage within the pertinent linguistic community is (say) R(w), which happens also to be our basic use of "f". Given this non-normative fact, and given that the spread of true (hence valuable) beliefs will be promoted to the extent that members of a community use the same words in the same fundamental ways, then each individual *ought* to use w in accord with R(w), i.e. ought to use it as "f" is used.

Thus we have a strong correlation between three things: (1) that 'experts' (or most people) use w in accord with R(w); (2) that w means what it does; and (3) that w's use ought to conform with R(w). One might then, with some plausibility, identify (1) and (2)—i.e. suppose that w's meaning is constituted

---

[19] This position is advanced by Mark Lance and John Hawthorne in their book, *The Grammar of Meaning: Normativity and Semantic Content.*

by its use—and then proceed on this basis to explain w's normative character. However, one might instead decide to adopt the
view under present consideration; to identify the fact that w
means what it does with the instrumental normative fact that
each person ought, for the sake of smooth communication, to
use it in conformity with R(w); and to explain this fact in terms
of the actual tendency for R(w) to be obeyed.

But there are a couple of considerations that militate against
the latter decision. First, it would be hard to square with our
explanatory deployment of meaning-attributions—with our
being able to account for what someone has uttered by reference to what it means. The difficulty here is exactly the same as
the one outlined immediately above in connection with the
view that meanings are constituted by *epistemic* obligations.

And second, the meaning of a word is just *one* factor bearing
on how it would be most prudent to use it; there will often be
other relevant considerations, e.g. local, idiosyncratic goals of
the speaker; and the best way *all things considered* for him (given
his peculiar situation) to use w may well be characterized by
R*(w) rather than R(w). So it may happen that someone means
by w just what is standardly meant, but that he ought *not*, all
things considered, conform with R(w).[20] Now perhaps there is
such a thing as *the fact that w ought, taking account nothing but
its communal use, to be used in accord with R(w)*; and someone
might hope to ground meanings in normative facts of that kind.
But even this desperate manoeuvre won't do. For if we really
bring to bear nothing but w's communal use, and don't make
any assumptions about the nature and purpose and context of
communication, we won't be able to draw any conclusions
about how an individual ought to use the word. The obvious
moral is to stop looking for some way to reduce a word's meaning

---

[20] This develops an objection to the Lance-Hawthorne position that was
made by Stephen Schiffer in his 'A Normative Theory of Meaning', *Philosophy
and Phenomenological Research* 65: 187–93. He points out that even though it
may be rational in some context for someone to use 'inflammable' as we use
"non-flammable", they don't mean the same thing.

to the somewhat indeterminate and context-dependent normative import of communal usage, and to acknowledge that usage
itself as providing its underling nature.[21]

Finally, we need to consider:

(C)   Rules of use for words, responsible for our meaning
what we do by them.

Note that the view criticized under (A)—namely, that a word's
meaning derives from the *correctness of certain norms* governing
its use—should not be confused with the idea that its meaning
derives from the *commitment to certain norms* or, in other words,
from the *following of certain rules* for its use. The latter idea is
not implausible; and is perfectly consistent with what I have
been arguing in this chapter. For neither 'believing that one
ought to accord with R(w)' nor 'following the rule, to accord
with R(w)' are themselves evaluative notions; so in acknowledg-
ing that meaning reduces to implicit normative commitment,
i.e. implicit rule-following, we are not thereby taking it to be
constitutionally evaluative. Nor are we conceding that that
meaning won't be naturalizable; for a reduction of meaning to
rule-following does not preclude a further analysis of rule-
following in terms of law-like use-regularities. Let me indicate
how such an account could be developed.

6. A NATURALISTIC ACCOUNT OF IMPLICIT RULE-FOLLOWING

There is a common form of explanatory theory which consists of
postulating a system that is governed, in so-called 'ideal'

---

[21] It might be thought that norms of deference to 'experts' can provide some
basis for thinking that meaning is constitutionally normative. And we can grant
that someone's meaning what he does by a given word may be determined, in
part, by his being prepared to accept correction from certain other people. But,
in that case, what is meaning-constituting is *not* that he *ought* to defer in this
way, but rather the fact that he *does* defer. And this is a non-evaluative fact.

conditions, by certain natural laws, but which is subject to a variety of factors that cause deviations from the behaviour that would 'ideally' occur. Note, for example, the theories concerning ideal gases, ideally rigid bodies, and ideally flat surfaces. Questions of whether such a model is plausible in a given context, and of which 'ideal laws' and potential 'distorting factors' should be postulated, are settled by the standard principles of scientific methodology, i.e. by reference to empirical adequacy, simplicity, coherence with other successful theories, etc. Thus explanatory models of this kind are thoroughly empirical and naturalistic.

When such a system is part of an animal (capable of desires), *and* when its laws, L, are partly created (or moulded, or sustained) by correction, encouragement, or some other form of positive or negative reinforcement on the part of others in the community, *and* when the laws are explicitly recognized and are deployed in that moulding process, then it is quite natural to regard them as *rules*, i.e. to speak of the animal as implicitly following the rule, 'Conform with L'. Even when the last of these conditions is not satisfied, i.e. when there is no explicit recognition of the laws, it is still somewhat natural to speak of implicit rule-following. Such talk is not compulsory—no explanatory gains derive from it— but nor is there is any compelling reason to eschew it.

Language is one domain in which such an explanatory model is attractive. It is plausible (following Chomsky, see Chapter 7) to postulate a 'language faculty' governed by laws that operate only in 'ideal' conditions. In particular it is plausible to suppose that each word is governed by some such law of use—a law which, in conjunction with other factors, explains the circumstances in which the various sentences containing the word are accepted. The other factors entering into such explanations include the laws of use for other words, external stimuli, general psychological principles, and distorting influences.

If there is a *universal* language of thought, and if its terms are governed by ideal laws that are *innate*, then it is *not* especially natural to regard our propensity to conform with those laws as a matter of rule-following. Rather, one would tend to think of such Mentalese terms as meaning what they do *directly* in virtue of the ideal laws that govern them. But if our language of thought consists of learned public language terms, then, since their laws of use will have resulted in part from communal correction, talk of rule-following is in order, even if the laws/rules are not articulated by anyone. Moreover, even though the innate laws of use for Mentalese symbols are not rules, the correlated laws governing correlated public language words may nonetheless be reasonably regarded as rules, since they are established, in part, on the basis of communal correction.

Thus, in *all* cases it is plausible to suppose that meanings are engendered by ideal laws of use. And in *some* cases it is natural (although not explanatorily advantageous) to acknowledge, as an intermediate step, that the word's meaning derives from our implicitly following rules that correspond to those laws.

7. BRANDOM

Bob Brandom's theory of meaning—elaborated in his magnum opus, *Making It Explicit*[22]—coincides in many central respects with the view developed here. Both stories are reductive; more specifically, both claim, following Wittgenstein, that the phenomenon of *meaning* is grounded in non-semantic aspects of use; both also follow him in stressing that the functions of different words, and the rules for their use, diverge considerably from one another; thus both reject the orthodox idea that truth and reference play a basic role in meta-semantics; indeed both accounts promote a *deflationary* perspective on truth-theoretic notions.

But a glaring difference is that, according to Brandom, meaning is intrinsically and fundamentally *normative*, whereas,

---

[22] See also his *Articulating Reasons*, Harvard University Press, 2000.

according to UTM, it isn't. He maintains that the meaning of a word is constituted by facts to the effect that one *ought* to accept such and such sentences containing it in such and such circumstances, that one is *entitled* to infer certain things from others, and so on. In his picture, such normative facts are consequences of ("instituted by") our implicit commitments:—we implicitly take ourselves and others to be obliged to say this, permitted to infer that, etc.; and these attitudes, in some sense, 'bring it about' that we are in fact subject to such epistemic norms. Finally, at the explanatory/metaphysical base of Brandom's model, there are social practices of producing bits of language and responding to them, of encouraging certain things, discouraging others, etc. These rule-governed activities engender the implicit normative attitudes that institute the normative facts that, in turn, constitute the meanings of words.

Let us examine the relative merits of this 'normative' approach and my alternative ('regularist') form of use-theory (UTM). And let's begin with a point we have already encountered: that, whereas a word's meaning would seem to be causally potent, helping to explain all of the details of our deployment of it (including the actions that result from the beliefs and desires that are articulated in terms of it), its normative attributes are causally inert (since an 'ought' can't cause an 'is'). One might therefore wonder why Brandom did not opt for a slightly different model—one in which semantic facts are constituted directly by our implicit normative attitudes. If he had taken that position then, given that such implicit attitudes, which are non-semantic and not *explicitly* normative, are grounded in our rule-governed practices of word-use, he would have found himself with something more like UTM. (Although there would still be the issue of whether the rule-following could be reduced to regularities.)

The answer, perhaps, is that Brandom would not agree that his meaning-constituting normative facts are causally inert. For he supposes them to be 'instituted' by our attitudes. And if that form of 'bringing into being' is akin to *constitution* or *reduction*, then perhaps the normative facts would inherit the causal powers of the attitudes that 'institute' them? We should consider, therefore, what kind of relation 'institution' might be.

Maybe an analogy with games, such as chess, will help. In that sort of context, it would seem that we are at liberty to stipulate the rules, and that such decisions are what make it right to follow them. It is our *taking* it to be the case that white must make the first move, that one is permitted to castle in such-and-such circumstances, and so on, that is responsible for these norms actually being correct. And we might well think that the same goes for the 'game' of language.

But, on reflection, what obliges a pair of players to follow the rules of chess is not simply the fact that they have each decided to follow them and, as a consequence, are in fact following them. It is that they have *agreed* with one another to follow them. Thus the obligation to conform is rooted in the moral obligation to keep that agreement, together with the prudential fact that their enjoyment of the game depends on keeping it. Similarly, we can suppose that there is implicit mutual agreement within a community of speakers to follow certain rules of word use. Similarly, that agreement creates an obligation to follow and obey the rules, and it will pragmatically benefit speakers to be able to rely on others to do so. Thus it is misleading to suggest that our obligation to conform is brought into existence simply by our implicitly assuming that we ought to. Its real sources are agreement and welfare-dependence.

Thus it would seem that there are fundamental normative facts of the form,

> In such-and-such non-normative circumstances, one is required (or entitled) to do so-and-so

And the relation that Brandom calls 'institution' is simply the relation between the antecedent of such conditionals and their consequents. For example, agreeing to do a certain thing 'institutes', in Brandom's sense, an obligation to do it. But the basic normative fact—the conditional—is not grounded or instituted by anything non-normative. And if this is indeed the way in which our attitudes can give a word certain normative attributes, then one cannot plausibly argue that those attributes are themselves causally potent. So it remains an objection to Brandom's theory that they are alleged to constitute facts that *are* causally potent.

Another questionable feature of his model is that the normative phenomena that are supposed to be meaning constituting include familiar facts of epistemic rationality. I won't dwell on this matter now, since it is on the central topic of the next chapter. But let me quickly mention a couple of concerns about it. How someone *ought* to use a given term depends on his evidential situation; and that situation varies from one person to another within a linguistic community. Thus it varies amongst people who mean the same thing by the term. Consequently, not *all* of the evidential norms governing a word can bear on its meaning. Indeed, our discussion of 'norm institution' provides reason to doubt that *any* of these norms are relevant. For, insofar as the meaning-constituting obligation to follow certain rules of word use derives from implicit agreement and welfare dependence then, as we saw, that obligation is moral and/or pragmatic. But surely our obligation to conform to the principles of non-contradiction, modus ponens, induction, and other norms of *epistemic* justification, is not reducible to morality or self-interest.

An advantage of UTM is that it avoids these difficulties. We begin (explanatorily speaking) with law-like regularities of use. We take these facts to engender (as indicated in section 6) the implicit following of rules. We then divide such rules into those that embody a concern for rationality and those that vary from word to word, embodying decisions as to how our rational commitments are to be articulated. We argue that these word-specific rules are what constitute facts of meaning. And we suppose that the meanings of words—hence, indirectly, those word-specific rules—institute norms of rational acceptance, via explanatorily fundamental conditional norms of the form, 'S means F by w → S is obliged to conform with R(w)'.

Let me complete this brief discussion of Brandom's approach by responding to the objections that he makes to non-normative proposals such as the one just sketched. Following Kripke, he offers a double-barreled critique of the thesis that each word's meaning consists in dispositions or regularities with respect to its use.[23]

First, he argues that one cannot 'read off', from a person's activity with a predicate, which particular meaning he attaches to it, or which objects are within the predicate's extension and which are not. For the notion one might be tempted to invoke to that end, namely, 'the set of things to which the predicate would be applied to in *ideal* conditions', cannot be spelled out satisfactorily in non-semantic terms.

And second, he emphasizes that meaning has evaluative consequences: for example, if a word means DOG then one *ought* to aim to apply it only to dogs. But mere dispositions, mere law-like regularities of verbal behaviour, have no such consequences. So those sorts of 'pure fact' cannot be what meanings are constituted from.

Regarding the first of these arguments, our goal in Chapter 3 was to show that one should not expect to be able to 'read off' the meaning or extension of a predicate from its usage. For such an expectation could be reasonable only from the perspective of an implausible, inflationary view, whereby 'w is true of x' has some sort of reductive analysis, e.g. to 'w would be applied to x in ideal conditions'. Equivalently, just because a given meaning is engendered by a given use, one should not expect any explanation of *why* that is so; one should expect nothing more than *grounds* for maintaining that it is. So, given deflationism, the 'reading-off requirement' should be junked.

And that turns out to be pretty good news for Brandom too! For not only does he subscribe to deflationism (in the form of a

---

[23] S. Kripke *Wittgenstein on Following a Rule*.

'pro-sentential' theory of truth), but his *own* positive account of meaning, namely, that it reduces to epistemic norms of usage, would equally fall afoul of the 'reading-off requirement'. For we will not generally be able to read off what is meant by a word from such normative facts. Granted, from something of the form, 'One ought to apply w to fs and only to f's', one could arguably read off that w's extension is the set of f's. But many norms of word-use, especially, norms of *justification*, don't have that structure—e.g. "One ought to accept instances of '<p> is true ↔ p'."

A less immediately objectionable anti-regularist strategy for Brandom would have been to concede that the meaning of a word need not be readable-off from what constitutes it, but to argue instead (a) that meaning reduces to rule-following, and (b) that in order for the following of a certain rule to reduce to a certain regularity, it *must* be possible—but is *not* in fact possible—to read off the rule from the regularity. For *this* reading-off requirement—applying to analyses of rule-following facts rather than analyses of meaning facts—is not affiliated with inflationism.

But to that argument against regularism a different response would apply: namely, that it *is* possible to read off from the ideal law governing someone's activity, which rule he is following. If the ideal law is 'R(w)', then, provided its operation within a person results in part from communal moulding, the implicitly followed rule is 'To conform with R(w)'. And, as for the charge that this notion of 'ideal law' is not purely empirical or purely naturalistic, it was argued in section 6 that this complaint is mistaken. The notion is deployed throughout science in theories that are established by the standard empirical methods.

So let us turn to Brandom's second Kripkean argument for the impossibility of reducing meaning-facts to use-regularities. Again, there is a certain dialectical instability in his overall position. On the one hand he objects that no mere *factual regularity* in the use of w could entail, for example, that one *ought* to aim to apply it only to dogs. But on the other hand it is no easier to see how someone's normative *beliefs* about the use of w could entail that it *actually* ought to be applied in that way. Thus Brandom's second argument against 'regularism', just like the first one, would equally tell against his own position.

Luckily for both of us, the argument is flawed. For (as we saw in Chapter 3) our epistemic route to the conclusion,

> Such and such use-facts about w engender the
> desirability of applying it only to dogs

can proceed only *via* the recognition that those use-facts constitute 'w means DOG'. So neither implicit attitudes nor regularities can be criticized as candidate meaning-constituters on the grounds that we don't see, independently of their being *successful* candidates, how they could have those evaluative consequences.

Brandom might instead have objected that the peculiar failure of regularity-of-use reductions of meaning is *not* that they cannot account for the desirability of applying predicates only to the members of their extensions, but rather that certain *other* evaluative implications of meaning cannot be explained, viz. the correctness of certain norms of justification. Suppose w's meaning F implies that one ought to obey a certain acceptance-rule, 'Conform with R(w)', for sentences containing w. It might then be argued that if that meaning were *constituted* by the normative fact that one should follow this rule, then, trivially, anyone who means F by w *ought* to follow it; but the fact that some *regularity* (e.g. R(w)) governs someone's use has no such implication.

However, this argument is easily resisted. In the first place, the conditional specifying the normative implications of word-meanings are surely not completely vacuous, as the imagined Brandomian account would have them be. And in the second place, there is a very real possibility that the correctness of our basic epistemic norms, like our basic moral norms, is explanatorily fundamental. It may be, for example, that there is no explanation of why

> S means IF by w → S ought to accept
>   instances of "p", "w(p, q)" ⊢ "q",

but that, given that this is so, and given the independently supported fact that w's meaning IF would be constituted by a certain regularity, we can infer the normative import of that regularity.

Thus we need not be moved by Brandom's particular reasons for holding that meanings occupy a strangely autonomous normative realm, a realm of phenomena that cannot be reduced to 'factual' regularities. His arguments put into jeopardy neither the strategy of meaning-reduction elaborated in Chapter 2, nor the suggestion, backed by our analysis in section 6, that we are at liberty to interpose a level of rule-following between meanings and law-like use-regularities.

I have been developing the following explanatory picture: that certain laws underlie our basic rules of word-use; that such rule-following constitutes the meanings of our words (and hence sentences, see Chapter 8); that these meanings then trivially engender the truth conditions of sentences, via the schema 'u means *that p* → (u is true ↔ p)'; and that true belief is valuable, both pragmatically and morally; or, in other words, that we *ought* to aim to accept sentences only when their truth conditions are satisfied. The speculation I've been opposing here—namely, that truth and/or meaning are constitutively evaluative concepts—could be sustained only it were incorporated within a better overall explanatory model than this one. But we have looked at various ways that such an alternative might go, and have found none to be appealing.[24]

[24] Earlier (and inferior) versions of this chapter were published in *Philosophy, the Good, the True and the Beautiful* (Anthony O'Hear (ed.), Cambridge University Press, 2000); in *What Is Truth* (Richard Schantz (ed.), de Gruyter: Berlin and New York, 2001); and as chap. 8 of *Meaning*. But I have revised and extended those discussions in order to address a variety of problems. I am pleased to thank Ned Block, Paul Boghossian, Allan Gibbard, Wolfgang Kuenne, Michael Martin, David Owens, Barry C. Smith, Helen Steward, Albert Visser, and Michael Williams for bringing some of these problems to my attention.

6

Meaning Constitution and Epistemic Rationality

1. INTRODUCTION

Certain rules of belief-formation appear to be basic. It is hard to see how our following them could be either explained or rationalized in terms of other such rules. Nonetheless, we take them to be rational (justified, warranted, reasonable, legitimate, etc.). Consider the rules: to believe that an observed surface is red when it seems red, to reason in accordance with modus ponens and scientific induction, to follow the counting and adding procedures which underlie arithmetic, to infer 'It is true that p' from 'p', to believe that bachelors are unmarried. We *ought* to follow and to obey these rules, or refined versions of them.[1] However, as far as we can tell, that normative status is not grounded in yet deeper norms of the same kind. So where could it come from? How could a rule for acquiring beliefs be both basic and legitimate?

The answer that I want to explore (and to oppose) in this chapter is that our fundamental epistemic norms are engendered by the conditions for grasping concepts and understanding words. The central idea is that basic rules for the acquisition and retention of beliefs are warranted (perhaps always, but at least sometimes) *because* following them is required in order for

---

[1] NB: one can be *following* a given rule and yet, inadvertently, not always *obeying* it.

us to possess our particular stock of concepts.[2] Alternatively, putting it in terms of language rather than thought: our following a basic rule for the acceptance of certain sentences is justified because our doing so is required for us to mean what we do by some of the words in those sentences. Or, as it is sometimes said: we *stipulate* that our terms are to mean whatever they have to mean in order for the rules governing them to be truth-promoting.[3]

This approach presupposes that a necessary condition of our possessing certain concepts is following specifiable beliefs-rules concerning them, and (equivalently) that a necessary condition

---

[2] Notice that both the question and the proposed answer assume a distinction between *giving* a reason (or justification) for something and *explaining why* something is reasonable (or justified). Evidently, doing the former will put us in a position to provide the latter; for our explanation can be simply that such-and-such a reason was given. But what is being assumed—since the rules at issue are basic, i.e. not supportable in terms of reasons or justifications—is that an 'explanation of reasonability or justification' may be provided in some other way.

[3] Versions of this 'semantogenetic' account of basic epistemic norms are suggested in the work of Hilbert, Poincaré, and the logical positivists. In the last few years the idea has been elaborated and defended by the following philosophers amongst others: Paul Boghossian in "Analyticity Reconsidered" (*Nous* 30: 3, 1996), in "How Are Objective Epistemic Reasons Possible" (*Philosophical Studies* 106, 2001), and in "Blind Reasoning" (*Proceedings of the Aristotelian Society,* suppl. vol., 2003); by Christopher Peacocke in *A Study of Concepts* and in "How Are A Priori Truths Possible?" (*European Journal of Philosophy,* August 1993); and by Bob Hale and Crispin Wright in "Implicit Definition and the A Priori" (P. Boghossian and C. Peacocke (eds.), *New Essays on the A Priori,* 2000). These writers concentrate on semantogenetic approaches to the explanation of *a priori* knowledge, but are aware of their broader application. Beyond these exponents of the view, it seems fair to say that most philosophers have some sympathy for the vague idea that our justification for accepting certain things is explained by the fact that they are, roughly speaking, 'true by definition' or 'conceptually true'.

I have criticized this way of thinking in "Implicit Definition, Analytic Truth and Apriori Knowledge" (*Nous* 1997; repr. as chap. 6 of *Meaning*) and in "Stipulation, Meaning, and Apriority" (in *New Essays on the A Priori*). The present chapter is a heavily revised version of the latter essay, and supersedes it. Certain parts are almost the same (e.g. the discussion of stipulation in sections 3 and 4). And some of my previous criticisms of the semantogenetic strategy are here simply re-articulated in a more forceful way. But there is a lot of new material, including the concern with epistemic norms in general (not just with those that engender *a priori* knowledge), the focus on issues of explanatory order, the expanded critique of recent work by Boghossian, Peacocke, Hale, and Wright, and the quite different sketch, in my penultimate section, of an alternative to the semantogenetic approach.

of our meaning certain things by our words is our following
certain identifiable rules of sentence-acceptance regarding those
words. And since that presupposition was defended in Chapter 2
and is one of the main theses of this book, I won't of course be
questioning it. What I will be questioning is whether a rule's having that concept-constituting character can ever *explain* its normative status, i.e. can ever be *why* we are justified in following it.
By the same token, I will be questioning whether our justification
for following certain rules of sentence-acceptance can ever be
explained by the fact that our doing so is meaning-constituting.[4]
In addition, I will be questioning whether concept-constituting
(or meaning-constituting) rules can ever be identified with the
epistemic principles whose rationality one might wish to explain.

2. SEMANTOGENETIC JUSTIFICATION

Here is an initially natural way of putting the strategy under
consideration. We are at perfect liberty to decide what our
words will mean; consequently we are entitled to stipulate that a
given word, w, will mean whatever would make *correct* a certain

---

[4] Remember (from section (a) of chap. 2) that *accepting* a sentence, in my
technical usage, is a psychological (but non-semantic) attitude of relying on it in
theoretical and practical inference. This attitude sometimes issues in an utterance,
but not always. Nor is every utterance of a sentence a result of its being accepted.

Remember also (from section 6 of chap. 5) that an explanation of meaning in
terms of *rules* of use does not (in my view) preclude a deeper explanation in
terms of regularities, or propensities, or laws, of use. For I would argue that a person's implicitly following a certain rule is constituted by his conforming to an
ideal law, where the notion of 'ideal' is not evaluative but is cashed out *naturalist-
ically*, as in the case of 'ideal gases', 'ideally rigid', etc. If someone insists that
genuine rule-following must proceed on the basis of some explicit formulation
of, and causal response to, the rule—and therefore that meaning cannot, on pain
of circularity, be a matter of rule-following—then he should put scare-quotes
around my use of the expression, "rule-following" and he should understand my
'rules' of use to be nothing but idealized laws. In that case, the principal issue of
this chapter would be articulated as the question of whether the rationality of a
basic epistemic rule (like modus ponens) is explained by the meaning-constituting
law-like fact that we tend to obey it.

acceptance-rule, @w, that involves this word;[5] if we do so, then we are entitled to suppose that w has that meaning; therefore, since its having that meaning entails the correctness of the rule, we are entitled to regard the rule as correct. Again:

> (1) We are entitled to mean anything we want by w.
>
> ∴ (2) We are entitled to stipulate that w is to mean what will make correct the acceptance-rule, @w.
>
> (3) Having done so, we are then entitled to hold that w does mean what will make @w correct.
>
> ∴ (4) We are entitled to hold that @w is correct.
>
> ∴ (5) We are entitled to follow @w.

Let us begin our examination of this explanatory model, and variants of it, by focusing on the notion of *stipulation* and on its role in motivating steps (2) and (3). In what conditions is it possible, in general, to stipulate something? What particular form must these conditions take in the special case of *semantic* stipulation, for example, in the case where we stipulate that w is to have a meaning relative to which @w is correct? And, from the fact that something has been stipulated to be a certain way, does it follow either that it really is that way, or that its being that way can be justifiably maintained?

3. STIPULATION

To stipulate that something be the case is, in a sense, to 'command' that it is to be so—to state that it shall be so with the

---

[5] An acceptance rule, @w, may take various forms. It may simply dictate accepting some specified sentence containing w, and in that case what is supposedly stipulated is that the word's meaning render this sentence *true*. It may dictate the following of certain rules of inference, and in that case what is stipulated is that the word's meaning make these rules *truth-preserving*. It may dictate accepting a certain sentence containing it in certain environmental circumstances, and in that case what is stipulated is that the sentence be *true in those circumstances*. And there may well be further cases. I am using the general term "correct" to cover whichever truth-theoretic notion is appropriate.

expectation of being able thereby to bring it about that it is so. Thus a teacher might stipulate which questions the students are to answer in order to pass his course; a dictator might stipulate who her successor will be; the owner of a dog might stipulate what it should be called; and we might for convenience introduce a new term, "autofanticide", under the stipulation that it is to mean "the killing by a time-traveller of his infant self".

Some stipulations are successful and others are not. That is, some actually bring about the commanded state of affairs and others don't. For example, perhaps NN is stipulated to be the next leader but then dies before the stipulation can take effect. Now one might be tempted to respond that any *genuine* stipulation *must* succeed, and to say that it would be speaking loosely—an oversimplification—to characterize the content of the dictator's stipulation as the stipulation that NN will be the next leader. Was its content not, somewhat more accurately, that NN will be the next leader *unless this is prevented by his death, or by externally enforced regime change, or..., and so on*? However, on this alternative way of conceiving of stipulation it would often be very hard, and perhaps impossible, to specify exactly what is stipulated. Nor, on reflection, does it seem at all deviant to say of a stipulation that it was not realized. Thus it is both less problematic and more natural to continue to suppose that stipulations need not succeed; they may or may not be frustrated.

Thus S can stipulate that p, yet, because of infelicitous circumstances, not be successful in bringing it about that p. However, S cannot stipulate that p unless he believes he is able thereby to bring it about that p. Therefore he cannot, at the time of stipulation, be aware of circumstances that that will evidently prevent it coming about that p. For example, I cannot stipulate that I will be the next King of England, or that "Giorgione" will stand for the largest prime, because I know that I'm not in line for the throne and that there is no such number.

4. *SEMANTIC* STIPULATION

For any successful stipulation one can raise the question of how it was implemented. Often the answer is fairly obvious. One of the conditions of a person's authority over others is that they follow her instructions; she is then in a position to stipulate that certain things are to be done. But there are cases in which it is more obscure how a stipulation works, and these more problematic cases include *semantic* stipulations. No doubt I *can* stipulate what "autofanticide" is to mean in my idiolect, or that my puppy's name is to be "Pooch"; but *how?* How does it come about that my 'commanding' these things will result in their being so? The issue here is often overlooked or dismissed, as though the phenomenon were entirely transparent. But although it is indeed obvious that we can and do stipulate such matters, the question of how this works is genuine and important.

Once the issue is confronted, the main difficulty we face in settling it is not hard to identify. It's that we aren't sure *what it is* for two expressions to have the same meaning, or for a certain word to be the name of a certain thing. We aren't clear which underlying facts would *constitute* those semantic relations. Consequently we don't see how our decisions manage to bring them into being. Note that this is so even when all one wishes to stipulate are the meanings and referents of words in one's own idiolect.

A virtue of the *use* theory of meaning is that it can help us to address this problem in a plausible way—a way that provides a reasonable explanation of the phenomenon of semantic stipulation.[6] Suppose that for two expressions to mean the same thing

---

[6] In the case of various well-known rivals of the use-theory, e.g. the Fodorian "informational" approach and the Millikanian/Dretskian "teleological" approach, it is relatively hard to see how semantic stipulation could be accommodated.

is for them to have the same basic use. In that case, a stipulation about what some new word is to mean is simply a 'commanding of oneself'—a decision—to give it a certain use. For, example, I might resolve to use "autofanticide" in the same way that I already use "the killing by a time-traveller of his infant self". And I might do that by treating these expressions as intersubstitutable, i.e. by following the rules of inference:

$$\frac{\pounds(\text{the killing}\dots\text{etc.})}{\therefore\quad\pounds(\text{autofanticide})} \qquad \frac{\pounds(\text{autofanticide})}{\therefore\quad\pounds(\text{the killing}\dots\text{etc.})}$$

(where the sentence-schemata, "$\pounds(\ )$", may create intensional contexts). Thus we can begin to understand how it is possible to stipulate the meaning of a word.

In addition, the character of *naming*—i.e. reference stipulation—is illuminated by the use theory of meaning. For my holding true

> *This* (ostended) puppy is Pooch

constitutes my using "Pooch" in a particular way; and this basic use provides the word with the meaning it has. Now in general

> w means N $\rightarrow$ (x)(w refers to x $\leftrightarrow$ x = n),

where N is the singular concept expressed by the name "n". And in particular

> w means POOCH $\rightarrow$ (x)(w refers to x $\leftrightarrow$ x = Pooch).

Therefore, in using the word "Pooch" as I do, and thereby meaning by it what I do, i.e. meaning POOCH by it, I make it the case that

> (x) ("Pooch" refers to x $\leftrightarrow$ x = Pooch)

and, in particular, that

> "Pooch" refers to this puppy $\leftrightarrow$ this puppy = Pooch.

Therefore, given the fact of identity articulated on the right-hand side, I bring it about that

"Pooch" refers to this puppy.[7]

It remains, however, to specify how we are able to implement the particular sort of stipulation deployed within the strategy of semantogenetic justification, namely, stipulations of the form: 'Word w is to have whatever meaning will make truth-theoretically correct the acceptance-rule, @w.' In considering this matter we must bear in mind two morals from the discussion so far: first, that a word's meaning consists in its basic use; and second, that an act of stipulation requires the belief that it will help to bring about the stipulated state of affairs. So we should ask ourselves whether there is any way in which I might start using the new term w that I can plausibly believe will result in its possessing a meaning relative to which @w will be correct.

Well, one thing I might do to that end is simply to *follow* the rule @w. That way of using w would provide it with a meaning. Moreover, in following @w—in holding true the sentences it tells me to—I would be taking it to be correct. Thus I would indeed believe that I am giving a meaning to w relative to which @w is correct. So a good strategy for implementing the stipulation, 'Let w mean whatever will make correct the rule @w', is simply to follow that rule.[8]

---

[7] Notice that my stipulation—that this puppy is to be named "Pooch"—is put into effect by a combination of facts, one of which is entirely up to me (i.e. that I accept, underived, the sentence "This puppy is Pooch") and some of which are not (e.g. the non-linguistic fact that this puppy *is* Pooch). One might be tempted to think that even this puppy's *being* Pooch results, at least in part, from my linguistic decision. But this would be a mistake. In the first place, necessary facts of identity (another example is that Hesperus = Phosphorus) are not susceptible to explanation and, a fortiori, are not the results of our cognitive activity. In the second place, it is no more natural to think that we make Pooch into this puppy than that we give Pooch four legs. And to accept that sort of thing is to endorse a radical and highly implausible ('world-making') form of anti-realism.

[8] For example, if I follow the rule that merely dictates acceptance of the particular sentence, "A", then I accept "A"; and so, in light of the truth schema, I also accept " 'A' is true"; thus I take the rule to be truth-theoretically correct.

5. *PURELY* MEANING-CONSTITUTING
STIPULATION

Although the stipulation, 'Let me mean by w whatever will make correct the rule @w', insofar as it is implemented by my following that rule, will suffice to give a use to w, and hence a meaning to it, this particular stipulation may be *more* than is required to give w that meaning; it may contain elements that are not needed. For it may be that @w dictates, amongst other things, my acceptance of various sentences that don't contain w; and it may be that I am *already* committed to accepting those sentences. Therefore, instead of stipulating that w mean whatever will make @w correct, I might have equally well stipulated that w mean what will make correct a certain *weaker* rule—a rule that does not bother to tell me to do what I would be doing anyway. Consider, for example, a decision to introduce the word, "bachelor" via the stipulation that it is to mean whatever will make true both "The dodos are extinct" and "The bachelors are the unmarried men". This may be implemented by my continuing to accept "The dodos are extinct" (for the usual empirical reasons) and by my now beginning to accept (unsupported) "The bachelors are the unmarried men". However, although the meaning of "bachelor" will indeed be fixed by this rule, the first part of it will be redundant. The real work of meaning-constitution is done by my underived acceptance of "The bachelors are the unmarried men".

This example illustrates an important general point about meaning-constitution, one that we encountered in section (g) of Chapter 2. What provides w with its meaning is not merely some fact to the effect that a certain acceptance-rule, @w, is followed, but is rather a fact to the effect that this is *the* rule governing w's use, i.e. that it is explanatorily necessary and sufficient with respect to w's overall deployment. Only *such* rules, and only stipulations regarding *their* correctness, are purely meaning-constituting.

From this fact about meaning-constituting rules we may argue, as follows, that they must be *cognitively fundamental*—neither supported nor subject to rational critique.

Suppose @w were followed as a result of deducing its correctness from another rule for the acceptance of w-sentences. Then our following @w would clearly not be explanatorily basic with respect to w's overall use, so it could not be purely meaning-constituting. Similarly, if it were followed as a result of a non-deductive inference from premises that are free of w. For in that case, our following the rule would partly be the product of an inference that has nothing to do with w, an inference dictating that *some* rule of the form @_ is to be followed. All that would need to be assumed about w, is that we are following a certain *conditional* rule: namely, to follow @w if something of the form @_ is to be followed.

Not only must our following of an acceptance rule be *underived*—indeed, unsupported by any form of evidence—if it is to qualify as one of w's *basic* rules of use (and hence to qualify as purely meaning-constituting), it must also be beyond epistemic assessment. For suppose, having been committed for a while to a certain acceptance rule, @w, we came to suspect that simpler and better total theory could be obtained by revising it. This matter might be rationally debated; there could well be different people on different sides of the issue, all understanding one another, all meaning the same thing by w. Therefore the rule of governing w's use (which includes its use in such debates) could not be @w. Rather, w's purely meaning-constituting rule would have to be epistemically undebatable. Thus, a better story would be that the debate is fundamentally about something that has nothing to do with w, namely, the question of whether one should follow *some* rule of the form, @_. We might then plausibly identify w's rule of use with a conditional: if something of the form @_ is followed, it is to be @w.

6. *IMPLICIT* PURELY MEANING-CONSTITUTING STIPULATION

Very few (if any) of the rules whose justification we are investigating—e.g. those of arithmetic and of classical logic— were, at some specific moment in time, suddenly and deliberately adopted by way of explicitly stipulating the meanings of constituent terms, such as "and", "not", "number", etc. Therefore, if the semantogenetic strategy is to have any application to those cases, it will have to be shown that they nevertheless involve 'stipulations' of a certain sort—we might call them "*implicit* stipulations"—and that these can have the same semantic (and hence epistemological) potential as explicit ones.[9]

Let us see how this can indeed be shown. To stipulate something is to command that it be so in the expectation of thereby bringing it about that it is so. In the case of *overt* semantic stipulations, the commands and subsequent decisions concern the uses of words: we implement them by making sure that our further uses of these words proceed from our deliberately following such-and-such acceptance-rules. However, even in the absence of an *articulated* commitment of this sort, our overall practice with a word, w, may be based on the *implicit* following of a certain acceptance-rule. In order to identify which rule this is, we have to figure out (by inference to the best explanation) which rule is such that our implicitly following it provides the most plausible source of everything else that we do with the word. And we can suppose

---

[9] If one didn't mind courting confusion, one might speak of an 'implicit, implicit, implicit definition' of "f"—one "implicit" indicating that the defining rule does not require accepting a sentence of the biconditional form, "x is f ≡ ...x...."; another conveying that "f" was not introduced by an overt decision to follow that rule; and the third meaning that the rule is not articulated or formulated, not even unconsciously.

that this rule-following implements an implicit stipulation to the effect that w is to mean what will make that rule correct.

A couple of complications in this picture are important to keep in mind. First, the question of what constitutes the meaning of a given word, w, must be addressed *holistically*, that is, in the context of parallel inquiries into which rules engender the meanings of the other words in the language. An answer in the case of w can be plausible only to the extent that it is part of the simplest *global* way of explaining linguistic usage in terms of the combination of all the basic rules associated with the various words, together with other factors, such as environmental conditions and general psychological principles.

And second, the meaning of w will inevitably depend *constitutively*, and not just *epistemologically*, on the meanings of certain other words; for the rule that constitutes w's having its meaning will require the acceptance of sentences that contain other terms besides w. In some cases the basic acceptance-rules that are, in turn, attributed to these other words (in the best overall account) do not concern w, so w's meaning is *asymmetrically dependent* on their meanings. But in other cases it is simplest to attribute to w and some of the other words a *single* basic acceptance-rule that governs their use in relation to one another, showing thereby that their meanings are *interdependent*.[10]

Notice that when w's meaning depends asymmetrically on the meanings of certain other words, w's basic rule of use can dictate an acceptance policy towards a sentence made entirely from those other words only if that policy is already dictated by *their* meaning-constituting rules. In this sense a purely meaning-constituting rule of use must be 'conservative'.[11] It does not follow, however, that we cannot deploy a new term by means of

[10] See chap. 2, section (i), for elaboration of these points.

[11] If a rule is to respect pre-established meanings it is not enough to forbid it to dictate the acceptance of sentences in the old vocabulary unless they were independently acceptable. It must, in addition, not provide a *new way* of arriving at those sentences, e.g. it must not designate a sentence as acceptable a priori that used to be acceptable only on the basis of certain experiences.

a rule that changes the acceptance status of certain pre-existing sentences. The implication of this way of introducing a term would be merely that its meaning would not be asymmetrically dependent on the old vocabulary.

7. ILLUSTRATIONS FROM SCIENCE, ARITHMETIC, AND LOGIC

The question arises, in regard to any one of our acceptance-rules, as to whether our following it is purely meaning-constituting, or whether it is the product of various factors, only one of them perhaps a purely meaning-constituting rule of use.

Consider for example the case of a physical theory, T, which postulates a previously unconceptualized phenomenon, f-ness. It is natural to factor our acceptance of "Tf" into a pair of components: on the one hand there is a certain a posteriori belief; on the other hand there is an a priori decision to articulate that belief in certain terms. Another way of expressing these two factors is that there is, first, an a posteriori commitment to accept some instance of the schema "T_" and, second, an a priori commitment, conditional on the first commitment, to accept "Tf". Alternatively, one might (following Russell, Carnap, Ramsey, and Lewis[12]) regard "Tf" as the conjunction of (i) an a posteriori existential claim (T's Ramsey sentence)

(RamT) $\exists\Phi(T\Phi)$

to the effect that *there is some* property with the characteristics that the theory attributes to f-ness; and (ii) an a priori conditional claim

(ConT) $\exists\Phi(T\Phi) \Rightarrow Tf$

---

[12] See B. Russell, *The Analysis of Matter*, 1927; R. Carnap, *Der Logische Aufbau der Welt*, 1928; F. Ramsey, "Theories", 1929, repr. in his *Foundations*, ed. H. D. Mellor, 1978; and D. Lewis, "How to Define Theoretical Terms", *Journal of Philosophy* LVII: 427–66.

to the effect that *if* there is any property that satisfies T then f-ness does.[13]

In light of the general picture of meaning-constitution that we have been developing, it is plausible to suppose that the meaning of "f" is fixed (purely), not by our acceptance of the full theory "Tf", but rather by our unsupported acceptance of the conditional component, ConT.

For notice that neither the supported nor the unsupported acceptance of "Tf" will do. As argued in section 5, it cannot be our *empirically based* acceptance of "Tf" that engenders "f"'s meaning; for that would preclude rational disagreement and debate about the theory. But, as we saw in section 6, nor can it be that a stipulated acceptance of "Tf" (as neither supportable nor revisable) is what does the meaning-fixing job; for "Tf" has consequences articulated in an observational vocabulary which is understood independently of T's theoretical term. Therefore, an unsupported acceptance of "Tf" would dictate conditions of acceptance for certain observation sentences that are inconsistent with following the rules that constitute their meanings; it would infringe on the rights of the established meanings of the observation terms to tell us when the sentences composed from them should or should not be accepted.

Consequently, the stipulation that "f" shall mean whatever is needed for "Tf" to be true is *not* purely meaning constituting.

---

[13] For the sake of definiteness I will usually express the two factors in the way proposed by Russell, Carnap, Ramsey, and Lewis. But it may be that some other way of doing it will prove to be preferable.

As Anil Gupta observes (in "Deflationism, the Problem of Representation, and Horwich's Use Theory of Meaning") ConT cannot plausibly be a *material* conditional, for the conditional commitment we want to articulate with it cannot come merely from regarding its antecedent as false. This point is also made by Tim Williamson (in his "Understanding and Inference", *Proceedings of the Aristotelian Society*, suppl. vol., 2003), who notes that we then face the question of whether T entails ConT (hence, of whether T is factorizable into ConT and RamT). But we can settle this question affirmatively by requiring that, even though the conditional is not material, it nonetheless has the property that it is true whenever its antecedent and consequent are true. This will be so, for example, if it is given the Stalnaker analysis: $(p \Rightarrow q) \equiv (q$ is true in the closest possible world in which p is true$)$.

Rather, what provides "f" with its meaning is the fact that the basic rule for its use is our acceptance of the conditional, "∃x(Tx) ⇒ Tf". Thus we can see how people can disagree as to whether a scientific theory is correct, yet nonetheless agree on the meanings of its terms: for they may disagree about RamT yet agree on ConT.

Let us now turn to the case of arithmetic. Consider the stipulation that "the number of _s" is to mean whatever will make true Hume's Principle

(HP)   (f)(g)[The number of f's = the number of g's *iff* the f's and the g's can be put into one-to-one correspondence].

As in the case of a physical theory, this can be divided into two parts. First there is

(RamHP)   (∃%)(f)(g)(%f = %g ↔ f∼g),

where "%" stands for a variable ranging over functions from properties to objects, and "f∼g" abbreviates "the f's and the g's can be put into one-to-one correspondence". This asserts that there is *some* function from properties to objects that satisfies a Hume-style principle. Second there is the conditional

(ConHP)   (∃%)(f)(g)(%f = %g ↔ f∼g) ⇒
(f)(g)(the number of f's = the number of g's
iff f∼g)

which asserts that *if* there is such a function then Hume's Principle holds.

We have no less reason here than in the case of a physical theory to suppose that it is our acceptance only of this conditional, ConHP, that is required for "the number of _s" to mean what it does. After all, the Ramseyfied Hume's Principle, RamHP, is statable in an antecedently available and comprehensible vocabulary, one that is entirely free of number-theoretic expressions. Therefore it will be found plausible, or not, in virtue of the established meanings of these more basic terms. Thus our acceptance of RamHP is a *prior* commitment—one which might well be justified, but which is not required for "the number of _s" to mean what it does. So it would seem that this meaning-fact stems from ConHp rather than HP itself.

Further grounds for the conclusion that HP itself is isn't meaning-constituting is that it can be rationally debated and revised. Disputes about the existence of numbers (and the existence of infinitely many things) seem to be perfectly coherent, indeed not especially uncommon. And surely all parties to such disagreements understand each other. What constitutes their shared understanding is, presumably, a shared view of how the numerical terms are used within HP; and this amounts (arguably) to a shared acceptance of ConHP.[14]

---

[14] For a demonstration that Hume's Principle yields the axioms of arithmetic, and for a defence of the view (just criticized) that it is what implicitly defines "the number of_s", see Crispin Wright's *Frege's Conception of Numbers as Objects*. See also Bob Hale's, "Grundlagen $64", *Proceedings of the Aristotelan Society*, 1996/7. And see their joint essay "Implicit Definition and the A priori", in *New Essays on the A priori*.

In that essay, Hale and Wright argue that amongst the various non-numerical statements entailed by HP, some, including statements implying, in effect, that there are infinitely many objects, were already fully understandable, though not yet demonstrable or assertible, prior to our acceptance of HP. But they argue that HP's acceptance is nonetheless *conservative* and hence constitutes a meaning for "the number of _s" that is asymmetrically dependent on the non-numerical notions deployed in HP. For, they say, we may regard its number-theoretic left-hand side as merely re-articulating ('carving up in a new way') the content expressed by the right-hand side, and thereby disclosing certain implications of our prior commitments that could not previously have been recognized, e.g. that there are infinitely many objects.

One can object, however, that since a word's meaning is constituted by our basic rules for its use (i.e. for the acceptance of sentences containing it) there is no possibility of a word's meaning remaining unaffected by the unsupported (and unsupportable) adoption of some *further* rule for its use. In particular, if certain non-numerical sentences are acceptable only in light of a basic commitment to HP, then that commitment must help engender their meanings.

If, on the other hand, the basic rules for the acceptance of non-numerical sentences are *not* affected by the introduction of numerical terms (via HP)—if, for example, the non-numerical sentence implying that there are infinitely many objects can be recognized as correct in advance of accepting HP, then we are confronted by two possibilities. Either our acceptance of some of these non-numerical

Proceeding to the case of logic, one might well suppose—again by analogy with the two-factor account of empirical theories—that, in order to give the logical terms, "not", "and", "all", etc., their classical meanings, it is not necessary to deploy them in classical reasoning but merely to make a certain conditional commitment: namely, that one *would* so deploy them *if* one were to accept that there existed logical entities for which classical reasoning is correct. Granted the parallel is not perfect. For, whereas scientific theories have non-theoretical consequences, the truths of classical logic have no consequences that are free of logical terms; therefore, our basic acceptance of classical logic cannot be inconsistent with antecedently established meanings. But here too there is a deeper ground for resisting the idea that full logical practices are what constitute the meanings of logical terms: namely, that such a supposition could not accommodate the fact that our logical rules may be challenged and revised by people who perfectly well understand what they are disagreeing with.

We should conclude, therefore, that the words, "if", "or", "every", and so on, derive thir meanings, not from our following the (let's say) *classical* logical rules governing their use, but rather from our appreciation of their role in those rules—an appreciation that can be shared by someone who does not follow them. To put it another way, we should acknowledge that their meanings are constituted, not from the first-order disposition to reason classically, but rather from a second-order conditional

sentences requires general epistemological principles, e.g. of symmetry or of simplicity, which go beyond meaning-constituting rules or it doesn't. In the former case, we should certainly say that arithmetic resembles an empirical theory, in that what constitutes the meaning of "the number of _s" is our basic acceptance of the conditional, ConHP, rather than our acceptance of HP itself. But even in the latter case, we might well take that position. For although unsupported acceptance of HP would not be inconsistent with prior meanings, to suppose that it is meaning-constituting would imply, quite implausibly, that no one who argued for a rejection of HP could really understand it.

Note that the present remarks are focused on the Hale/Wright picture of meaning-constitution. Their *epistemological* contention—namely, that since HP is meaning-constituting, its truth is known a priori—is criticized below, in section 12.

disposition—namely, given a disposition to follow classical logical rules, to implement that practice with those particular words.[15]

8. 'NON-MEANINGS' AND 'BAD MEANINGS'

We have been elaborating and illustrating the idea that each word's meaning stems from a basic and explanatorily adequate rule dictating the acceptance of certain sentences containing it. But among the philosophers who endorse something like this general idea, many insist that one or another substantial qualification of it is necessary.

For example, it is often supposed that a rule of inference can yield a *genuine* meaning (or concept) only if it is *truth-preserving*. Let me explain why I think that no such requirement is called for.

One possible motivation for it is the view that any word, w, derives its meaning from a stipulation that it is to mean whatever will make truth-theoretically correct some rule, @w. For if there is no such meaning, then the stipulation cannot succeed; so (it might seem) the word cannot acquire a meaning. But this last step is a non-sequitur. Why assume that only *successful* stipulations can engender meanings? Why not allow, rather, that what we do in the *attempt* to implement a stipulation—namely, our

---

[15] Against this idea, Boghossian argues (in "Blind Reasoning") that our acceptance of a 'conditionalized' form of classical logic would require a prior grasp of the very meaning(s) to be constituted. And on the basis of this contention he maintains that it must be the full-blown rules of classical logic that engender the meanings of our logical terms. However, there are two substantial difficulties with this proposal. In the first place—as we have seen—the conclusion leaves us unable to explain the rational (perhaps empirical) revision of logic. And in the second place, Boghossian's argument is compelling only given the assumption that our meaning-constituting rules are followed *explicitly*. For only then will our following the conditionalized rules of logic presuppose a prior understanding of the conditional. But that assumption can well be denied. Surely many, perhaps all, of our meaning-constituting rules are followed *implicitly*.

following @w—gives a meaning to w, even though that meaning does not have all the characteristics we wanted it to have?

A second possible motivation for the correctness requirement
on meaning-constituting rules is the principle that meaning
determines reference. For one way of understanding how this 'determination' takes place is to suppose that the reference of a term
is whatever will make correct the rules that engender the term's
meaning.[16] However that interpretation of the "meaning determines reference" principle is far from compulsory. No doubt, if
two expressions have the same meaning, then, leaving aside
context-sensitivity, they must have the same reference. In this
sense the principle is uncontroversial. But (as we saw in Chapter 3)
it gives us no reason to expect that meaning DETERMINES reference, in some stronger sense, i.e. that there is some way of *reading
off* the reference of a term from how its meaning is constituted.

Thirdly, one might think that a truth-preservation requirement is needed in order to explain our intuition that certain
bizarre but imaginable rules could not provide meanings.
Consider Prior's infamous term, "tonk", which he introduced
tongue-in-cheek via the 'rules' of inference

$$\frac{\text{P}}{\therefore \ \text{p tonk q}} \qquad \frac{\text{p tonk q}}{\therefore \quad \text{q}}\ ^{17}$$

Surely there is no such concept as TONK, and, if meaning-
constituting rules have to be truth-preserving, that would
explain why. But there is an obvious alternative explanation.
Namely, that despite initial appearances to the contrary, we

[16] This appears to be Peacocke's reason for imposing the requirement. See
section 11 for further critical discussion.

[17] See Arthur Prior, "The Runabout Inference Ticket", *Analysis* 21: 38–9.

Boghossian (in his "How Are Objective Epistemic Reasons Possible?") cites the
need to explain why "tonk" is meaningless as his reason for maintaining that any
meaning-constituting rule of use must be truth-preserving. However, in his later
paper, "Blind Reasoning", this restriction is abandoned, and the meaninglessness of
"tonk" is explained along the lines that I go on to mention here, and which I describe
at greater length in "Implicit Definition, Analytic Truth and Apriori Knowledge".

have not in fact been presented with genuine *rules* for the meaning-constituting use of "tonk", i.e. rules that can really be followed in a meaning-constituting way. To see this, notice that following them in a meaning-constituting way—*implicitly* following them—would require a fair degree of conformity with them; and this would involve a propensity to believe *every proposition*, including any instance of 'p and not p'; but that would be inconsistent with the meaning-constituting rules of use for "not". Moreover, since it is essential to *belief* states that they play a distinctive role in our deliberations—in our deciding to do one thing rather than another—such a propensity would be inconsistent with the very notion of *belief*.

Thus there are no persuasive grounds for doubting that *every* basic rule of acceptance gives us a genuine meaning, including rules that are not truth-theoretically correct. But now a further question must be confronted: is there a distinction, amongst genuine meanings, between those that are 'epistemologically legitimate' and those that are 'defective'? Some philosophers have argued that there is indeed such a distinction, that only a restricted class of acceptance-rules yield "epistemologically reasonable" meanings.

This view is based on examples of allegedly conceivable meaning-constituting rules, such as:

(POM) $\dfrac{\text{x is English}}{\therefore \quad \text{x is a pom}}$ $\dfrac{\text{x is a pom}}{\therefore \quad \text{x is pretentious}}$

and

(FLURG) $\dfrac{\text{x is an elliptical equation}}{\therefore \quad \text{x is flurg}}$ $\therefore \quad \dfrac{\text{x is flurg}}{\text{x can be correlated with a modular form.}}$[18]

---

[18] POM is a variant of Michael Dummett's BOCHE (*Frege: Philosophy of Language*). FLURG comes from Boghossian's "Blind Reasoning". As Wiles showed (in the course of proving Fermat's Theorem), it is possible, but extremely difficult, to demonstrate that each elliptical equation can be correlated with a modular form.

The thought, presumably, is that since it would be illegitimate to follow such rules underived, then it would be illegitimate to possess the concepts whose possession would be engendered by doing that.

But these examples don't in fact threaten the idea that the following of *any* rule of acceptance—as long as it is cognitively basic and explanatorily adequate—will constitute a legitimate meaning. For neither of them articulates rules that could be followed in that way. We have already seen that the alleged "tonk" rules do not provide a basis for denying that all acceptance-rules engender genuine meanings; for, since they cannot be followed thoroughly, they are not real implicit rules. Similarly, no meanings have been given to "pom" and "flurg", because the alleged rules governing their use—if they are understood to be unsupported—are not implicitly followable. For, in order to do that, we would have to acquire a tendency to apply the predicates, "pretentious" and "correlated with a modular form", on the basic of considerations that are inconsistent with our following the rules that constitute our meaning what we do by those predicates.

Thus we have seen no reason to agree that there are possible basic acceptance-rules that fail to engender legitimate meanings.[19]

---

[19] It might be thought that, even it I am right that it is *impossible*, rather than merely *irrational*, to follow the "tonk", "pom", or "flurg" alleged rules, there are other cases of rules that really *can* be followed, but (as we may eventually come to see) *shouldn't* be: for example, the rule dictating acceptance of *any* instance of the naïve truth schema, "<p> is true → p" (since we would then be saddled with the 'liar' contradictions).

It must be remembered, however, that the sort of rule-following at issue here is *implicit*, rather then *explicit*; and that the latter may be possible even when the former is not. For our implicit following of rule @w is constituted by our conformity with it being an *ideal law*, i.e. by the fact that we would (ideally) conform in any counterfactual circumstances (see fn. 4). So the fact that there are instances of the naïve truth schema which we will (or would) not be prepared to accept, shows that the simple rule (to accept *all* instance of that schema) is not the one that we implicitly follow.

9. JUSTIFICATION

Now, at last, we are ready to address issues of epistemology; we are in a position to examine the alleged relations between the normative status that an acceptance-rule may have, and the phenomena of stipulation and meaning-constitution. To begin with, it is evident that someone may stipulate that something is to be the case without being justified in believing that it will be the case. Remember the stipulation that NN will be the next leader. The dictator's presuppositions, including her assumption that NN will not die before she does, may happen *not* to be justified. Similarly, if I have stipulated that "f" is to mean whatever will make "Tf" true, my view that "f" now has such a meaning might well not be justified. For, as we have seen, in some cases "f" can have such a meaning only if an *empirical* condition, "$\exists x(Tx)$", is satisfied; and it may be unreasonable of me to hold that this is so.

But let us restrict our attention to stipulations that are *purely* meaning-constituting. Suppose we stipulate that w is to mean what will make correct the rule @w; we try to implement this stipulation by following that rule; and we do thereby imbue w with meaning. In such a case, it certainly strikes us as *legitimate* to follow @w. But why does it strike us that way? And do we have an explanation of that normative status?

One natural strategy for answering these questions is, first, to claim that we have the right to mean whatever we want and, second, to observe that this amounts to an entitlement to follow the appropriate meaning-constituting rule.

But whatever right we have to mean what we want surely *derives from* our entitlement to use words the way we want. So insofar as our concern is to explain the latter entitlement, it is unclear why there should be any point in bringing meaning-constitution into the picture. This is a serious defect of the semantic model that I set out initially (in section 2). Looking back, one can see that the purported explanation rested on the premiss, "We are entitled to mean anything we want by w". But this is something to be explained on the basis of our entitlement to follow the constituting rules.

Here's an alternative way of trying to show that any purely meaning-constituting rule is justified. One might contend that a requirement for a rule to be able to constitute a *genuine* meaning is that it be truth-theoretically correct, e.g. truth-preserving; and one might argue (in the spirit of reliabilism) that our epistemic reason to follow it resides in that correctness.

But, as argued in section 8, we might well question whether a basic rule involving w must actually be correct in order for our following it to give a meaning to w? In stipulating that the rule be correct, and stipulating that w have the meaning that will make it correct, we no doubt feel convinced that the rule is correct and that w has that meaning. But whether these convictions are actually *true* is a further matter. The stipulation will not be successful if they are not; but since a use for w will nonetheless have been instigated, a meaning for it will nonetheless have been established.

Moreover, even if this objection were set aside, even if we were to concede for the sake of argument that a rule can engender a meaning only if it is correct, we would still not be able to *explain*, on the basis of @w's meaning-constituting character, our justification for following it. For insofar as such an explanation is thought to derive (internalistically) from our *recognition* of the link between meaning-constitution and correctness, this would contradict our presumption that @w is basic, i.e. not justified by argument. And insofar as the explanation of the rule's legitimacy is thought to derive (externalistically) from the mere *fact* that @w is meaning-constituting and therefore truth-preserving, one may object that two separate explanatory arrows go directly from the truth-theoretic correctness of @w to, on the one hand, its being justified and, on the other hand, to its constituting a meaning. There is no explanatory arrow from its constituting a meaning to its being justified.

Beyond the just-mentioned difficulties in seeing how the meaning-constituting character of a rule could possibly explain its legitimacy, there are two further serious objections to the semantogenetic approach.

One is that, on the face of it, epistemic norms (such as the rationality of modus ponens and of inferences from "p" to "It is true that p") tell us something about what we are *obliged* to accept (or to believe) *given* the meanings of pertinent terms. But in that case one must distinguish between, on the one hand, the legitimacy of our meaning what we do by a word, together with the correlated legitimacy of our following the rule that constitutes this meaning-fact, and, on the other hand, the obligations that flow from giving the word that meaning. Insofar as the epistemic norms we are concerned to explain are of the second type, then the semantic model explains (at best!) the wrong thing. For its focus is on our *unconditional* following of @w, whereas our real concern is with the following of it *given what it means*. Moreover—and this is an important, separate point—the normative status it purports to explain is merely our *entitlement* to follow that rule, whereas our real concern is with our (conditional) *obligation* to follow it.[20]

[20] It might well be supposed that if someone follows a certain rule, and is entitled to do so, then he is obliged to act as the rule dictates. And, on this basis, an advocate of the semantogenetic strategy can argue, in response to part of my objection, that he *is* able to account for the obligations that relate to epistemic norms such as modus ponens. For, given what we standardly and justifiably mean—that is, given a certain entitled rule-*following*—he can explain our obligation to *obey* that rule. He may well deny that there really exists any *requirement* to *follow* those rules (which is what I accused him of not being able to explain), and contend that the only requirements that need accounting for are those to *obey* the rules we are justifiably following.

But this response strikes me as inadequate. In the first place, it is evident that rationality does *not* leave open which epistemic rules to follow. We are to be criticized, not merely for *violating* modus ponens, or the principle of non-contradiction, but also—indeed: more harshly—for not even trying to conform to them. Add, in the second place, the obligation one has to obey a rule that one is legitimately following (e.g. to read the newspaper over breakfast) is analogous to the obligation one has to try to satisfy any legitimate desire. In both cases the 'ought' is a mere matter of prudence, a matter of acting in one's own self-interest. But someone's obligation, if he means what is standardly meant by "if", to obey modus ponens, is surely more serious. In failing to do so he is not merely betraying his own interests, but doing something objectively wrong. This difference in normative force between epistemic rules and other rules that we may legitimately follow at will is explained by the fact that we are obliged, given what we mean, to *follow* certain epistemic rules.

A final grave difficulty is that, since (as was argued in section 7) meaning-constituting rules are all, in a certain sense, 'conditionalized', *their* rationality is not at all what we are interested in explaining. Our concern, rather, is with the rationality of modus ponens, Hume's Principle, the truth schema, induction, etc. But since none of these rules is meaning-constituting, even if the semantogenetic model were right it wouldn't apply to any of them.

10. BOGHOSSIAN

In order to clarify this critique of semantogenetic accounts of justification, and to show its relevance to current thinking in the area, let me apply it to versions of the approach that have recently been proposed by Boghossian, Peacocke, and jointly by Hale and Wright.

Paul Boghossian's initial version of the strategy went along the following lines.[21] We can be justified in supposing that

If w has a meaning, then the rule, @w, is correct

since this follows from our stipulation that w is to have the meaning (if there is such a meaning) that will make @w correct. And we can be justified in supposing that

w has a meaning

(at least in certain cases). Moreover the argument from these premises to the conclusion

@w is correct

is valid. Therefore, we are justified in supposing that @w is correct.

However, this account provokes a couple of concerns that should be (and can be) addressed. In the first place, it is unclear

---

[21] See his "Analyticity" (in *A Companion to the Philosophy of Language*, edited by R. Hale and C. Wright and "Analyticity Reconsidered". I have altered his formulations in order to conform with the terminology of this chapter.

how our warrant for the two premises can explain our warrant for the conclusion unless it is assumed either that we actually reason to that conclusion from those premises or, at least, that such a rationale is in principle available to us. But this assumption conflicts with the presumption that our warrant for following @w is *epistemologically basic*. Remember we are trying to account for *fundamental* epistemic norms.

And, in the second place, if we have stipulated that w is to mean (if anything) what will make @w correct (and if we can assume that w is meaningful), then it must be that we *believe* that w means something that will make @w correct (and we believe, equivalently, that @w is correct). But it does not follow that these beliefs are *justified*. That conclusion would surely require some sort of *normative* premiss, e.g. that we are *justified* in making the stipulation.

Boghossian's subsequent development of his position removes these concerns.[22] One important modification—taking care of the first worry—is to dispense with any reliance on the phenomenon of stipulation. He moves to the more direct claim that our deploying a term via an acceptance-rule (e.g. our following certain inference rules) suffices to provide it with a meaning, and he maintains that it is the meaning-constituting character of such a rule which provides it with its justification. As for explaining how this happens—which will address the second worry—a number of distinct answers may be read into Boghossian's various discussions of the issue.

One of his proposals goes like this. In order for an acceptance rule for w to be meaning-constituting it must be *unsupported*; for any derivation of it would have to involve w, whose meaning would, per impossibile, already have to have been constituted. Thus w's meaning-constituting rule *cannot* be supported on the basis of deeper considerations. But in that

---

[22] See his more recent "How Are Objective Epistemic Reasons Possible?" and "Blind Reasoning".

case (since 'ought' → 'can') we are *not obliged* to support it; we shouldn't be blamed for failing to do so.[23]

But it must not be forgotten that our question was how to explain the rationality of basic (i.e. unsupportable) epistemic norms. So there can be no progress in supposing that the meaning-constituting character of a rule explains its rationality *via the intermediate step that such a rule is basic.* To put this complaint another way: if we are able to argue that unsupportable rules are thereby legitimate, then would it not be simpler and better to apply this maxim *directly* to our basic norms, without bringing in irrelevant and distracting considerations of meaning-constitution?

Moreover, one might well have qualms about that maxim— about the thesis that if an acceptance-rule *cannot* be supported then it *needn't* be, and is legitimately followed without support. For can we not imagine that some of a person's (or a community's) *basic,* i.e. unsupportable, epistemic norms are nonetheless irrational?

If so, if the maxim is indeed subject to counter-example, then there must be some defect in the argument leading up to it. And on closer scrutiny a flaw does in fact emerge. For having shown (given that @w is meaning constituting)

Not possible: (p and q),

where "p" means "@w is followed", and "q" means "@w is supported", it is rightly inferred that

Not obligatory: (p and q)

and therefore that

Legitimate: not (p and q).

---

[23] Boghossian himself comes to the view that there must be something wrong with this line of thought. For he holds, as we saw in section 8, that certain meaning-constituting rules (e.g. those for "pom" and "flurg") are irrational to follow. But he never specifies exactly *where* the line of thought goes astray. Of course, if (as I argued) there are in fact no such 'defective' concepts, then Boghossian's own concern about his proposal would be eliminated. But the critique developed below would still undermine it.

But from here there is a slide to

> Legitimate: (p and not q),

i.e. that it is legitimate to follow the rule in the absence of any support for doing so. And that is the fallacious move. For a denial of its conclusion (i.e. the illegitimacy of following the unsupported rule) is perfectly consistent with the preceding step (i.e. the legitimacy of not both following and supporting it). One might as well argue that since it isn't possible to keep incompatible promises, it is legitimate to make them and then break them!

A second strategy, also suggested in Boghossian's work, for linking meaning-constitution with justification, is to invoke the following argument:

> We are entitled to give a word whatever (non-defective) meaning we like. Therefore we are entitled to give it any use that will provide it with a (non-defective) meaning.

But we saw (in section 8) that there may well be no such things as defective meanings. Moreover, even if there are, the present argument would appear to put matters in the wrong explanatory order. Surely, our evaluation of a certain meaning as irrational or not, or as useful or nor, must derive from an evaluation of the rules of use that constitute them. We do not have basic norms dictating that such-and-such meanings are good, or bad, from which we can deduce and hence explain the value of the correlated rules. Rather, it is the other way round. If only certain meanings are legitimate, that would be because only certain basic uses are legitimate. So, although we might indeed be able to *infer* the rationality of a basic use from the fact that this use constitutes a non-defective meaning, we cannot *explain* its rationality in that way.[24]

---

[24] As Anna-Sara Malmgren pointed out to me, the reason that norms of meaning are explained by norms of use is not simply that meaning is constituted by use. For, surely, the obligation not to inflict pain does not stem from an

In light of these difficulties, a third strategy that might be attributed to Boghossian is to suppose that the warrant for following a certain rule, @w, will sometimes be explained by the conjunctive fact (1) that it is meaning-constituting, and (2) that it is either 'conditionalized' (in the sense of section 7) or 'unconditionalizable' (on pain of circularity, since 'conditionalization' would require a prior grasp of logical concepts). But this strategy does not seem satisfactory either.

In the first place, one might well wonder whether the first conjunct is doing any explanatory work. For, on Boghossian's view, any conditionalized or unconditionalizable rule, @w, is rational, independently of whether it is meaning-constituting.

In the second place, one might well wonder whether any sort of *explanation* of our warrant is given here, rather than a mere *characterization* of a certain class of rational rules. Granted, he does offer an explanation of why it would be irrational to deploy an unconditional rule if a conditionalized version of it is available. Thus we might be able to see why a certain potential source of irrationality is avoided by following a conditionalized rule. But that doesn't yield the result that following it is rational, for there may be further sources of irrationality to be reckoned with. Nor does it explain why the unavailability of a conditionalized version of a certain rule makes it legitimate to follow the unconditionalized version.

In the third place one might well wonder whether many—or even *any*—of the epistemic norms that we most want to explain (or at least to be covered by our characterization) will actually be covered: for example, the rationality of classical logic, arithmetic, the truth schema, induction, etc. For on the one hand these principles are not conditionalized; but on the other hand

---

obligation to refrain from bringing about whatever neurological state (if any) constitutes pain!

The right picture would seem to be that if there are basic norms concerning properties at a given metaphysical level, then they will induce (and explain) norms concerning correlated properties at both more basic and less basic levels.

they do seem to be conditionalizable. Only in the case of logic is this point of view questioned by Boghossian, and even in that case it can be argued (as in section 7) that conditionalization is possible after all.

In the fourth place—again suggesting that the epistemic norms with which we are concerned are not addressed—these norms concern what rules we *must* follow; whereas a Boghossian-style account delivers merely that one is *entitled* to follow them. (This point is elaborated in footnote 20.)

And in the fifth place, in a similar vein, our epistemic norms (such a modus ponens) dictate what is to be done, *given* that one has the relevant concepts (such as IF . . . THEN . . .), whereas a Boghossian-style account of a use-rule is geared to deliver an unconditional evaluation of it.

11. PEACOCKE

Christopher Peacocke's account of epistemic norms is conducted at the level of *thought* rather than at the level of *language*, but it is also a version of the semantogenetic strategy.[25] He has argued that it may be a condition of possessing a certain concept **F** (where **F** is the concept expressed by the English term "f") that one be fundamentally committed to certain belief-forming rules which contain it. In other words, it may be constitutive of the identity of concept **F** that it play a specific role in the cognitive economy of those who possess it, a role that includes following (as 'primitively compelling') the belief-forming rule, @**F**. This idea is equivalent to the idea that the term w is implicitly defined to mean **F** by our underived commitment to acceptance-rule, @w, and I have no quarrel with it. However, Peacocke claims, in addition, that this phenomenon provides an explanation of some of our epistemic norms. And this runs up against versions of the difficulties that I have been emphasizing.

[25] See his *A Study of Concepts* and "How Are A Priori Truths Possible?".

Why *ought* we to follow those primitively compelling belief-forming rules that are concept-constituting? Peacocke's answer is to claim that a rule can be concept-constituting only if it is truth-theoretically correct. And this claim is based on his view of how the nature of a concept *determines* the referent (semantic value) of that concept:

> "Determination Theory" (DT):
>> The referent of a concept is that which will make truth-theoretically correct the primitively compelling belief-forming rule that provides the concept's possession condition [26]

But, paralleling points made above, there are two objections to this way of trying to account for the normative status of our primitively compelling, concept-constituting, belief-forming rules.

First, DT seems too strong. One may grant that if concepts **F** and **G** have the same possession condition, then they must have the same referent (if any). In this sense of "determine", the nature of a concept uncontroversially determines its referent. But this is not sufficient to justify DT: for it does not preclude the possibility of the referent of **F** and **G** being something that renders their shared possession condition *in*correct. Moreover, consider a component of thought that *is* governed by a primitively compelling belief-forming rule, but one that cannot be made correct by any judicious selection of referent. It is hard to see any point in refusing to call this admitted constituent of beliefs a *concept*—a concept whose identity is given by that rule.

But, setting aside this first criticism, suppose that DT were accepted. Then the fact that @**F** is concept-constituting would *depend* on the fact that it is truth-theoretically correct. In addition,

---

[26] Assuming that each concept has a referent—which, for the case of *predicative* concepts, is perfectly plausible (since, at worst, their extension is the null set)—this entails that a concept's possession condition must be truth-theoretically correct.

it might be argued (via reliabilism) that a separate consequence of @F's truth-theoretic correctness would be our *justification* for following it. But even if these points were right, there would be no explanatory link between the rule's being concept-constituting and it being legitimate. Rather, both of these characteristics of @F would be independently explained by its correctness.

Thus we have no account of how the concept-constituting character of a belief-forming rule can be responsible for our obligation to obey it.[27]

12. HALE AND WRIGHT

Bob Hale and Crispin Wright have developed a semantogenetic account of rationality that is focused on a priori knowledge, particularly, on our knowledge of what they take to be the basis of arithmetic, namely, that the number of A's equals the number of B's just in case there is a one–one correspondence between the A's and the B's (Hume's Principle). Their strategy is first to present general conditions that must be met in order that it be possible for us to stipulate that the term "f" means something that will make "#f" true, and second to argue that these conditions are satisfied in the case where "f" is "the number of _s" and "#f" is Hume's Principle. With this background they go on to maintain that we have implicitly made that stipulation about the meaning of "the number of _s"; that, as a result, Hume's

---

[27] Peacocke's version of the semantogenetic strategy is also subject to some of the other criticisms developed in section 9. First, possession conditions will have to be 'hedged', i.e. 'conditionalized', to enable substantive commitments involving their corresponding concepts to be debated; so even if a rule's being a possession condition were to account for its rationality, that could not bear on the rationality of the principles (of e.g. logic and arithmetic) whose normative force we are most concerned to explain. And second, there's the point that our epistemic norms don't tell us what concepts we are supposed to possess, which would be the upshot of Peacocke's account, if it were successful; they tell us, rather, what we are supposed to do, vis-à-vis our beliefs, *provided* we possess the pertinent concepts.

Principle is true, and hence that our commitment to it is justified a priori.

But, for now familiar reasons, these last steps are highly questionable. In what exactly does our justification reside? Is the idea that we *reason* to the conclusion that Hume's Principle is correct, inferring it from our awareness of the stipulation we have made and from our awareness that whatever is stipulated must be correct? Surely not! For in the first place, insofar as this reasoning would begin with an act of introspection, it would arguably yield (at best) an a posteriori justification. Second, it is not true that all stipulations are successful. And third, the idea that we justify our acceptance of Hume's Principle by means of some *argument* conflicts with the assumption that our acceptance of it is epistemologically basic.

So perhaps Hale and Wright are supposing that, regardless of our reflections on the matter, our stipulation explains why Hume's Principle is true, and the truth of Hume's Principle explains why our commitment to it is justified. But this would be no good either. The stipulation that "f" is to mean what is needed to make "#f" true is implemented by our giving "f" a certain use, by our accepting (as basic) "#f" by our *taking* it to be true. But this attitude on our part cannot ensure that "#f" really *is* true; for it is not up to us whether or not there is to be such a thing as the non-linguistic fact that #f. Moreover, even if (for the sake of argument) this worry is set aside—even if it is assumed that any *stipulation*, properly so-called, must be correct—no semantic explanation of our warrant for accepting "#f" would be forthcoming. For insofar as our underived acceptance of "#f" is what constitutes our stipulation of "f"'s meaning—i.e. that it is to mean whatever will make "#f" correct—we cannot hope to explain the rationality of that acceptance in terms of the existence of the stipulation. For, in the first place, the explanatory order is the other way around. And, in the second place, our premiss would have to be the *rationality* of the stipulation; its mere existence would not be sufficient.

Finally, we should note a further unsatisfactory feature of Hale and Wright's strategy, which it shares with those of Boghossian and Peacocke. It ignores the fact that our epistemic norms concern what rules ought to be followed *by those who understand our language*. It is oriented instead towards explaining why we are entitled to understand our words as we do, and why we are entitled to use them in whichever ways are required for such an understanding. But that orientation is off-target.[28]

13. THE ACTUAL ORIGINS OF BASIC EPISTEMIC NORMS

I think we must conclude that the semantogenetic strategy does not work. But if we can't account for the normative status of basic epistemic rules in terms of their meaning-constituting character, how *can* we account for it? What *else* might explain our obligation to follow them?

Let me prepare the ground for an answer to this question by emphasizing a couple of distinctions. To begin with, there is the difference to which I have just alluded between those norms that concern the circumstances in which sentences should be accepted *given what they mean*, and those norms that assess such matters *unconditionally*.[29] The latter, since the meaning of a word is constituted by the rules governing its use, entail specifications

---

[28] See section 7 for a further criticism of the overall position defended by Hale and Wright. I argue there that their construal of the conservativeness requirement on meaning-constituting stipulations is too weak, and that this mistake invalidates their inference that our acceptance of Hume's Principle, rather than a conditionalized form of it, is what engenders the meaning of 'the number of _s'. If, as I suggest, the conditionalized version is indeed what constitutes that meaning, then we have an additional reason to deny that the rationality of Hume's Principle (and hence arithmetic) can be explained semantogenetically.

[29] To put it another way, the distinction is between those norms that concern the circumstances in which beliefs should, and should not, be adopted *by someone who possesses their component concepts*, and those norms that concern which concepts it is desirable to possess.

of which meanings ought to be expressed in our language and which ought not to be; so we might call them "semantic norms". Within the former category—i.e. norms that are relativized to the possession of pertinent meanings—there is a bifurcation, between those that assess, conditional on the *public* meanings of words, an *individual's* basic rules of word use (i.e. the rules that constitute meanings *within his idiolect*) and those, such as induction, that assess rules that go beyond what is meaning-constituting. We might call the first of these types, "communication norms", since their function (or so I will suggest) is to minimize, for the sake of precise communication, variations amongst individuals in their basic rules of use for a given word. Only the rest are strictly speaking "epistemic norms", since they alone concern the substantive beliefs a person should and should not have, who fully possesses the concepts they contain.

Let us focus, to begin with, on what I'm calling *communication* norms. The rule governing an individual's use of a word will often diverge somewhat from the rule governing its usage by most other people in his community (or the rule that governs its usage by "experts" to whom other people tend to defer). In such a case, provided the discrepancy is not too great, the individual is nonetheless credited with meaning the same as everyone else.[30] However, such individual differences in rules of basic use are instrumentally undesirable, diminishing the exactness and efficiency of communication and therefore impeding the transfer of true (hence valuable) beliefs. Consequently, we invoke norms dictating that if one means such-and-such by a word, then one's basic acceptance-rule for it ought to be so-and-so, where 'so-and-so' is the usage of 'experts' (or of the majority) which constitutes its public meaning such-and-such. Thus an individual's basic rule of use is by no means beyond criticism. Indeed, the whole point of our invoking communication norms is to bring such rules into conformity with one another.

---

[30] See chap. 2, section (h), for further discussion.

Turn now to the case of *epistemic* norms: norms dictating that anyone who fully understands certain terms ought to follow certain acceptance-rules, where those rules go beyond what is required for understanding. Arguably, the (conditional) requirement to respect *modus ponens*, arithmetic, and the truth-schema are of this sort, since (as we saw in section 7) what constitutes the meanings of pertinent terms are not the rules themselves, but mere conditionalized versions of them. But especially clear cases are provided by the rules of induction/abduction. Reason requires us, given some body of data, to find 'simpler' explanations of it more plausible than 'complex' ones. Thus certain principles characterizing the relevant notion of simplicity, and specifying its bearing on the credibility of hypotheses, are rational. But since they don't concern particular words, they cannot be meaning-constituting.

So how might such fundamental epistemic norms be accounted for? Of course, the purpose of this chapter has been not so much to give an answer to this question as to criticize the most prominent one—the semantogenetic approach. Still, a merely negative line of argument is bound to seem more compelling if it can be conjoined with some prima facie plausible alternative account. And I think that there is indeed such an alternative, namely, that the correctness of these norms *cannot* be explained because they are explanatorily *fundamental*. Not only are we not able to justify rules such as modus ponens and induction, we can't even explain why they are justified. Now, it might be felt that such a conclusion makes a mystery of epistemic normativity; or, even worse, that it opens the door to relativism or scepticism. But no such response would be warranted. After all, *some* normative explanatory premises would surely be needed in order to account for the rationality of our basic epistemic rules; and if we would be left with no intolerable mystery about how *these* could stand in the absence of any explanation of them—if we would not thereby feel pushed into scepticism or relativism— then why should we be puzzled or anxious if it turns out to be a fundamental normative fact that our rules of modus ponens, truth introduction, induction, etc., are rationally required.[31]

Moreover, even though an explanation of such normative facts may well be impossible, we may at least be able to raise and answer the question of how we have come to embrace and impose these norms—of why we *regard* them as correct. For here it is plausible to invoke our desire for true beliefs and our partial dependence on other people for their acquisition. These factors explain why we want others to follow the basic epistemic rules that we are convinced are the right ones, i.e. to follow the ones that we are most inclined to follow ourselves. And since we all (innately?) have fundamental deductive, inductive, numerical, and observational inclinations that are similar to one another, and we all appreciate that we are similarly prone to deviate from them under the influence of factors such as distraction, wishful thinking, etc., this explains our agreement as to which epistemic rules ought to be followed.[32]

---

[31] One might be tempted to suppose that all such epistemic norms may be explained on the basis of a single principle: namely, that our fundamental belief-acquisition rules ought to be *reliable* (i.e. engender *truth*). It is questionable, however, how reliable our epistemic rules actually are. One problem is that they often (indeed, very often) dictate beliefs that turn out to be false. Another is that some of them dictate *degrees* of belief rather than full belief—and it is unclear, in those cases, how reliability is to be assessed.

[32] This agreement is manifested, most immediately, in our accord with respect to the evaluation of *specific* acceptances; for we often don't quite know how to articulate *general* rules that dictate them.

One must distinguish the assessment of *following* such *rules* of use, from the assessment of *conformity* with them. An epistemic norm of the form:

If S means F by w, then S's use of w ought to *conform with* rule $w

is the product of two more fundamental norms, namely:

If S means F by w, then S ought to *follow* rule $w

and

If S ought to follow rule $w, then S ought to conform with $w.

The discussion in the text above focuses on the first of these two more fundamental elements. However, another way of violating an epistemic norm, is to violate its second element. Thus one might be *following* exactly the right rule of use for a word, given its meaning, but nonetheless *fail to satisfy* that rule, for one reason or another, e.g. tiredness, inebriation, complexity of subject matter, etc.

Finally, let us briefly consider how it might be possible to account for what I am calling *semantic* norms: for the fact that it is desirable to possess certain concepts but not others; for the fact that certain meaning-constituting rules of word-use should (or may) be followed *unconditionally*, and others should (or may) not be. Here, the appropriate form of account would seem to be instrumental. For there appears to be no other sense in which it is *valuable* to deploy a language in thought and communication, and, more specifically, to deploy one that expresses a rich stock of useful meanings. In other words, given the nature of our world and of ourselves, and the advantages to be gained from representing certain facts and from living together harmoniously, certain basic use-propensities are worth having and others are not worth having.

However, under this vague rubric we must distinguish between (a) providing an internalistic, practical *justification*, via means/ends reasoning, for following a given meaning-constituting rule of word-use; and (b) offering a mere *explanation* of the 'objective desirability' of following such a rule, in terms of the beneficial effects of doing so. Only certain meanings are sufficiently superficial that we will be able to *rationalize* the introduction of terms to express them. Abbreviations, for example, may be justified in this way. But in the case of more fundamental meanings—those whose rules of use cannot be *explicitly* followed (on pain of circularity)—the desirability of their incorporation within our language cannot be explained in terms of any such rationale. One cannot motivate or defend, for example, our deployment of the concept RED, by an argument to the effect that we will benefit from following such-and-such a rule. For that style of argument would motivate the *explicit* following of the rule; but our meaning what we do by "red"—i.e. (roughly) our accepting "That is red" in the presence of red things—cannot come about in that way. Thus, in the case of RED and all other similarly deep concepts, no such means/ends rationale for possessing them may be given. We might nonetheless be able to

construct an explanation of their 'objective desirability'. For
that sort of account may be taken to reside in a demonstration
that possession of such concepts promotes our well-being. But
even this weaker story cannot be expected in every case. For we
don't have a conception of 'our well-being' that is independent
of our nature. And our nature surely includes the possession of a
certain stock of fundamental concepts.

14. CONCLUSIONS

An epistemic norm specifies (in effect) how one ought to use
certain words (i.e. which sentences containing them should be
accepted) *given* what those words mean. Some such norms
appear to be basic, i.e. not supported by others. In those cases
we might wonder how their correctness might be explained.
And we might be tempted to answer, as many philosophers
have been, that it is the meaning-constituting character of the
legislated usage that explains why that usage is required of us.
But I have been arguing that this semantogenetic view of epistemic norms is mistaken.

For, in the first place, when our following a certain rule of use
is meaning-constituting, the unconditional legitimacy of our
following it is a *semantic* norm, not an *epistemic* one. Second,
that normative status does not derive merely from the fact that
our allegiance to the rule is meaning-constituting, but depends,
in addition, on the *legitimacy* of our deploying the resulting
meaning. Third, despite this *inferential* route between these
norms, the proper *explanatory* route between them is evidently
from the legitimacy of following the rule *to* the legitimacy of
possessing the concept that would thereby be established, rather
than the other way round. Fourth, the normative phenomenon
with which we are concerned is the *requirement* to reason in certain ways, not merely the *legitimacy* of doing so. And fifth, the
norms of logic, arithmetic, etc., with which we are primarily

concerned are too substantive to be meaning-constituting; so even if the semantogenetic model were correct, it couldn't do what it was intended to do.

Here's an alternative picture. Amongst the various norms telling us which sentences should and should not be accepted given the circumstances and given what we mean, some are associated with meaning-constituting rules and some are not. For those norms that are, the explanation of why we embrace and impose them resides in the instrumental value of the improved communication that is fostered by communal compliance. And for those norms that are not—e.g. those mandating modus ponens, the truth schema, explicit definitions, and inductive-abductive generalization—the explanation of why we embrace and impose them resides in our shared ingrained inclination to follow those rules (and to discount judgements made in certain unfavourable conditions) in conjunction with our need to rely on the reasoning of others. The *correctness* of these norms remains unexplained and is probably unexplainable, but that should be no cause for panic or puzzlement.[33]

[33] I am indebted to Paul Boghossian for the stimulus of our many conversations about these issues. No one has done more than he has to refine and improve the semantogenetic view of epistemic norms. I would also like to thank Marcus Giaquinto and Anna-Sara Malmgren for their helpful comments on an earlier draft of this chapter.

7

Meaning and its Place in the Language Faculty

1. METHODOLOGICAL BACKGROUND

Some projects are incoherent: their alleged aims self-contradictory or not well defined.[1] Others, though coherent, are impractical or unfeasible: we have no reason to think they can be properly carried through. And some, though both clear and doable, are not worthwhile: their completion would yield results of too little value.

Studies of language, which vary enormously from one to another with respect to their subject matter, ambitions, methods, and potential products, well illustrate these three respects in which a project may be sound or suspect. Such studies can be concerned with language in general, or with some particular language; their focus may be historical, sociological, neurological, cultural, evolutionary, philosophical, literary, or psychological; and their goals can be descriptive, explanatory, normative, or pedagogical. Thus dozens of ways of investigating language are imaginable, but few can be expected to satisfy our three desiderata.

---

[1] This chapter was stimulated by Noam Chomsky's "Internalist Explorations", *Festschrift for Burge*, edited by M. Hahn and B. Ramberg (reprinted in his *New Horizons in the Study of Language and Mind*). However, the Chomskian point of view that I discuss here is also articulated in various other works of his, including *Knowledge of Language*; *Language and Thought*, and "On the Nature, Use and Acquisition of Language", W. Lycan (ed.), *Mind and Cognition: A Reader* 627–46.

One that does appear to satisfy them is the scientific investigation into which internal properties of a person are responsible for his or her linguistic activity, for the individual's capacity
to speak and understand a language. This endeavour, which
Chomsky has termed "I-linguistics", is clearly coherent, for it
is simply one part of the global scientific enterprise. Moreover,
the prospects of arriving at knowledge in this domain are
initially quite reasonable and have been bolstered by the development of increasingly successful theories, and the value of
such results can be no less than that of reaching a scientific
understanding of any other significant aspect of the natural
world.

Of course the legitimacy of I-linguistics, judged with regard to
coherence, feasibility, and value, has no tendency to imply the
illegitimacy of other studies of language. But, if we are not to
waste time and energy, it is important to focus attention on
these desiderata and on how hard it is to satisfy them, and to
concentrate our efforts on projects that do.

Certain 'philosophical' accounts—those that are self-
consciously *non*-scientific—are particularly vulnerable in this
regard, as Chomsky has frequently pointed out.[2] However, the
theory I elaborate in the present work has nothing to fear from
such scrutiny. Granted, its primary focus is on our *pre*-theoretical
conceptions of meaning, truth, rule-following, sentence, belief,
etc., and on obtaining a perspective from within which the
many confusions about these matters, to which we so easily fall
prey, may be understood and removed. And granted, a scientific
I-linguistics can be expected to deploy somewhat different
notions, specially geared for explanation and prediction. But
insofar as these new notions are streamlined, technical modifica-
tions of the pre-existing ones, the very same puzzles and paradoxes that plague ordinary thought about meaning will equally

---

[2] There is a striking convergence of opinion between Chomsky and later
Wittgenstein regarding the dubious legitimacy of certain philosophical theories
of language.

arise within scientific theorizing about it. And so the solutions developed in earlier chapters can make a substantial contribution to I-linguistics.

2. EVIDENCE

Since the aim of I-linguistics is to discover the causal basis of an individual's linguistic activity—his speech and understanding— those phenomena will provide the primary evidence for any theory within the field. This is not to draw an invidious distinction between what may and may not give support to an I-linguistic theory. Insofar as such a theory is *scientific*, there can be no such distinction: any fact in any domain *might* somehow prove relevant, and a great variety of facts *have* proved relevant. The point is merely that since the goal is to explain certain phenomena, then those phenomena must be amongst the facts that are accommodated.

More specifically, what must ultimately constrain our theory are vocal sounds that a person produces, the circumstances in which they are produced, and the characteristic reactions to sounds that are heard. Such facts are plainly relevant and uncontroversially observable, insofar as they presuppose relatively few of the psychological hypotheses whose correctness might be at issue. Thus, although they by no means exhaust the data that might well be deployed in support of an I-linguistic theory, they will provide an essential epistemological foundation for it.

Notice however that although the ur-data in I-linguistics will tend to be fairly behavioural, we cannot expect to be able to predict and explain *specific items* of linguistic behaviour; for any such item will be the product of an unmanageably large array of interacting causal factors including, not merely the individual's knowledge of his language, but also his beliefs, what he desires to express, and his levels of alertness, intoxication, etc.

Following Chomsky, it seems reasonable to postulate that a person's 'knowledge of language' is embodied in a distinct mechanism or faculty and that the focus of I-linguistics should be on the character of this faculty. The more-or-less behavioural facts one might expect roughly to correlate with the properties of a person's language faculty are extremely crude, vague, qualified, approximate generalizations regarding the way that his or her words sound, and the tendency for them to be deployed in certain distinctive combinations in certain circumstances, for example:

[B]   Peter often says things of the form "x seems to be sleeping", but rarely of the form "x seems sleeping".

Peter is very often disposed to assent to "That's red" in the presence of red things.

Peter is normally inclined to agree to "Mary intended to take her medicine" if he agrees to "Mary was persuaded to take her medicine".

Such crude behavioural patterns are presumed to result from the operation of the language faculty in 'normal conditions'. More specifically, it might be tentatively supposed that Peter's language faculty immediately engenders such facts as that

[D]   The sentence "x seems to be sleeping" is grammatical, but "x seems sleeping" is not.

"That's red" is applied to red things.

"Mary intended to take her medicine" is accepted if "Mary was persuaded to take her medicine" is accepted[3].

and that these in turn, given further, normal facts about Peter, account for his observable behaviour patterns.

[3] These formulations cannot be quite right. For the facts determined by the language faculty will be *theoretical*, i.e. not exactly expressible using ordinary language expressions such as "grammatical", "applies" and "sentence".

It is not unnatural to characterize such immediate output of the language faculty as items of *knowledge,* for example:

[K]   Peter knows that sentences of the form "x seems to be sleeping" are grammatical and that sentences of the form "x seems sleeping" are not.

Peter knows that he applies the word "red" to red things.

Peter knows that he applies "intended" if he applies "was persuaded".

and to suppose that what explains such items of knowledge, namely, the *fundamental* content of the language faculty, is also a body of knowledge. For insofar as Peter's language faculty is governed by certain law-like regularities, R, which result in certain facts, D, we may speak of Peter's *implicitly* knowing R and D.

However, our describing the laws and immediate products of the language faculty as states of 'knowledge' is more of a *façon de parler* than a substantive theoretical move. We are entitled to recharacterize the fact *that Peter's language faculty entails that "John is sleeping" is grammatical* as the fact *that Peter implicitly knows that "John is sleeping" is grammatical.* But the latter formulation makes no additional commitments, has no explanatory advantages, and does nothing to illuminate the nature of the fact 'known'.[4]

The immediate products, D, of the language faculty, (which can be regarded as states of implicit knowledge) are the objects of deeper explanation: they are the 'data' for a linguistic theory which characterizes the internal structure of that faculty. The virtue of focusing on such 'data' rather than verbal behaviour, is

---

[4] As Chomsky puts it, 'In English usage, having a language is called "knowing a language"' [Section 1 of "Internalist Explorations"]. Similarly we can say that having a faculty governed by the law that R(FL) can be described as "knowing that R(FL)".

that they are more sharply formulated and bear more directly on what we want to find out about, namely, the basic nature of that component of the mind/brain. However, this advantage is acquired at a certain risk, which should not be forgotten. For it is an uncertain theoretical hypothesis that the inclination to engage in some particular verbal behaviour is the joint product of some (theoretically articulated) output of a 'faculty of language', together with other factors that determine whether or how that output-state will be manifested on any given occasion. This is indeed a reasonable conjecture, for it is indeed plausible to suppose that a person's speech behaviour, although affected by such factors as environmental conditions, beliefs, tiredness, desire to speak, honesty, etc. is also an expression of his 'knowledge of a language'. But it should not be forgotten that both the faculty-of-language postulate, and specific theses about its immediate deliverances, are theoretical conjectures whose plausibility derives from the observation of behavioural tendencies together with assumptions about the interaction between the language faculty and other mental and physical factors.[5]

3. A VERY SIMPLE PICTURE

In developing this idea let us assume with Chomsky (a) that each human being indeed has a faculty of language, FL, a component of his mind/brain constituting the primary causal/explanatory

---

[5] In stressing the crucial evidential role of behavioural facts I do not mean to impugn the value of other kinds of data. Of particular importance is an individual's intuitive judgements regarding the grammaticality (or degree of grammaticality) of sentences presented to him, and regarding the appropriateness of producing them. Note however that the utility of such information presupposes the theoretical assumption that we each have intuitive access to the products of our own language faculty. This assumption can be reasonable only to the extent that the linguistic theories to which it leads can also accommodate the behavioural data.

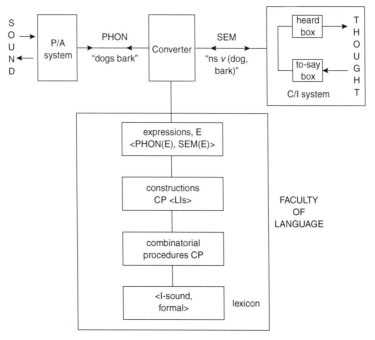

basis of his linguistic activity; (b) that the possible states, L^1, $L^2, \ldots$, of FL are, by definition, possible I-languages; (c) that each such state, L, is a computational procedure that generates infinitely many I-expressions, E_1, $E_2, \ldots$; (d) that each such expression, E, is a pairing <PHON(E), SEM(E)> of phonetic and semantic objects, which, through their respective interaction with the perceptual/articulatory system (P/A) and the conceptual/intentional system (C/I), determine an association of a sound with a thought; (e) that these PHON-SEM pairs are constructed from lexical items, LI(1), LI(2), ...; and (f) that these lexical items are stored in a lexicon which is accessed by the computational procedures that form I-expressions.[6]

Figure 2 provides a simple model of how things might work, a model which incorporates all these assumptions, but which nevertheless is not adopted by Chomsky, as we shall see.

[6] See Chomsky, "Internalist Explorations", sections 2 and 3.

In this very simple picture (which I'll call vsp) each lexical item consists in an I-sound paired with formal properties that indicate the 'functional type' to which it belongs. Thus some lexical items will be *schemata* containing 'slots' into which items of specified functional types may be inserted to yield terms that may in turn be inserted into other schemata, and so on. A 'construction' specifies certain lexical items to be combined in that way, and specifies in which order this is to be done, for example:

Apply LI(15) to the sequence <LI(3), the result of applying LI(7) to the sequence <LI(22), LI(1), LI(4)>>

Thus a construction is a pair consisting of an abstract combinatorial procedure, CP, for example:

Apply u to <v, the result of applying w to <x, y, z >>

and a sequence of lexical items, for example:

<LI(15), LI(3), LI(7), LI(22), LI(1), LI(4)>

on which the procedure is to be imposed. The expression E that is computed from such a construction is a pair consisting of a phonetic object, PHON(E), and a semantic object, SEM(E). An important difference between these two components of E is that in PHON(E) the information about how the LIs have been combined is largely deleted. All we have, roughly speaking, is a modified string of I-sounds. But in SEM(E) that structural information is retained—encoded by means of bracketing. The phonetic object, PHON(E), determines (via P/A) how the expression sounds. And vice versa. So when that sound occurs, the correlated semantic object, SEM(E), which consists in a combinatorial procedure imposed on a sequence of I-sounds, enters the 'heard box' and passes into thought.[7] It is an expression of the

---

[7] One could perhaps simplify further by getting rid of the 'CONVERTER'. But it is worth explicitly noting that it is one thing for FL to deliver a list of pairs of PHONs and SEMs, and another thing to have a device which, with access to that information, takes a given PHON as input and outputs the appropriate SEM (and vice versa).

person's language of thought. Finally, each I-sound expresses (or embodies) the concept it does in virtue of its basic conceptual role, which consists in the fact that certain specified thought-formulations, which employ that I-sound, are maintained in certain circumstances.[8] Each SEM derives its content from the concepts expressed by the LIs from which it was constructed and from the combinatorial procedure imposed on those LIs. (See section 7 for further discussion of the compositionality of meaning). Note that there may be an innate predisposition towards the instantiation of particular conceptual roles.

For example (and simplifying enormously for the sake of illustration), a person's lexicon might contain the lexical items <"dog", (f1, f5)> and <"bark", (f2, f4, f9)> and <"*ns v*", (f15)>. The formal features, f1, f2, ..., fN, might be such that an expression can be formed by applying something with f15 to a pair of terms with f1 and f4. Thus we have a permissible construction consisting of the procedure, "Apply the first item to the second and third items" imposed on the sequence of three LIs

$$<\text{"}ns\ v\text{"}, \text{f15}>$$
$$<\text{"dog"}, (\text{f1}, \text{f5})>$$
$$<\text{"bark"}, (\text{f2}, \text{f4}, \text{f9})>$$

---

[8] Those circumstances may sometimes be articulated in terms of inputs to the central conceptual system from some peripheral system of representations, e.g. vision. And those representations, not composed of I-sounds, will express their own concepts.

As detailed in chap. 2, when I speak of a term (e.g. an I-sound) "having a conceptual role" or "being governed by a basic regularity", I have in mind a fact about it to the effect that the acceptance of certain postulates or inference rules involving the term is explanatorily basic with respect to its overall deployment, e.g. (very roughly):

> Peter's acceptance of instances of "<p> is true iff p" is the explanatory basis of his overall use of "true".

> Peter's acceptance of inferences from "p" and "q" to "p and q", and vice versa, is the explanatory basis of his overall use of it.

The idea is that the meanings of I-sounds are constituted by such law-like regularities, which are exemplified in C/I. Moreover, according to VSP, these don't need to be explicitly articulated in FL (or anywhere else).

This construction determines a certain phonetic object, "dogs bark", and a certain semantic object, "*ns v* (dog, bark)".[9] The first of these determines (given the character of the P/A system) a certain sound. The second passes into the C/I system: to think that dogs bark is for this object to have a particular 'location' in that system, i.e. for it to be in the 'belief box'. Its elements, namely "dog", "bark" and "*ns v*", express or embody the concepts they do in virtue of their conceptual roles, or, more specifically, in virtue of certain of their deployments (in postulates, inference patterns, etc.) being explanatorily basic.[10]

4. MENTALESE

Let us now consider various objections and alternatives to this picture. One modification of VSP, suggested by the work of Jerry Fodor, involves the idea that the language of thought is the same for everyone—a universal 'Mentalese'.[11] This idea can be represented by amending the above model slightly. We might suppose that each lexical item contains, not merely an I-sound paired with formal properties, but also a symbol ('word') of Mentalese. And we can suppose that the SEM part of an expression is made up of the Mentalese components, rather than the I-sounds, of the LIs from which it is constructed. Thus, one

---

[9] One might wonder why we should suppose that in order to get "dogs bark" we need to recognize as a lexical item, not merely "dog" and "bark", but also "*ns v*". The answer is that the combinatorial procedures can then be articulated in purely argument-functional terms, as just indicated. Moreover, there don't have to be any principles that specify what these procedures are allowed to be. Any way of combining any lexical items will be permitted as long as it squares with their formal properties. That Fregean conception of grammar is the essence of Chomsky's syntactic "minimalism".

[10] An utterance will seem ill-formed to the extent that the hearer's P/A system responds to it by outputting a phonetic representation that does not sufficiently coincide with the PHON of any of the expressions constructed in his FL.

[11] See, e.g., J. Fodor, *The Language of Thought*.

possible I-expression would be the PHON-SEM pairing

$$<\text{``dogs bark''}, \text{``}n^* \ v \ (\$, \#)\text{''}>$$

where "$n^* \ v$", "$\$$", and "$\#$" are the Mentalese translations of "$ns \ v$", "dog", and "bark".

However, as Chomsky has pointed out, this sort of move has various disadvantages.[12] In the first place it is evidently less simple than VSP, postulating an additional inner language. In the second place it is not plausible to suppose that languages are so easily translated into a universal Mentalese. Experience with translating spoken languages into one another suggests that exact translation is rarely possible, because words in one language tend not to have exactly the same meanings as words in another, which they would have if they could each be translated into Mentalese. This argument breaks down if Mentalese is imagined to be so rich that it has separate terms for all the subtle variations of meaning exhibited in ordinary languages, but in that case the first objection (regarding the extra complexity of the Mentalese hypothesis) becomes even more telling.

Amongst the considerations that might nonetheless be thought to militate in favour of Mentalese are

(1) the explanatory value of a language in which to have the thought processes involved in learning one's first spoken language,

(2) the need to integrate linguistically encoded information with representations from the visual system,

(3) the fact that an individual, growing up in isolation and never acquiring a spoken language, would nevertheless be capable of elementary reasoning.

However, these considerations may be accommodated by supposing that the terms of a normal person's language of thought include, not only I-sounds, but also a strictly limited

---

[12] See Chomsky, "Internalist Explorations", section 4.

number of universal Mentalese terms (expressing such very basic concepts as RED, OBJECT, LATER THAN, etc.). Indeed, there is mounting experimental evidence from cognitive science—see especially the work of Susan Carey and Elizabeth Spelke[13]—to the effect (a) that concepts such as these operate within innate, special-purpose 'core knowledge' systems (of the sort that animals also possess) and so are in fact expressed in Mentalese; and (b) that they are later supplemented with a variety of further concepts which are acquired only with a public language, which are mentally articulated in that language, and which are deployed in central processing. This concession towards the Mentalese hypothesis is perfectly consistent with VSP. For we can continue to maintain that most of a person's language of thought is composed of the I-sounds of his or her spoken language. Moreover, the association of the few Mentalese terms, e.g. "red*", with their spoken-language equivalents can be constituted in the conceptual system, e.g. by there being an inferential relation between "x is red*" and "x is red". Thus there is no need for complex lexical items that would pair each I-sound with a Mentalese term.[14]

---

[13] S. Carey and E. S. Spelke, "Domain Specific Knowledge and Conceptual Change", in L. Hirschfeld and S. Gelman (eds.) *Mapping the Mind: Domain Specificity in Cognition and Culture*, 1994, 169–200; E. S. Spelke, "What Makes Us Smart? Core Knowledge and Natural Language" in *Language in Mind*, edited by Dedre Gentner and Susan Goldin-Meadow; S. Carey, *The Origin of Concepts*, MIT Press.

I am not suggesting that either Carey or Spelke would fully endorse theses, (a) and (b), esp. in the cryptic, simplified formulations given here.

[14] Some further considerations that might be thought to favour the Mentalese hypothesis are:

(a) the presumed fact that thoughts, unlike sounds, are not ambiguous.
     But a given I-sound might have two distinct conceptual roles, and its tokens indexed to keep track of them: e.g. some beliefs may be formulated with "bank(1)" and some with "bank(2)". In that case, the process of understanding an instance of "I went to the bank" will involve, first, FL's assigning to it the unique SEM determined by that PHON; and, second, C/I's determining (on contextual/pragmatic grounds) the right conceptual role, i.e. guessing which of the two groups of sentences containing "bank" that are already in the belief box are sentences to which the present instance of 'bank' is inferentially relevant, and then indexing it accordingly.

5. REFERENTIALISM

A second way of departing from VSP is to suppose that each I-sound derives its content—i.e. embodies the thought constituents that it does—*not* in virtue of a fundamental, internal, conceptual role, but rather in virtue of standing in some *referential relation* to some aspect of the external world. This idea may be thought to be motivated by Davidson's contention that the compositionality of meaning (the fact that the meanings of sentences are explained by the meanings of their words) can be accommodated only by supposing that the meanings of sentences consist in truth conditions and that the meanings of words consist in their referents.[15] And the idea is further supported in the work of Fodor and others suggesting how this reference relation might be 'naturalized', i.e. analysed in non-semantic, scientifically respectable terms.[16] Thus Fodor maintains that a predicate has as its meaning the abstract concept (i.e. content), DOG, in virtue of the fact that tokenings of that predicate in the belief-box are nomologically correlated with the presence (to the speaker) of dogs. This alternative to the 'internal conceptual role' account of concept-identity can be affixed either to my VSP, in which concepts are internally expressed by I-sounds, or to the Mentalese variant, in which concepts are expressed by Mentalese terms.

(b) the possibility of more-or-less approximate translations.
   But couldn't these be constituted merely on the basis of similarities of basic conceptual role?

(c) the existence of thoughts that we are able to express in public only by means of metaphors and other evocative language.
   But, even if there are such thoughts, they provide no reason to postulate a 'deeper' language (i.e. Mentalese) in which they *can* be literally expressed.

For more on the pros and cons of Mentalese, see *The Mind of a Savant* by Neil Smith and Ianthi Tsimpli.

[15] D. Davidson, "Truth and Meaning", in *Truth and Interpretation*.

[16] See, e.g. Fodor's *Psychosemantics*, Dretske's *Knowledge and the Flow of Information*, Stampe's "Toward a Causal Theory of Linguistic Representation", Papineau's *Reality and Representation*, and Jacob's *What Minds Can Do*.

Either way, there are two objections. In the first place, the motivation for the referential approach, insofar as it comes from the need to account for the compositionality of meaning, is defective. For, as we shall suggest in section 7 (and substantiate in the next chapter) it is both possible and preferable to explain compositionality in other terms.

And in the second place, the referential approach to concept identity does not provide a framework in which the characteristic uses of words (sounds) can be explained. For in order to do that we must be able to explain the use in relation to one another of the concepts expressed by those words: e.g. Peter's unshakeable conviction that bachelors are unmarried, that if John is taller than Bill then Bill is not taller than John, that the sentence "dogs bark" is true if and only if dogs bark, that if electrons exist they are negatively charged, etc. It is very hard to see how these convictions could be explained merely in virtue of referential relations that are constituted by the tendency to think "That's a bachelor", "a man", "bigger", "married", "true", "an electron", "charge", "negative", "atom", etc. . . . ." in the presence, respectively, of bachelors, men, instances of 'bigger than', etc.

Nor can the referentialist afford to retreat to the claim that his view is not *attempting* to address the above explanatory questions, but merely to provide an account of concept-identity. For this would be to concede that the view contributes nothing at all to one of the important goals of I-linguistics; and it is unclear how any other goal of I-linguistics would be furthered either. Moreover, it is fairly obvious that theories of concept constitution *must* play a vital role in such explanations; for it is clear that the event of *having* a certain thought, e.g. Peter's maintaining, on a particular occasion, *that it is raining*, is due in part to the *nature* of that type of thought, together with auxiliary facts regarding sensory input, background theories, etc. In other words, we really must suppose that the facts that identify which concept is expressed (or embodied) by a given internal term (i.e. an I-sound, or a Mentalese symbol) are facts that play a fundamental role in explaining the overall deployment of that term within C/I. The referential properties of a term will not be able to do this explanatory work.

6. DEFINITIONS

A third alternative to VSP involves the idea that the *meanings* (in a pretheoretical sense) of I-sounds are explicitly encoded in the faculty of language. They are not, as in VSP, merely constituted by behaviour of I-sounds in the belief system, C/I. Rather, C/I is capable of 'interpreting' the specifications, given in the language faculty, of each term's meaning, thereby ensuring that the term is deployed appropriately. This picture is favoured by Chomsky, who implements it by supposing (a) that lexical items consist, not merely of I-sounds (and their formal properties), but of I-sounds (and formal properties) *paired with I-meanings*; and (b) that the input to, and output of, the C/I system, namely SEM(E), is constructed, *not* from I-sounds (as in VSP), but from I-meanings. Thus we have something like Figure 3.[17]

This picture, whereby pretheoretical meanings are encoded by items (I-meanings) in the faculty of language, may be developed in various alternative directions, depending on the answers given to the following pair of questions:

(Q1)   What is the form of an I-meaning? Does it look somewhat like a classical definition in which an I-sound's meaning is articulated within a 'universal basic-concept language' via a synonymous expression composed from the terms of that language? Is it rather the representation of a regularity of use, i.e. a conceptual role? Or is there perhaps some further possibility?

---

[17] Chomsky does not explicitly present this model: it is my reconstruction of what he suggests in sections 2, 3, and 4 of "Internalist Explorations".

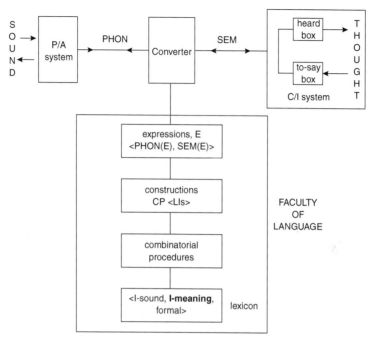

FIGURE 3

(Q2) What is the relation between the I-meanings and the constituents of thoughts? Is it that I-meanings themselves are constituents of belief-formulations and are manipulated within the conceptual system? Or is it rather that the I-meanings determine the use of the terms that are deployed within the conceptual system, terms such as I-sounds or words of Mentalese?

Regarding Q1, it seems more plausible to suppose that, in general, I-meanings take the relatively liberal, flexible form of the specification of a regularity of use, rather than the relatively constrained form of an orthodox explicit definition. For it is notoriously difficult to provide satisfactory, proper definitions of just about anything. Therefore it seems more realistic to imagine that each lexical item pairs an I-sound with the representation of a basic regularity of use, which will not in general (though it may sometimes) take the form of an explicit definition.[18]

Turning to Q2, the issue is whether we should suppose that the terms in which we think are literally composed of the specifications of their conceptual roles, or whether, rather, these instructions for their use—their I-meanings—are acted on by C/I to result in the terms' being used accordingly. A merely apparent advantage of the former view, that the terms deployed in thought consist in their 'definitions', is that wherever the term is, the C/I system will know what to do with it; for the C/I system will react to a term depending on its intrinsic characteristics. But on reflection we can see that there is no need for this sort of mechanism. Suppose the conceptual role of a mental term "f" consists in the underived acceptance within C/I of certain sentences, "#f", containing it. Then that fact alone, together with other general principles about the system, will constrain and influence the deployment of "f". It is not as if each *token* of "f" exhibits some characteristic, meaning-fixing behaviour, so that it is plausible to locate the cause of this behaviour within each token. It is rather that the variety of facts about "f"'s deployment are best explained by the properties of *some* of its tokens, namely, the acceptance of certain belief-formulations containing them. Thus it is gratuitous to suppose that each token carries its definition around with it.

Assuming these particular answers to Q1 and Q2, it remains to compare VSP with a Chomskian model that incorporates them. We have, on the one hand, the picture I presented initially—VSP—in which the basic internal conceptual roles of I-sounds are merely exemplified in C/I; and, on the other hand, a Chomskian model in which *in addition* these conceptual roles are explicitly represented within the lexicon of FL as I-meanings. Clearly, the postulation of I-meanings involves an extra layer of complexity, and therefore must be justified in

---

[18] For example, the regularity governing "bachelor" may be a disposition to accept, underived, "The bachelors are the unmarried men".

terms of explanatory advantages. But it is unclear what these advantages could be.

One possibility is that considerations of learnability and innateness would favour the existence of I-meanings. The claim, more specifically, might be that since we learn our language so quickly and on the basis of such little evidence, it must be that we have available to us only a very limited stock of psychologically possible I-meanings, which are waiting innately in the language faculty for particular I-sounds to be associated with them. Consider the public term "red" which, by age 4, is associated with some Mentalese symbol, "red*", in the visual system, where "red*" is keyed to the detection of red light. It might be held that this development is so quick and natural that there must be an innate proclivity towards that pattern of use, *arising from a characterization of it being present innately in the faculty of language*. But clearly we can distinguish the hypothesis of there being an innate proclivity towards a certain restricted set of conceptual roles, from the further hypothesis that these are spelled out in the faculty of language, rather than merely instantiated in the C/I system. All the explanatory work is being done by the innateness hypothesis: the postulation of I-meanings appears to be otiose.

Another idea might be that in order to explain why a term has a certain conceptual role we should suppose that there must somewhere exist an explicit characterization of that role, instructions to which the term can be made to conform. But it is hard to see any merit in this explanatory strategy. In the first place, the existence of the explicit characterization would itself call for explanation. In the second place, the conceptual role of a term will often consist in nothing more complex that the presence in the belief-box of certain thought-formulations which contain that term; and this can well be something much simpler than the explicit characterization of that role, so there is no explanatory rationale for supposing that the exemplification of role stems from some specification of it. We can suppose rather that a person, simply by holding true what he hears, provides such terms with their conceptual roles. And in the third place, it is possible, indeed plausible, that certain conceptual roles are innate. In such a case innate Mentalese terms might well possess them. Again there is no need for anything in the faculty of language to articulate those roles.[19]

Finally, it might be suspected that *the symmetry of sound and meaning* should dictate that since I-sounds are represented in FL, I-meanings must also be represented there. However, although it can be valuable to treat sound and meaning similarly, the analogy must of course break down somewhere. And one point at which it appears to collapse is this. A vocal sound is a short event correlated with the P/A system's temporarily entering into a certain characteristic state—its outputting a certain PHON. A meanings on the other hand—a way of understanding such a sound—is a long-lasting background condition of the C/I system. Thus, although we can speak of understanding a word at just the same time as it is being heard, what is happening in C/I is an event—the arrival of a SEM—caused by the sound (i.e. by the corresponding PHON) within a salient background state of C/I—a state that constitutes knowing what such sounds mean and that is responsible for providing the event with distinctive consequences (e.g. beliefs) within C/I. Thus we have, at bottom, an association between a sound-*type* and a background state of C/I. There is no need for something correlated with each *instance* of a given sound-type to give characteristic

[19] There are at least two ways for a priori belief to arise from within the VSP perspective. One way is through the innateness of certain conceptual roles. For example, it may be an innate feature of C/I that there is a Mentalese token "%" such that "p%q" is inferred from "p" and "q", and vice versa; and in that case the belief that if dogs bark and pigs fly, then pigs fly, is a priori. Another kind of a priori commitment may arise by virtue of the pragmatic decision to hold true a certain sentence (so that it is not held true for empirical reasons). For example, "Bachelors are unmarried" is maintained for the sake of a socially useful distinction, not in order to accommodate experience. Needless to say, such accounts of how beliefs might be engendered independently of experience would not qualify as *justifications*. See chap. 6 for extensive discussion.

meaning-instructions to C/I. Rather, when the sound appears C/I is already in the state required to understand it.[20]

Thus the asymmetry between the ways that sound and meaning relate to FL stem from the radical difference in nature between sounds and thoughts. A sound event is a distinctive pattern of air vibrations. What is correlated with it, i.e. a thought constituent, is an entity whose identity as the thought constituent it is depends *not* on its intrinsic properties, but on its role in the conceptual system. For example, in the language of thought model a thought constituent consists not merely of a certain mental term, but depends on the basic role of that term, i.e. the fact that certain sentences containing the term are (non-inferentially) 'in the belief box'. Consequently, in order to produce a particular sound element, the articulatory system must be sent the appropriate 'instruction'—the appropriate PHON. But in order to produce a certain thought constituent it does not matter what element ('symbol') is generated in C/I: what is crucial is the *role* of that element. That conceptual role does not need to be specified every time the symbol possessing it is produced. Once the conceptual role of a mental symbol has been established then, insofar as an element of SEM keys that symbol, it will key the appropriate thought constituent. This being so, there is no reason why the elements of SEM should not be I-sounds. Indeed, for the sake of economy, the elements of thought might also be assumed to be I-sounds (as in VSP). These elements will qualify as particular thought elements in virtue of having particular conceptual roles. And each such role, having once been learned, is tied to an I-sound. There is no need for these ties to be articulated in the faculty of language.

[20] One might be tempted to try a further simplification, that is to eliminate not merely I-meanings, but I-sounds as well! But this is clearly not feasible. For there must be information of some sort passed between P/A and C/I, so there have to be terms in which that information is articulated. Moreover, there must be a system capable of taking the output of P/A—roughly, a string of sounds—and determining its compositional structure. Thus, neither I-sounds nor FL can be dispensed with.

Thus the postulation of I-meanings offers no explanatory advantages. Therefore VSP is preferable to any of the pictures that involve I-meanings, whether they articulate orthodox definitions or conceptual roles, and whether they themselves are the terms of thought, or merely determine the deployment of those terms.

7. COMPOSITIONALITY

A fourth point of conflict between VSP and certain alternatives has to do with the compositionality of meaning. What explains the fact that we know the meanings of an unlimited number of sentences? Under the influence of Chomsky and Davidson some philosophers and linguists hypothesize that the language faculty is the site of unconscious inferential processes in which conclusions about the meanings of complex expressions are explicitly inferred from premises about the meanings of their parts and from further premises about the ways those parts have been combined.[21] In addition it is often supposed (following Davidson) that such inferences are possible only if the conclusions regarding the meanings of sentences are articulated as claims about the *truth conditions* of these sentences, and only if the premises about the meanings of the words are articulated as claims about the referents of those words. For, in that case, Tarski-style demonstrations of the truth conditions of sentences may be converted into derivations of their meanings.

However, there are a number of good reasons to reject these ideas:

First, what needs to be computed is SEM(E), a semantically structured correlate of PHON(E). But this is done simply by combining I-meanings (in Chomsky's picture) or I-sounds (in

---

[21] I don't mean to suggest that either Chomsky or Davidson holds this view, only that their remarks on compositionality have led others to adopt it. See, e.g., R. Larson and G. Segal, *Knowledge of Meaning*.

VSP) in a certain order as legislated by some combinatorial procedure, under the constraint of their formal properties.

Second, there is no explanatory need for any conclusion of the form

> "PHON(E) means that p"
> or "PHON(E) is true if and only if p"
> or "SEM(E) means that p"
> or "SEM(E) is true if and only if p"

to be *explicitly* drawn. Not that the speaker cannot be said to know such things. But this knowledge is merely implicit in the fact that he deploys SEM(E) as he does in his conceptual-intentional-belief system.

Third, one might wonder how it can be that the content of SEM(E) is determined by the contents of its parts—i.e. why there is no possibility that the underlying property in virtue of which a complex mental expression has its meaning will fail to square with the properties in virtue of which the lexical items have their meanings (given the way these items have been combined). But this can be explained trivially, in a way that has nothing to do with truth conditions. It suffices to suppose that the content-property of a complex mental expression, SEM, is *constituted by*—one might even say *identical to*—its property of being constructed as it is from LIs with certain meanings.[22]

Suppose for example that the term "%" embodies the concept FIDO in virtue of having underlying property P^1, and that the term "#" embodies the concept BARKS in virtue of having the underlying property P^2. Then how can we be sure that the SEM, "#(%)", will possess that underlying property P^3 which would constitute its embodying the complex concept FIDO BARKS? How can we be sure that "%"'s having P^1 and "#"'s having P^2 will together guarantee that "#(%)" has P^3? Don't we need,

---

[22] This 'deflationary' approach to compositionality, sketched in the following couple of paragraphs, is developed more fully in chap. 8.

as the Davidsonians maintain, to suppose that these content-constituting characteristics, P^1, P^2, and P^3, are referential and truth conditional properties? I am claiming that we don't. For it suffices to suppose that P^3 is the property

> x results from applying a term with P^2
> to a term with P^1.

And similarly in other cases. We can suppose that what *constitutes* the content property of a SEM is its 'construction property', i.e. its property of resulting from the imposition of a certain syntactic/semantic structure (or combinatorial procedure) on lexical items whose own contents are provided by specified content constituting characteristics.

I have argued that the concept-constituting characteristic of a lexical item should be identified with its basic conceptual role. But it is worth noting that this conclusion is completely independent of considerations of compositionality. Indeed, as we have just seen, the determination of the conceptual content of a complex by the contents of its parts is trivially accommodated without making any assumptions whatsoever about what sort of property of a primitive is responsible for its embodying the concept it does.

8. CONCLUSION

For over 40 years Chomsky's research program has been subjected to a stream of philosophical criticism deriving for the most part from the failure to appreciate that when familiar words are deployed in scientific theories they may acquire new and technical meanings. Thus he is accused of not discussing *language* properly so-called, of contradicting himself in referring to *unconscious rule-following*, of confusion about *representation* and *knowledge*, of blindness to the externalist character of *meaning*, and so on. But he emerges unscathed from these criticisms, which are based on elementary equivocation, and do little but bring philosophy into bad repute.

This of course is not to suggest that Chomsky's framework for I-linguistics is correct. It is to say that its assessment must appreciate its *scientific* character: it must concern the question whether or not we can find any simpler explanation of the phenomena within its domain. In that spirit I have tentatively proposed a model, VSP, in which the association of sounds with meanings is achieved by virtue of the conceptual roles of those sounds, i.e. their basic acceptance properties. I have argued that VSP compares favourably to various alternatives, including those suggested by Fodor, the Davidsonians, the referentialists, and Chomsky himself.[23]

[23] This chapter is a slightly revised version of a paper that appeared in *Chomsky and his Critics* (edited by Louise Anthony and Norbert Hornstein, Blackwell, 2003). I am very grateful to Ned Block, Susan Carey, Robyn Carsten, Tim Crane, Michael Harnish, Rita Manzini, Alec Marantz, Barry C. Smith, Neil Smith, and especially to Noam Chomsky, for their comments on that paper.

8

Deflating Compositionality

1. DAVIDSON'S PROBLEM

What kind of assumptions about the words of a foreign speaker would put us in a position to interpret each of the unlimited number of things he might say, and how could such assumptions be verified? Like Quine, Davidson supposed that answers to these questions would constitute a more-or-less complete philosophical account of meaning. However, unlike Quine, who took for granted that the hard issues here are confined to the second question—Can verifiably correct translation manuals ever be found?—Davidson focused equal attention on an aspect of the first one—How could interpretations of the infinitely many complex expressions of a language be derived (as they surely must be) from finitely many assumptions about the meanings of the simple terms?[1] What form would our hypotheses about the meanings of someone's words and sentences have to take in order that the latter be deducible from the former? And for that matter, how does the understanding we have of our *own* language derive from our understanding of its basic elements.

Davidson's approach to his new problem was ingenious and seductive: we should solve it by piggy-backing on Tarski's work on truth.[2] For Tarski showed us how the truth conditions of

---

[1] For Quine's account of meaning and translation see his *Word and Object*; for Davidson's views see the essays in his *Inquiries into Truth and Interpretation*, especially "Truth and Meaning", first published in *Synthese* 17: 304–23.

[2] To the other problem, that of how we might *justify* the use of a given manual of interpretation, Davidson's solution is similar to Quine's. The method

various formalized sentences could be deduced, in predicate logic, from premises specifying the referents of names and atomic predicates, and from further premises specifying, for each connective, how the referent (or truth-value) of any complex that is formed with it depends on the referents (or truth-values) of the connected expressions. Therefore, if we identify a sentence's possessing the meaning it does with its having a certain truth condition, and if we identify a word's possessing the meaning it does with its having a certain referent (or, in the case of a connective, with the fact about how the truth-values/referents of the complexes formed with it depend on the truth-values/referents of the connected expressions), then Tarski-style deductions of truth conditions become precisely what we were looking for—namely, derivations of sentence-meanings on the basis of assumptions about word-meanings.[3]

Consider for example how to arrive in such a way at an interpretation of the Italian sentence "Gira Marte". We start with the three semantic premisses:

The name "Marte" refers in formal Italian to Mars.[4]

(k) (The predicate "gira(x)" is true in formal Italian of k $\leftrightarrow$ k rotates).

based on Davidson's 'Principle of Charity' differs only in detail from Quine's strategy of radical translation.

[3] The sort of meaning on which I have been focused in this book is *the literal semantic meaning, within a given language, of an expression type.* In that vein, the central question of this chapter is how a person's knowledge of the meaning, in *that* sense, of a complex expression is derived from his knowledge of the meanings of its words. A further question—obviously related—concerns the *proposition* that is fully articulated by a sentence-token, and asks how it is derived from features of its words and from their syntactic mode of combination. I won't be addressing that further question here, except to note the plausibility of supposing that we arrive at the proposition expressed by a given token on the basis, in part, of our knowledge of the meaning of the type to which it belongs. Thus the question at issue here is the more basic one.

[4] The route through '*formal* Italian' is necessary because Tarskian deductions of truth conditions can be carried out only for sentences in some logically regimented, i.e. formalized, part of the language. Ordinary sentences are then dealt with by attributing to them the same truth conditions as their formalizations.

The result of applying a predicate to a name is true in formal Italian ↔

the predicate is true in formal Italian of the referent in formal Italian of the name.

And we also have the syntactic premise

The result of applying "gira(x)" to "Marte" is "gira (Marte)".

From these assumptions we infer that

"gira(Marte)" is true in formal Italian ↔ Mars rotates.

Then we invoke the fact that

The formal Italian, "gira(Marte)", gives the meaning of the ordinary Italian sentence, "Gira Marte",

which puts us in a position to conclude that

"Gira Marte" is true in Italian ↔ Mars rotates.

More generally, Davidson conjectured that for *every* sentence of a natural language we could infer what it means—and hence explain why it means what it does—by showing, along Tarskian lines, why its logical formalization (or regimented equivalent) has the truth condition that it does. And this idea became widely accepted, instigating several decades of 'normal science' in semantics.

2. TROUBLES FOR TRUTH-THEORETIC SEMANTICS

The research projects engendered by the Davidsonian paradigm fall into two groups. First, there have been concerted attempts to show how the strategy could be applied to *all* sentences, including those built with devices that Tarski did not investigate. How, for example, might we deduce the truth conditions of sentences containing adverbs, or that-clauses, or attributive adjectives, or conditional-probability constructions, on the basis of premisses concerning the referents of their words? To that end, how could such sentences be formalized in first-order predicate logic? Over the last 30 years clever solutions have been found to several problems of this sort, although many kinds of sentence still remain intractable.

The second set of issues that have needed to be addressed includes various foundational questions. For instance, does the truth condition of a sentence in fact suffice to determine its meaning? In other words, is there any reading of "s is true *if and only if* p" in which it will be strong enough to ensure "s means that p"? Considerable efforts to find or devise such a construal have not yet produced an acceptable one.[5]

In addition there's an issue as to whether a natural language sentence could in fact have the same meaning as the best formulation one can give of it in predicate logic? For example, is it plausible that "John might win" has precisely the same meaning as "$(\exists x)[\text{PossWorld}(x) \ \& \ \text{Wins}(\text{John}, x)]$", and that the sense of "Mary is walking slowly" is identical to that of

---

[5] One sometimes hears it said, on behalf of Davidson, that he was not really attempting to *analyse* "s means that p", but rather to *eliminate* this obscure (intensional) notion by showing that we can make do instead with the relatively unproblematic (extensional) "s is true if and only if p". But remember that the problem he set was to specify which assumptions about a person would enable us to tell what beliefs his assertive utterances are expressing, i.e. to say what he means. So if the answer, roughly speaking, is that these assumptions will engender the 'truth conditions' of his utterances, then it is obligatory to face up to the challenge of articulating precisely what sort of truth-conditional claim about a sentence would amount to a specification of the belief that its utterance would manifest, i.e. to a specification of what it means. It seems clear that Davidson himself *does* face up to this challenge, and that he is himself responsible for some of the best attempts to meet it. For example, there is the idea that "s is true if and only if p" be understood as "It is a law of nature that (s is true $\leftrightarrow$ p)", or that it be understood as (roughly) "It follows from any truth theory verified via the Principle of Charity that (s is true $\leftrightarrow$ p)". However, a problem with all such construals, which take the form "$\Box$ (s is true $\leftrightarrow$ p)", is that if the analysans is satisfied, and if we can find some "q", as it would seem we always can, not synonymous with "p" yet such that $\Box$ (p $\leftrightarrow$ q), then even though s does not mean that q, we can nonetheless infer that $\Box$ (s is true $\leftrightarrow$ q).

"$(\exists x)[\text{Walking}(x) \ \& \ \text{By}(x, \text{Mary}) \ \& \ \text{Slow}(x)]$"? No doubt the members of such pairs necessarily have the same truth value, but the structural and semantic differences between them are nonetheless so great that one might well wonder whether they could count as exact synonyms of one another.

The expectation that these technical and foundational difficulties will eventually be overcome derives largely from the conviction that there is no decent alternative to the Davidsonian truth-theoretic perspective, and therefore that it *must* be more-or-less right. It seems to me, however, that there *is* a good alternative—a 'deflationary' alternative—whose correctness would undermine the purpose of the Davidsonian research programme and make it unnecessary to swallow its various implausible commitments.[6]

3. A DEFLATIONARY APPROACH TO COMPOSITIONALITY

The alternative I have in mind may be described as deflationary, for its basic idea is that Davidson's problem (of how we might derive interpretations of complex expressions) has a trivial solution. This solution assumes the principle of compositionality: that the meaning of a complex is determined by the meanings of its parts and by how those parts are combined. But it involves no general explication of meaning (e.g. in terms of reference and truth conditions) and hence, unlike Davidson, offers no

---

[6] Certain alternatives to Davidson's approach are variants of the same idea and are subject to similar objections. A prominent example, developed by Richard Montague (see, for example, his *Formal Philosophy: Selected Papers of Richard Montague*) is based on identifying the meaning of a sentence with a function from possible worlds to truth values. But again one might well be sceptical of whether all natural language constructions can be covered, of whether even this notion of 'truth condition' is rich enough, and of whether the highly formalized 'equivalent' sentence could really mean exactly the same thing as an ordinary English sentence. No such problems arise within the deflationary framework that I will be urging.

substantive explanation of *why* the principle of compositionality holds.

For illustration, look again at how we might reach an interpretation of "Gira Marte". We can begin with premises specifying the meanings of its primitives:

> "Marte" in Italian means the same as *our* "Mars".

> "gira_" in Italian means the same as *our* "_rotates".

Then, in light of the principle of compositionality, we can infer

> The result of applying "gira_" to "Marte" in Italian means the same as the result of *our* applying "_rotates" to "Mars".

And finally, given the syntactic facts

> The result of applying "gira_" to "Marte" = "Gira Marte"

> The result of applying "_rotates" to "Mars" = "Mars rotates"

we can deduce the interpretation

> "Gira Marte" in Italian means the same as *our* "Mars rotates".

And, in general, whenever some foreign expression is constructed by imposing a certain combinatorial procedure (i.e. a certain syntactic structure) on certain words, then we can interpret it in our language with the expression that results from imposing exactly the same procedure on synonyms of those words.[7]

If this sort of approach will do, then Davidson's programme and its attendant difficulties can be put behind us. We can

---

[7] Notice that although we translate a foreign complex expression using one of our own that has the same structure—i.e. one that results from the same combinatorial procedure—the resulting *order* of synonymous words need not be the same. For the basic elements of a language include *schemata*, e.g. "gira_" and "_rotates". Therefore word order will partially derive from where the 'slots' in these schemata are located. Thus an identity of combinatorial procedure is quite consistent with a difference of word order.

abandon the desperate struggle to find a conception of 'truth condition' sufficiently strong to capture meaning. We will then be able to avoid the problematic commitment to cram every natural language construction into the narrow and gratuitous mould of predicate logic. And in that case there will be no need to claim, rather implausibly as we have seen, that the predicate logic formalization of a natural language sentence will perfectly preserve its meaning. What a relief!

4. DAVIDSON'S PRE-EMPTIVE OBJECTIONS

But *will* the deflationary approach do? Davidson himself was always aware of it. So it is worth our while to examine his reasons for rejecting the idea and to consider how persuasive they are.

In the first place, he argues (in his essay "Radical Interpretation"[8]) that a manual of translation does not itself fully specify meanings, and so cannot constitute an interpretation. For one can know (e.g. on the basis of testimony) that two expressions should be intertranslated—i.e. that they have the same meaning as each other—without having any understanding of either one of them.

However, the problem we were set was to specify the assumptions we might make that would enable us to interpret a foreign language. And one good answer is that a correct manual of translation into our own language will do the trick. Granted, the information it provides will suffice only given an as-yet unexplained further fact, namely that we understand our own language. But the explanation of that further fact is not that we make additional explicit assumptions—assumptions, this time, about our *own* words. For, if that were what understanding one's own language amounted to, the question would arise as to how the terms in which the additional assumptions are articulated

---

[8] Reprinted in his *Inquiries into Truth and Interpretation*. See esp. 129–30.

could themselves be understood, and we would be on the verge of a vicious regress. Rather, as argued in Chapter 2, the understanding we have of our own terms must be seen as a species of know*how*, consisting in our propensities for when and where to deploy them. I'll be returning to this matter later. But the crucial point for now is the illegitimacy of insisting, given a translation of some foreign expression, that further explicit assumptions about our own expressions are needed because we ought to strive for an explanation, solely in terms of explicit propositional knowledge, of how we manage to arrive at its meaning.

But, for the sake of argument, let us bow to Davidson's objection—at least to the letter of it—and take up his challenge to specify what knowledge (whether explicit or implicit) would suffice to understand a language (whether someone else's or one's own). This creates no particular difficulty for the deflationary strategy, because it is a simple matter to implement the approach in terms of meaning-facts rather than translation-facts. We can begin by adopting the convention that each capitalized English expression is to refer to the meaning of the original lower-case expression: thus "Mars" means MARS, "_rotates" means ROTATES(x), "Mars rotates" means MARS ROTATES, and so on.[9] Then we can invoke the principle of compositionality in a Fregean form: namely, that the result of applying one term to others (to produce a complex expression) *means* the result of applying the meaning of the first term to the meanings of the others.[10]

[9] Note that although the term "MARS" is introduced to name the meaning of "Mars", it is not synonymous with "the meaning of 'Mars'". It is a substantive, contingent fact that "Mars" means what it does, i.e. that "Mars" means MARS.

[10] Frege's picture, which I am embracing here (and in chap. 7, section 3), is that (i) each primitive term has a certain functional character (it is either an object, or a first-level function, or a second-level function, etc.); (ii) complex expressions result from applying terms to each other in a way that is consistent with their functional character; (iii) the referent and the meaning of each term has the same functional character as that of the term itself; and (iv) the referent and meaning of each complex is determined by a sequence of functional application that parallels the way that the complex expression itself is determined. See his "Concept and Object" and "Function and Concept" in *Translations from the Philosophical Writings of Gottlob Frege*.

From these premisses, together with assumptions about how "Mars rotates" and "Gira Marte" are composed from their component words, we can infer that they both mean the result of applying the function ROTATES(x) to the argument MARS, i.e. that they both mean ROTATES(MARS). Thus we can derive (and hence explain), for each sentence of a language (including our own), a fact concerning what it means.

At the beginning of his "Truth and Meaning" Davidson dismisses that particular way of trying to give a

> ... useful account of how the meanings of sentences depend upon the meanings of the words (or other structural features) that compose them. Ask, for example, for the meaning of "Theaetetus flies". A Fregean answer might go something like this: given the meaning of "Theaetetus" as argument, the meaning of "flies" yields the meaning of "Theaetetus flies" as value. **The vacuity of this argument is obvious. We wanted to know what the meaning of "Theaetetus flies" is; it is no progress to be told that it is the meaning of "Theaetetus flies".** This much we new before any theory was in sight. In the bogus account just given, talk of the structure of the sentence and of the meanings of words was idle, for it played no role in producing the given description of the meaning of the sentence.[11] [emphasis added]

But the Fregean answer does *not* merely apply the logical law of identity to the meaning of "Theaetetus flies", which would indeed be vacuous. Rather, it incorporates the principle of compositionality by maintaining that the meaning of the result of applying a function-expression to certain argument-expressions equals the result of applying the meaning of the function to the meanings of its arguments. Thus it characterizes the meaning of "Theaetetus flies" by describing it as *the result of applying*

---

[11] *Inquiries into Truth and Interpretation*, 20.

the meaning of "flies" to the meaning of "Theaetetus". Therefore, contrary to what Davidson says, our assumptions about the structure of a sentence, and about the meanings of its words, play an *essential* role in our characterization of the meaning of that sentence.

What *is* true is that we have not yet *identified* the meaning of "Theaetetus flies". We have specified it merely via the construction description, "the result of applying FLIES(x) to THEAETETUS"; but we have not said what that result is, what the description describes.[12]

It is worth emphasizing, however, that no such identification is needed as far as interpretation is concerned. Our deflationary strategy for arriving at an understanding of foreign sentences works completely independently of any assumptions on that score. Nevertheless, it's not too hard to come up with a natural answer. If we apply FLIES to THEAETETUS what we get is a further meaning-property, namely, THEAETETUS FLIES. This meaning-property is possessed by certain complex expressions—by whichever sentences mean the same as "Theaetetus flies". And it is constituted by the construction-property

> being the result of applying a word meaning FLIES to a word meaning THEAETETUS

Going deeper: given that the pair of meanings, FLIES and THEAETETUS, are reduced to specific non-semantic properties, U1 and U2, (e.g. use-properties a la UTM), then what comes from applying the first of these meanings to the second will be the meaning that is constituted at a more profound level by

> being the result of applying a word that has U1 to a word that has U2

---

[12] For a sympathetic elaboration of Davidson's complaint that the deflationary approach fails to specify *directly* what the meanings of complexes are, see James Higginbotham's "A Perspective on Truth and Meaning", in *The Philosophy of Donald Davidson*.

Thus the meanings of complex expressions are quite definitely identified.[13]

A little later in the same article, Davidson makes a further criticism of the deflationary approach:

> This is the place to scotch another hopeful thought. Suppose we have a satisfactory theory of syntax for our language, consisting of an effective method of telling, for an arbitrary expression, whether or not it is independently meaningful (i.e. a sentence), and assume as usual that this involves viewing each sentence as composed, in allowable ways, out of elements drawn from a fixed finite stock of atomic syntactic elements (roughly, words). The hopeful thought is that syntax, so conceived, will yield semantics when a dictionary giving the meaning of each syntactic atom is added. Hopes will be dashed, however, if semantics is to comprise a theory of meaning in our sense, for **knowledge of the structural characteristics that make for meaningfulness in a sentence, plus knowledge of the meanings of the ultimate parts, does not add up to knowledge of what a sentence means**. The point is easily illustrated by belief sentences. Their syntax is relatively unproblematic. Yet, adding a dictionary does not touch the standard semantic problem, which is that **we cannot account for even as much as the truth conditions of such sentences** on the basis of what we know of the meanings of the words in them.[14] [emphasis added]

---

[13] For further discussion and defence of the deflationary view of compositionality, see my "The Composition of Meanings", *Philosophical Review* 106, 1997, 503–31, reprinted as Ch. 7 of *Meaning*. Notice that a trivial derivation of compositionality—one might consider it an 'explanation' in some very weak sense—results from our identification of the *meaning*-property of a complex expression with the *construction*-property of that expression, i.e. its property of the form, 'e results from applying such-and-such combinatorial procedure to words with so-and-so meanings'.

[14] *Inquiries into Truth and Interpretation*, 21.

The central contention here is that knowledge of the syntax of a sentence—for example, a belief attribution—plus knowledge of what its words mean, will not enable us to infer the sentence's truth condition. But I can find no construal of this claim in which it constitutes a good objection to deflationism.[15]

Does it mean that the imagined knowledge about a sentence, s, cannot yield any conclusion of the form "s is true if and only if p"? If so the claim is mistaken. Once we have determined, via the deflationary approach described and illustrated above, that a sentence means the same as our "John believes that dogs bark", we may straightaway conclude that it is true if and only if John believes that dogs bark. We simply invoke the schema "s means the same as our "p" → (s is true ↔ p)".

So, perhaps Davidson's intention is to complain that the proposed account does not yield a *compositional* account of truth conditions, a Tarski-style deduction of them from premises about the referential properties of words. In that case, my response is that part of the point of the deflationary approach is to obviate the need for such an account. For we can interpret foreign speakers perfectly well without it, merely on the basis of the unexplained principle that meaning is compositional.[16]

[15] A different (but not wholly unrelated) argument against the deflationary picture is suggested by Jerry Katz (see his *Sense, Reference, and Philosophy*, 194). He points out that certain sentences—e.g. Chomsky's notorious "Colourless ideas sleep furiously"—would appear to have no meaning despite being constructed by combining meaningful words in syntactically legitimate ways. One might reply, however, that such sentences seem 'weird' because they are very obviously a priori false (or very obviously a priori true), and not because they are meaningless. Do we not say that it is impossible for ideas to sleep and impossible for sleeping to be done furiously? Moreover, any desire for a more restrictive notion of meaningfulness, could be accommodated simply by adding further conditions to the deflationary criterion. And this would have no tendency to jeopardize our non-truth-theoretic answer to Davidson's question of how the meanings of complexes are derived from the meanings of their parts.

[16] Note that the quoted passage appears *before* Davidson's presentation of his own solution to the problem of how interpretation of an entire language is possible; it occurs in the context of critical discussions of various initial attempts to solve it. His arguments that these attempts all fail are intended to give support to the truth-theoretic alternative solution that he goes on to articulate. But in that

Finally, Davidson's point might be that knowledge of the syntax of a sentence, s, plus knowledge of what its words mean, do not together suffice for us to be able us to say, for a variety of conditions, whether s would be true in each of those conditions. And it is indeed clear that in order to decide if s would be true in certain specified circumstances, characterized, say, by "C", it will not be enough to translate s into our sentence "A". We will also have to figure out whether "A" holds in the given circumstances. And that will require the identification of relevant rules of inference enabling us to determine whether "A" does or does not follow from "C". But, notice that the same would be true from within a Davidsonian framework. Even if we are given that s is true if and only if A, there will be a need to consult logical rules in order to settle whether "A" (and hence s) would be true in the circumstance, *that* C, i.e. whether "A" follows from "C".

One might think that an advantage of the Davidsonian approach—stemming from the fact that it deals, in the first instance, with regimented or formalized sentences—is that the needed rules are well established; they will be the standard rules of predicate logic. Whereas it is comparatively uncertain what rules of inference, applying to structurally explicit *natural* language sentences, are available to be invoked by the deflationist. In fact, however, *both* approaches must confront this uncertainty. For remember (from section 1, especially footnote 4) that the Davidsonian is compelled to recognize the existence of 'transformation principles' associating ordinary sentences with their underlying 'semantic structures'—i.e. with sentences in a

---

case these arguments cannot legitimately presuppose that we already accept that solution.

Thus Davidson's proposal to deploy truth-theoretic notions, instead of meaning-theoretic notions, in the derivations of sentence-meanings is not motivated—appearances to the contrary—by any antecedent argument that the latter notions are intolerably obscure (or are unsuitable for some other reason), but rests merely on the allegation (which I am criticizing) that purely meaning-theoretic derivations cannot be given.

regimented part (or formalized extension) of the language—and such principles do not differ substantially from rules of deduction. Therefore, a commitment to there being ordinary language inference rules is necessary on either strategy.

I conclude that Davidson's resistance to the deflationary view of compositionality was always unjustified, and remains so. In order to interpret the expressions of a language it suffices to assume that meaning is compositional. There is no need to explain that fact by analysing sentence-meanings in terms of truth conditions. Indeed, there is no reason to suppose that it *can* be substantively explained. Consequently, the truth-theoretic picture has nothing to recommend it.

Once we abandon the idea of explaining compositionality in truth-theoretic terms, then two further Davidsonian ideas are put into doubt. In the first place, one of the main motivations for identifying semantic structures with expressions of first-order predicate logic is removed. And, in the second place, we might begin to wonder about the need to draw any distinction at all between semantic and syntactic structures. Let me stress, however, that these two further anti-Davidsonian speculations are not integral to the deflationary position on compositionality that is elaborated here. It implies that we should take them seriously. But their correctness will hinge on whether the various phenomena (including inferences and structural ambiguities) that are standardly explained by invoking predicate-logic semantic structures can be better explained without them. The above discussion suggests that the prospects for finding such better explanations within a non-standard 'syntactic semantics' are by no means negligible. For we see that standard, i.e. predicate logic, explanations of inferences are usually radically incomplete and that syntactically oriented rules of logic are also needed. But an attempt to settle these issues would take us beyond the scope of this work.[17] The central anti-Davidsonian

---

[17] Let me, however, address an argument offered by Katz (see his *Sense, Reference, and Philosophy*, 192) against the idea that semantic structure might be

claim here is quite independent of them. It is simply this: that however the semantic structure of a sentence is articulated, whether it be in terms of a predicate logic structure, a syntactic structure, or something else—the meaning of the sentence need not, and should not, be derived truth-theoretically; for it can be obtained, as illustrated above, merely on the basis of assumptions about its structure, the meanings of its words, and the principle of compositionality.

5. WHY COMPOSITIONALITY ISN'T A CONSTRAINT ON CONCEPT CONSTITUTION

Besides Davidson, two other philosophers who have drawn overly strong conclusions from the compositionality of meaning are Jerry Fodor and Ernie Lepore. In a series of papers and books, culminating in "Why Compositionality Won't Go Away", they argue that

> ... [C]ompositionality is the sovereign test for theories of lexical meaning. So hard is this test to pass, we think, that it filters out practically all of the theories of lexical meaning that are current in either philosophy or cognitive science. Among the casualties are, for example, the theory that lexical meanings are statistical structures (like stereotypes); the theory that the meaning of a word is its use; the theory that knowing the meaning of (at least

identified with syntactic structure. He points out that sentences constructed syntactically in different ways may nonetheless be taken to have the same meaning, e.g. (simplifying his illustration) "The dog the cat scratched barked" and "The cat scratched a dog, which barked". One might reply, however, that we have a variety of more and less coarse-grained conceptions of 'the same meaning'; and that, although, according to one of them, the provable equivalence of sentences like these establishes (by definition) their 'sameness of meaning', there is nonetheless a more fine-grained conception, captured by identity of syntactic construction properties, relative to which they do not qualify as synonyms.

some) words requires having a recognitional capacity for (at least some) of the things that it applies to; and the theory that knowing the meaning of a word requires knowing criteria for applying it.[18]

Their strategy of argument is very simple. Suppose someone maintains that the meaning of a word (or the content of a Mentalese term) is engendered by its inferential role, or associated stereotype, or an associated recognitional capacity, or to put it schematically, by it's G-property. To refute such claims, Fodor and Lepore have repeatedly offered the following objection: meanings are compositional; G-properties are not—here they plug in one of the targeted theories, e.g. inferential roles, stereotypes, criteria, ...; therefore meanings aren't engendered by G-properties. Or, more explicitly:

(1) A complex's meaning what it does is determined by its structure and the meanings of its words.

(2) A complex's G-property is *not* determined by its structure and the G-properties of its words. (This is supported by examples, e.g. the stereotype associated with "pet fish" (a goldfish, perhaps) is not determined by the stereotypical pet (a dog) and the stereotypical fish (a salmon)).

(3) Therefore, the meaning of an expression is not engendered by its G-property.[19]

---

[18] See their "Why Compositionality Won"t Go Away: Reflections on Horwich's "Deflationary" Theory', *Meaning and Representation* (Blackwell: 2002). See also J. Fodor, "There Are No Recognitional Concepts; Not Even RED", *Philosophical Issues*, 9, edited by E. Villanueva (Atascadero, Calif., Ridgeview Publishing Co., 1998); J. Fodor and E. Lepore, "Why Meaning (Probably) Isn't Conceptual Role", *Mind and Language* 6: 4, 1991; Fodor and Lepore, "The Pet Fish and The Red Herring: Why Concepts Arn't Prototypes", *Cognition* 58(2): 243–76; and Fodor and Lepore, *Holism*. These essays are reprinted in *The Compositionality Papers*, edited by Fodor and Lepore: The quoted passage is on p. 41 of that book.

[19] For some reason Fodor and Lepore do not consider whether Fodor's own *informational* account of concept constitution would be 'filtered out' by their

But there is a gap in this line of thought. No matter what is substituted for "G", the argument is valid only in the presence of a further premiss: the following Uniformity Assumption

> If the meanings of *words* are engendered by their G-properties, then so are the meanings of *complexes*.

Without that assumption the most one can conclude from (1) and (2) is that *either* the meanings of words aren't engendered by their G-properties, *or* the meanings of complexes aren't. Thus it would be perfectly coherent for someone to deny the Uniformity Assumption and maintain that whereas the meanings of *words* are engendered by (say) the laws governing the acceptance of sentences containing them, the meanings of complexes are constituted in some other way.[20]

For example, it might well be maintained that

> The word "pet" means what it does in virtue of the fact that L_1("pet").

> The word "fish" means what it does in virtue of the fact that L_2("fish").

> The schema "*a n*" means what it does in virtue of the fact that L_3("*a n*").

---

compositionality condition. In fact it would be. For consider concepts such as HOT SNOW and ROUND SQUARE. Since these are never exemplified, it cannot be that the terms expressing them do so in virtue of causal correlations between exemplifications of the concepts and tokenings of the terms—the mechanism which, according to Fodor, is the one involved in fixing the meanings of primitives such as "hot" and "round". For further discussion, see my "Concept Constitution", *Philosophical Issues*, 9.

[20] A slightly different interpretation of the argument offered by Fodor and Lepore sees it as directed against claims regarding the identity of meaning-*entities*, e.g. "DOG = such-and-such inferential role", rather than, as I have assumed, against theories of how meaning-*properties* are constituted, e.g. "w means DOG in virtue of having such-and-such inferential role". But the same objection can be made to this variant: namely, that we need not identify the meanings of *complex* expressions with entities of the same sort that we identify *word*-meanings with.

but that

> The complex "pet fish" means what it does *not* in virtue of its being governed by some further law, L_4; but, rather, in virtue of its being the result of substituting words meaning what "pet" and "fish" do into a schema meaning what "*a n*" does.

Given the supposed reductions of the meaning-properties of these three elements, it follows that "pet fish" means what it does in virtue of its being the result of substituting words governed by the laws L_1 and L_2 into a schema governed by L_3. The expression's possession of this property will help explain its overall use, i.e. the fact that the sentences containing it are accepted when they are.

This exemplifies the deflationary dictum that we *presuppose* compositionality in specifications of how the meanings of complexes are constituted. From this perspective we should resist the impulse to begin by identifying the kind of fact in virtue of which (i) complexes and (ii) lexical items, mean what they do; to continue by proving that the former facts will indeed be determined by the latter; and to conclude that the compositionality of complex expressions has thereby been explained. That is the inflationary aspiration embodied in Davidson's truth-theoretic semantics; and the same mistake (in the form of their Uniformity Assumption) vitiates the strategy of argument deployed by Fodor and Lepore.[21]

[21] Mark Sainsbury, in "Two Ways to Smoke a Cigarette", *Meaning and Representation*, suggests that there is no real conflict between my deflationism and the position of Fodor and Lepore, because what they criticize are various 'theories of meaning', in the sense of 'theories that deduce the meanings of sentences from specifications of the meanings of words', whereas deflationism concerns the constitution of meaning-facts at some underlying level. But, in the first place, insofar as the 'specifications of meaning' to which Fodor and Lepore are objecting include specifications of use, or associated stereotypes, etc., it is hard see how Sainsbury's distinction is to be applied. In the second place, as we have seen, the deflationary perspective does involve a wholly non-reductive 'theory of meaning', albeit a trivial one, in its explanation of how interpretation takes place. This

In subsequent defence of that assumption, and hence of their overall strategy, Fodor and Lepore cite what they aptly call "the principle of *reverse* compositionality", according to which the fact that a complex means what it does determines the structure of that complex and the meanings of its constituents. This principle implies, for example, that an expression can mean PET FISH *only* if it is constructed from terms meaning PET and FISH. Their line of thought is then

(1)   that compositionality and reverse compositionality are both plausible;

(2)   that the conjunction of these facts is best explained by supposing that the meanings of words are *components* of, i.e. present within, the meanings of the complex expressions they form; and

(3)   that this suggests that the Uniformity Assumption is indeed correct.[22]

Now one might well accept their first step, at least with respect to our most fine-grained conception of meaning. And one might also accept the second step, at least if it is taken to say that the meaning of a complex 'contains' (in some suitable non-spatial sense) all and *only* the meanings of its component words. But surely (2) does not lead to (3). Suppose, given the need for a non-spatial notion of containment, one took the import of (2) to be that the meanings of complexes are ordered *sets* whose members are the meanings of words. In that case, word meanings, which we have no reason to identify with sets, would be very different kinds of entity from the meanings of complexes; and so one would expect the kind of property in virtue of which

was my basis for concluding that compositionality does not constrain a theory of primitive concept constitution. And, in the third place, Fodor and Lepore's Uniformity Assumption is equally objectionable in the context of either form of theory.

[22] See their "Why Compositionality Won't Go Away", *The Compositionality Papers*, 59–61.

a complex means what it does to be quite different from the kind of property in virtue of which a word means what it does. One might then be quite inclined to agree with the deflationist that the property that is responsible for a *complex's* meaning what it does *isn't* a use or inferential role, *isn't* a stereotype or prototype, and *isn't* a recognitional capacity, but is rather the property of being constructed in a certain way from words with certain uses, or associated prototypes, or recognitional capacities, . . . , or whatever other characteristic one takes to engender the meanings of words.[23]

It is not, of course, that there is nothing to choose amongst alternative theories of lexical meaning; but the need to accommodate the two compositionality principles won't be what decides the issue. The constraint we need in order to obtain a good theory comes, not from the *compositionality* of meaning, but rather from the *use import* of meaning, namely, that the overall use of a

---

[23] Although Fodor and Lepore believe that their Uniformity Assumption is correct and that it can be supported in the way just discussed, they maintain (in "Why Compositionality Won't Go Away", 58–9) that neither it, nor the argument of which it is a part, are really needed in order to see that compositionality substantially constrains the nature of lexical meaning. For they think that there is a separate line of thought that yields this conclusion: viz.

1. Anyone who understands certain complex expressions, e.g. "Flounders swim" and "John snores", must also understand other expressions built from the same elements, e.g. "Flounders snore". ('systematicity')
2. Therefore, the meaning of a term does not depend on the complex expression in which it appears. ('context-independence')
3. But the stereotype associated with the word "swim" in "Flounders swim" is not the same as the stereotype associated with that word in "John swims".
4. Therefore the meaning of "swim" is not engendered by an associated stereotype.

But note (a) that any alert defender of the stereotype theory of meaning will simply deny premiss 3 and will maintain that his theory, properly stated, is that the stereotype associated with the isolated word "swim", whatever it may be, is the meaning of that word *wherever* it occurs; (b) that even if the above argument were persuasive it could tell against only the stereotype theory, and would have no bearing on any of the other accounts of lexical meaning, e.g. the use theory, that were alleged by Fodor and Lepore to be precluded by compositionality; and (c) the argument does not really hinge on compositionality, but rather on context-independence, so it cannot be presented as a justification of their primary claim.

complex is explained, in part, by the meanings of its words and how they are combined. From this constraint we can infer that the property responsible for a word's having the meaning it does is the property that (in conjunction with other factors, including the meaning-constituting properties of other words) can best account for the inferential character, and the circumstances of acceptance and rejection, of all the various sentences in which it appears. And this, as I have argued in previous chapters, points us towards a certain form of *use* theory of word meaning. For, quite plausibly, a word's conformity with certain *core* regularities of use is the property that explains its *overall* usage. More specifically, we are led to conclude that the meaning of a word derives from the fact that our acceptance of certain specified sentences containing it (in certain specified conditions) is what explains its overall use.[24] But this is not to subscribe to a use theory of *sentence* meaning.[25] Therefore there is no obligation to devise some notion of the 'core uses' of complex expressions, to show that they are determined by the core uses of words, and thereby to *explain* compositionality. Our only obligation—but this is a fairly onerous one—is to discover which particular basic acceptance properties of words will provide the best explanations of their overall uses, i.e. of the uses of all the sentences containing them.[26] As for the *meanings* of those sentences,

[24] For a sustained explanation of this idea, see chap. 2.

[25] Katz complains (*Sense, Reference, and Philosophy*, 194) that insofar as this account does not associate a specific possible use with each meaningful sentence, then it cannot qualify as a "use theory of meaning". But, of course, this is not an argument against the theory—merely a terminological suggestion about what not to call it.

[26] It might be thought that I have skated over the *real* problem of compositionality, which is to show how it might be so much as possible for properties assigned to individual words (e.g. basic regularities in their use) to explain the overall usage of all the unlimited number of sentences that can be made from them. But this also is a pseudo-puzzle. For the law of use of a function term will specify the usage of any results of applying it to other terms. E.g. the meaning-constituting property of "and" is a tendency to infer "p and q" from "p" and "q", and vice versa. Therefore, just as laws governing the behaviour of protons, electrons, etc. would only qualify as such if they explain the properties of whatever is made out of them, it is trivial that the basic uses of words must have consequences for the usage of all the complexes into which they enter.

they derive from their construction out of words with certain uses. And there is nothing non-trivial to be said about how and why that happens.

6. ON KNOWING THE MEANINGS OF ONE'S OWN EXPRESSIONS

Let me end with a word on understanding one's *own* language. In order that I understand for example the English sentence "Mars rotates", it is conceptually (a priori) necessary and sufficient for me to *know* (in some sense) what it means—specifically, that it means MARS ROTATES. But it cannot be my *explicit* knowledge of this fact that constitutes my understanding of the sentence; for that would be too easy; I can explicitly infer it merely from the capitalizing convention for naming meanings. Rather, the needed knowledge is *implicit*: it consists in the fact that what "Mars rotates" means in my idiolect resembles its meaning in English. And that resemblance derives, in turn, from the fact that the basic uses of the words "Mars" and "_rotates" (and their mode of combination) are similar in my idiolect and in the public language.[27] Consequently, if someone implicitly knows

---

[27] Fodor and Lepore stress the importance of distinguishing, on the one hand, the contrast between *occurrent* and *dispositional* mental states and, on the other hand, the contrast between *conscious* and *unconscious* states. And they think that my use of "explicit" and "implicit" oscillates confusingly between these alternatives. But in fact I am pointing to a *third* contrast by means of that terminology. Explicit commitments are *articulated*, i.e. spelled out in the 'belief box' perhaps, whereas implicit commitments are not. E.g. my implicit knowledge that "Mars rotates" means, in my idiolect, MARS ROTATES consists merely in the *fact* that it has that meaning. Therefore, some explicit commitments are occurrent and some dispositional; and the same can be said of implicit commitments. Similarly, some explicit commitments are conscious and some unconscious; and the same goes for implicit ones (in that we are aware introspectively of some, but not all, of our linguistic dispositions).

The emphasis on *resemblance* between idiolectal and public language meanings is intended to explain how understanding an expression is a matter of degree. By "basic use in the public language" I have in mind *basic use by the relevant experts*.

the meanings of the elements of a sentence of his language (whether it be a sentence-type or a sentence-token) and also knows how those elements are combined, he thereby satisfies the condition for understanding the whole. There is no need for any inference, or for any other sort of process, to take him from those antecedent items of knowledge to the state of understanding the sentence.

Contrary to Fodor and Lepore[28] it is no objection to these theses that one may come across a hard-to-parse sentence-token (e.g. "Dogs dogs dog dog dogs"), be given information about its structure (e.g. "$[[Dogs_N \ [dogs_N \ dog_V]]_{NP}[dog_V \ dogs_N]_{VP}]_S$"), know what the words mean, and yet still not understand that sentence. For, the knowledge required for understanding a *word* does not amount to having some piece of *explicit* information about its meaning (e.g. that "dog" means the same as "chien") but is rather a matter of know*how*, of being governed by its law of use. And similarly, the required knowledge of structure cannot take the form of some theoretical characterization of it, but must also be implicit and manifested in use (e.g. being disposed to infer "Certain dogs dog dogs"). Once *this* sort of knowledge of word meanings and sentence structure is obtained, then understanding the sentence is guaranteed.

Nor is it reasonable to object that since understanding is a form of knowledge, and since knowledge yields further knowledge only by inference, our understanding of complex expressions *must* result from inference. This *conclusion* can't be right, because, regarding our understanding of the language of thought (whether it be an ordinary language or universal Mentalese), there would be no language in which to conduct the alleged inferences. Moreover, the *argument* for that conclusion isn't right; because it is only for *articulated* (though perhaps unconscious) knowledge—i.e. formulated in the language of thought—that transitions between states of knowledge are likely

---

[28] See "Why Compositionality Won't Go Away", 45–7.

to be mediated by inference; but understanding is *implicit* knowledge.

Finally, it is not relevant to point out that if, as a matter of empirical fact, we think in a universal Mentalese, then understanding a token of a public sentence will require translating it into that mental language, a process which might involve explicit (yet unconscious) inferences. This is beside the point; for, even if inferences are involved, they will enter merely into how we grasp the *structure* of the sentence token (and maybe into how we learned the meanings of its words). They will *not* be employed in the move from that grasp of structure, together with our knowledge of word meanings, to our understanding of the token. For there is no such move. To see this once again, suppose that properly understanding a token of "Mars rotates" is empirically constituted by unconsciously translating it into a specific sentence, "m", of Mentalese—a sentence consisting in a certain structure imposed on certain Mentalese terms. Now imagine someone who happens to translate "Mars rotates" into a *different* Mentalese sentence "m*"—so his understanding is defective. Then it must be (as a matter of conceptual necessity) that either the *structure* of "m" differs from the structure of "m*", or that the *terms* making up these Mentalese sentences are not all the same. In other words, either our subject hasn't on this occasion understood "Mars" or "_rotates", or he hasn't grasped how those words have been combined. Thus once the meanings of the words in a token, and the way these words are combined, have been properly (i.e. implicitly) identified, there is nothing more to be done. The conditions for understanding have been met.[29]

[29] This chapter grew out of a paper of the same name that I delivered at a conference at Reading University in May 1999, the proceedings of which are included in Emma Borg (ed.), *Meaning and Representation*, Blackwell, 2001. Thanks to Jim Edwards, Jerry Fodor, Richard Heck, Ernie Lepore, Josep Macia, Stephen Neale, Paul Pietroski, Barry C. Smith, and Mark Sainsbury for helpful discussions of the issues treated here.

Bibliography

Blackburn, S. (1984). 'The Individual Strikes Back', *Synthese* 58: 281–301.

—— (1986). 'Advertisment for a Semantics for Psychology', *Midwest Studies in Philosophy* 10, edited by P. French, T. Uehling, and H. Wettstein (Minneapolis: University of Minnesota Press).

Block, N. (1994–5). 'An Argument for Holism', *Proceedings of the Aristotelian Society* 95: 151–69.

Boghossian, P. (1989). 'The Rule Following Considerations', *Mind* XCVIII (392): 507–50.

—— (1996). 'Analyticity Reconsidered', *Nous* 30: 3.

—— (1997). 'Analyticity', in *A Companion to the Philosophy of Language*, edited by R. Hale and C. Wright (Oxford: Blackwell).

—— (2003). 'The Normativity of Content', *Philosophical Issues*, 13:1 (October) 33–45.

—— (2003*a*). 'How Are Objective Epistemic Reasons Possible', *Philosophical Studies* 106.

—— (2003*b*). 'Blind Reasoning', *Proceedings of the Aristotelian Society, suppl. vol.* 77, Issue 1, 225–48.

Brandom, R. (1994). *Making It Explicit* (Cambridge, Mass.: Harvard University Press).

—— (1996). 'The Significance of Complex Numbers for Frege's Philosophy of Mathematics', *Proceedings of the Aristotelian Society* 293–315.

—— (2000). *Articulating Reasons*, Cambridge, Mass: Harvard University Press.

Burge, T. (1979). 'Individualism and the Mental', *Midwest Studies in Philosophy* 4: 73–121.

Carey, S. (2006). *The Origin of Concepts* (Cambridge, Mass.: MIT Press).

—— and Spelke, E. S. (1994). 'Domain Specific Knowledge and Conceptual Change', in L. Hirschfeld and S. Gelman (eds.), *Mapping the Mind: Domain Specificity in Cognition and Culture* (Cambridge: Cambridge University Press), 169–200.

Carnap, R. (1928). *Der Logische Aufbau der Welt* (Berlin: Schlachtensee Weltkreis-Verlag).

Chalmers, D. (2002). 'The Components of Content' in D. Chalmers (ed.), *Philosophy of Mind: Classical and Contemporary Readings* (Oxford: Oxford University Press).

Chomsky, N. (1975). 'Quine's Empirical Assumptions', in Davidson and Hintikka (eds.), *Words and Objections*, Kluwer.

—— (1986). *Knowledge of Language* (New York: Praeger).

—— (1987). 'Reply to Review Discussion of *Knowledge of Language*', *Mind and Language* 2: 178–97.

—— (1990). 'On the Nature, Use and Acquisition of Language', W. Lycan (ed.), *Mind and Cognition: A Reader*, 627–46 (Oxford: Blackwell).

—— (1993). *Language and Thought* (Wakefield, R.I.: Moyer Bell).

—— (1999). 'Internalist Explorations', *Festschrift for Burge*, M. Hahn and B. Ramberg (eds.) (Cambridge, Mass.: MIT Press).

—— (2000). *New Horizons in the Study of Language and Mind* (Cambridge: Cambridge University Press).

Crane, T. (1991). 'All the Difference in the World', *Philosophical Quarterly* 41: 1–25.

Crimmins, M., and Perry, J. (1989). 'The Prince and the Phone Booth: Reporting Puzzling Beliefs'. *Journal of Philosophy* 86: 685–711.

Davidson, D. (1967). 'Truth and Meaning', *Synthese* 17: 304–23.

—— (1984). *Truth and Interpretation* (Oxford: Clarendon Press).

Devitt, M. (1996). *Coming To Our Senses* (Cambridge: Cambridge University Press).

—— (2002). 'Meaning and Use', *Philosophy and Phenomenological Research*, LXV:1 (July) 106–21.

—— and Sterelny, K. (1987). *Language and Reality: An Introduction to the Philosophy of Language* (Oxford: Basil Blackwell).

Donnellan, K. (1989). 'Belief and the Identity of Reference', in French, Uehling, and Wettstein (eds.), *Midwest Studies in Philosophy 13, Contemporary Perspectives in the Philosophy of Language II* (Notre Dame: University of Notre Dame Press), 275–88.

Dretske, F. (1981). *Knowledge and the Flow of Information* (Cambridge, Mass.: MIT Press).

Dretske, F. (1986).'Misrepresentation', in Radu Bogan (ed.), *Belief: Form, Context, and Function* (New York: Oxford University Press).

Dummett, M. (1958). 'Truth', *Proceedings of the Aristotelian Society* n.s. 59: 141–62.

—— (1973). *Frege: Philosophy of Language* (London: Duckworth).

—— (1978). *Truth and Other Enigmas* (Cambridge, Mass.: Harvard University Press).

—— (1991). *The Logical Basis of Metaphysics* (Cambridge, Mass.: Harvard University Press).

Evans, G. (1973). 'The Causal Theory of Names', *Proceedings of the Aristotelian Society*, suppl. vol. 47: 187–208.

Field, H. (1973). 'Theory Change and the Indeterminacy of Reference', repr. in his *Truth and the Absence of Fact* (Oxford: Oxford University Press, 2001).

—— (1977). 'Logic, Meaning and Conceptual Role', *Journal of Philosophy* 69: 379–409.

—— (1981). 'Some Thoughts on Radical Indeterminacy', *The Monist* 81: 253–73.

—— (2000). 'Indeterminacy, Degree of Belief, and Excluded Middle', *Nous* 34: 1–30.

—— (2001). 'Meaning Attributions' in his *Truth and the Absence of Fact*.

—— (2003). 'No Fact of the Matter', *American Journal of Philosophy*, December.

Fine, K. (1975). 'Vagueness, Truth, and Logic', *Synthese* 30: 265–300.

Fodor, J. (1975). *The Language of Thought* (New York: Thomas Y. Crowell Co.).

—— (1982). 'Cognitive Science and the Twin-Earth Problem'. *Notre Dame Journal of Formal Logic* 23: 98–118.

—— (1987). *Psychosemantics* (Cambridge, Mass.: MIT Press).

—— (2001). 'Language, Thought, and Compositionality', *Mind and Language*, 1–15.

—— and Lepore, E. (1991). 'Why Meaning (Probably) Isn't Conceptual Role', *Mind and Language* 6: 4, 329–43.

—— (1991). *Holism* (Oxford: Blackwell).

—— (1996). 'The Pet Fish and The Red Herring: Why Concepts Arn't Prototypes', *Cognition* 58(2): 243–76.

Fodor, J. (2002). *The Compositionality Papers* (Oxford: Oxford University Press).

Frege, G. (1952). 'Concept and Object', *Translations from the Philosophical Writings of Gottlob Frege*, P. Geach and M. Black (eds.), (Oxford: Blackwell) 42–55.

—— (1952). 'Function and Concept', *Translations from the Philosophical Writings of Gottlob Frege*, 21–41.

—— (1952). 'On Sense and Reference', *Translations from the Philosophical Writings of Gottlob Frege*, 56–78.

Gibbard, A. (1994). 'Meaning and Normativity', *Philosophical Issues 5: Truth and Rationality*, edited by E. Villanueva (Ascadero, Calif.: Ridgeview Publishing Company), 95–115.

—— (2002). 'Horwich on Meaning', unpublished manuscript.

Grice, P. (1957). 'Meaning', *Philosophical Review* 66: 377–88.

—— (1969). 'Utterer's Meaning and Intention', *Philosophical Review* 78.

—— (1989). *Studies in the Way of Words* (Cambridge, Mass.: Harvard University Press).

Gupta, A. (2003). 'Deflationism, the Problem of Representation, and Horwich's Use Theory of Meaning', *Philosophy and Phenomenological Research*, Vol. 67 (November) 654–66.

Hale, R. (1996/7). 'Grundlagen $64', *Proceedings of the Aristotelian Society*.

—— and Wright, C. (2000). 'Implicit Definition and the A priori', in P. Boghossian and C. Peacocke (eds.), *New Essays on the A Priori* (Oxford: Oxford University Press).

Harman, G. (1982). 'Conceptual Role Semantics'. *Notre Dame Journal of Formal Logic* 28: 252–6.

—— (1987). '(Non-solipsistic) Conceptual Role Semantics', in E. Lepore (ed.), *New Directions in Semantics* (London: Academic Press).

—— (1993). 'Meaning Holism Defended' in Fodor and Lepore 1993a. *Holism: A Consumer Update. Grazer Philosophische Studien* 46 (Amsterdam: Rodopi, B.V., 163–71).

Higginbotham, J. (1999). 'A Perspective on Truth and Meaning', in *The Philosophy of Donald Davidson*, edited by Lewis Hahn (La Salle, Illinois: Open Court).

Horwich, P. G. (1995). 'Meaning, Use and Truth', *Mind* 104.414: 335–68.

Horwich, P. G. (1997*a*). 'Implicit Definition, Analytic Truth and Apriori Knowledge', *Nous* 31: 423–40.

—— (1997*b*). 'The Composition of Meanings', *Philosophical Review* 106: 503–31,

—— (1997*c*). 'The Nature of Vagueness', *Philosophy and Phenomenological Research*, LVII: 4.

—— (1998*a*). *Meaning* (Oxford: Oxford University Press).

—— (1998*b*). Truth, 2nd edn. (Oxford: Oxford University Press).

—— (1998*c*). 'Concept Constitution', *Philosophical Issues* 9, edited by E. Villanueva (Atascadero, Calif.: Ridgeview Publishing Company).

—— (2000*a*). 'Stipulation, Meaning, and Apriority' in P. Boghossian and C. Peacocke (eds.), *New Essays on the A Priori* (Oxford: Oxford University Press).

—— (2000*b*). 'Stephen Schiffer's Theory of Vagueness', *Philosophical Issues, 10*: *Skepticism*.

—— (2006). 'The Value of Truth', *Nous*.

Jackson, F., and Pettit, P. (1993). 'Some Content is Narrow', in J. Heil and A. Mele (eds.), *Mental Causation* (Oxford: Oxford University Press).

Jacob, P. (1997). *What Minds Can Do* (Cambridge: Cambridge University Press).

Katz, J. J. (2004). *Sense, Reference, and Philosophy* (Oxford: Oxford University Press).

Kripke, S. (1980). *Naming and Necessity* (Cambridge, Mass.: Harvard University Press).

—— (1982). *Wittgenstein: On Rules and Private Language* (Oxford: Blackwell).

Lance, M., and Hawthorne, J. (1997). *The Grammar of Meaning: Normativity and Semantic Content* (Cambridge: Cambridge University Press).

Larson, R., and Segal, G. (1995). *Knowledge of Meaning* (Cambridge, Mass.: MIT Press).

Lewis, D. (1970). 'How to Define Theoretical Terms', *Journal of Philosophy*, LVII: 427–66.

Loewer, B. (1993). 'The Value of Truth', in E. Villanueva (ed.), *Philosophical Issues* 4 (Atascadero, Calif.: Ridgeview Publishing Company).

Loewer, B. (1997). 'A Guide to Naturalizing Semantics', in B. Hale and C. Wright (eds.), *A Companion to the Philosophy of Language* (Oxford: Blackwell).

Lycan, W. (1990). 'On Respecting Puzzles about Belief Ascriptions [A Reply to Devitt]', *Pacific Philosophical Quarterly* 71: 182–8.

McDowell, J. (1984). 'Wittgenstein on Following a Rule', *Synthese* 58(3): 325–63.

—— (1994). *Mind and World* (Cambridge, Mass.: Harvard University Press).

McGinn, C. (1984). *Wittgenstein on Meaning* (Oxford: Blackwell).

Millikan, R. (1984). *Language, Thought and Other Biological Categories* (Cambridge, Mass.: MIT Press).

Montague, R. (1974). *Formal Philosophy: Selected Papers of Richard Montague*, edited and with an introduction by Richmond Thomason (New Haven, Conn.: Yale University Press).

Neale, S. (2003). *Descriptions*, 2nd edn. (Oxford: Oxford University Press).

—— (2004). 'This, That, and the Other', Anne Bezuidenhout and Marga Reimer (eds.), *Descriptions and Beyond* (Oxford: Oxford University Press).

Neander, K. (1995). 'Misrepresenting and Malfunctioning', *Philosophical Studies* 79: 109–41.

Papineau, D. (1987). *Reality and Representation* (Oxford: Blackwell).

Peacocke, C. (1992). *A Study of Concepts* (Cambridge, Mass.: MIT Press).

—— (1993). 'How Are A Priori Truths Possible?', *European Journal of Philosophy*, August.

Prior, A. (1960). 'The Runabout Inference Ticket', *Analysis* 21: 38–9.

Putnam, H. (1975). 'The Meaning of "Meaning"', in his *Mind, Language and Reality: Philosophical Papers, 2* (Cambridge: Cambridge University Press).

—— (1995*a*). 'On Truth' in his *Words and Life*, edited by J. Conant (Cambridge, Mass.: Harvard University Press).

—— (1995*b*). 'Does The Disquotational Theory of Truth Solve All Philosophical Problems?' in his *Words and Life*.

Quine, W. V. (1953). 'Two Dogmas of Empiricism', in his *From a Logical Point of View* (Cambridge Mass.: Harvard University Press).

—— (1962). *Word and Object* (Cambridge, Mass.: MIT Press).

Quine, W. V. (1990). *Pursuit of Truth* (Cambridge, Mass.: Harvard University Press).

Ramsey, F. P. (1929). 'Theories'; repr. in his *Foundations*, ed. H. D. Mellor (London: Routledge & Kegan Paul, 1978).

Recanati, F. (2004). *Literal Meaning* (Cambridge: Cambridge University Press).

Rumfitt, I. (2000). 'Yes and No', *Mind*, vol. 109.436.

Russell, B. (1927). *The Analysis of Matter* (London: Allen & Unwin).

Sainsbury, M. (2002). 'Two Ways to Smoke a Cigarette', *Meaning and Representation*, edited by E. Borg (Oxford: Blackwell).

Salmon, N. (1981). *Reference and Essence* (Princeton, NJ: Princeton University Press).

—— (1986). *Frege's Puzzle* (Cambridge, Mass.: MIT Press).

Schiffer, S. (1972). *Meaning* (Oxford: Oxford University Press).

—— (1987). *Remnants of Meaning* (Cambridge, Mass.: MIT Press).

—— (2000*a*). 'Vagueness and Partial Belief', *Philosophical Issues, 10: Skepticism*, 220–57.

—— (2000*b*). 'Horwich on Meaning: Critical Study of Paul Horwich's *Meaning*', *Philosophical Quarterly* 50: 527–36.

—— (2002). 'A Normative Theory of Meaning', *Philosophy and Phenomenological Research* 65: 187–93.

—— (2003). *The Things We Mean* (Oxford: Oxford University Press).

Schlick, M. (1959). 'Positivism and Realism' in A.J. Ayer, *Logical Positivism* (Glencoe, Ill.: The Free Press).

Segal, G. (2000). *A Slim Book about Narrow Content* (Cambridge, Mass: MIT Press.

Sellars, W. (1969). 'Language as Thought and as Communication', *Philosophy and Phenomenological Research* 29: 506–27.

Smith, N., and Tsimpli, I. (1993). *The Mind of a Savant* (Oxford: Blackwell).

Spelke, E. S. (2003). 'What Makes Us Smart? Core Knowledge and Natural Language' in *Language in Mind*, edited by Dedre Gentner and Susan Goldin-Meadow (Cambridge, Mass.: MIT Press).

Sperber, D., and Wilson, D. (1995). *Relevance* (Oxford: Blackwell).

Stampe, D. W. (1977). 'Toward a Causal Theory of Linguistic Representation', *Midwest Studies In Philosophy* 2. edited by P. French, T. Uehling, and H. Wettstein (Minneapolis: University of Minnesota Press), 42–63.

Travis, C. (2001). *Unshadowed Thought* (Cambridge, Mass: Harvard University Press).

Unger, P. (1979). 'There Are no Ordinary Things', *Synthese*, 117–54.

White, S. (1991). 'Narrow Content and Narrow Interpretation', in S. White (ed.), *The Unity of the Self* (Bradford: MIT Press).

Williams, B. (1996). 'Truth in Ethics', *Ratio* 8: 227–42 (special issue, *Truth in Ethics*, ed. B. Hooker).

Williamson, T. (1994). *Vagueness* (London: Routledge).

—— (1997). 'Reply to Commentators', *Philosophy and Phenomenological Research*, LVII: 4.

Wittgenstein, L. (1953). *Philosophical Investigations* (Oxford: Oxford University Press).

Wright, C. (1980). *Frege's Conception of Numbers as Objects* (Aberdeen: Aberdeen University Press).

—— (1984). 'Kripke's Account of the Argument against Private Language', *Journal of Philosophy*, 759–78.

—— (1986). *Realism, Meaning, and Truth* (Oxford: Blackwell).

—— (1992). *Truth and Objectivity* (Cambridge, Mass.: Harvard University Press).

—— (1996). 'The Epistemic Conception of Vagueness', *Southern Journal of Philosophy*, suppl. vol. 33: 133–59.

—— (2002). *Rails to Infinity* (Cambridge, Mass.: Harvard University Press).

Provenance of the Chapters

Chapter 1
A variant is to be published as "The Nature of Meaning" in *The Blackwell Guide to Philosophy of Language*, edited by Michael Devitt and Richard Hanley.

Chapter 2
This is a revised version of "A Use Theory of Meaning", *Philosophy and Phenomenological Research*, LXVIII (2), 2004, 351–72.

Chapter 3
Not based on any previous publication.

Chapter 4
This is an expansion of "The Sharpness of Vague Terms", *Philosophical Topics*, 28(1) (special issue on Vagueness, edited by Christopher Hill), 2000, 83–91.

Chapter 5
Parts of this chapter were published in *Philosophy, the Good, the True and the Beautiful*, (Anthony O'Hear (ed.), Cambridge University Press, 2000); in *What Is Truth* (Richard Schantz (ed.), de Gruyter: Berlin and New York, 2001); and in Chapter 8 of my *Meaning*.

Chapter 6
This is a heavily revised version (with very little overlap) of "Stipulation, Meaning, and Apriority", in *New Essays on the A Priori*, edited by Paul. Boghossian and Christopher Peacocke, Oxford University Press, 2000.

Chapter 7

This is a slightly revised version of "Meaning and its Place in the Language Faculty", in *Chomsky and his Critics*, edited by Louise Anthony and Norbert Hornstein, Blackwell, 2003.

Chapter 8

This is based on "Deflating Compositionality", in *Meaning and Representation*, edited by Emma Borg, Blackwell, 2001.

I would like to thank the various publishers of these earlier articles for allowing me to include revised versions of them in the present work.

Index